FREDERICK DELIUS

Also by Sir Thomas Beecham

★

A MINGLED CHIME

Drawing by James Gunn, A.R.A.

Sir Thomas Beecham

FREDERICK DELIUS

———

VIENNA HOUSE
New York

To the memory of a beloved companion,
brave and beautiful, gracious and gay,
to whom the music of Delius was ever a joy
and a mystery.

Illustrations

Preface

Nearly thirty years have passed since I gave a conditional promise to Jelka, the wife of Frederick Delius, that I would one day write the story of her husband's strange and troubled life. Not, be it emphasized, a critical or explanatory account of his music, for much had already been written about that. Germany was first in the field in 1907 with a monograph by a well-known and respected musicologist Max Chop, and although numerous articles and pamphlets along similar lines appeared during the next fifteen years in England, it was not until 1923 that Philip Heseltine launched the first full-sized work upon the composer. The strain of superlative eulogy running throughout this slightly juvenile effort could hardly fail to recall the comical apostrophe of Charmian in the second scene of *Antony and Cleopatra*: 'Sweet Alexas, most anything Alexas, almost most absolute Alexas,' and nearly twenty years had to go by before we were gratified by the cooler and more scholarly production of Professor Arthur Hutchings. In the meantime two other books of a semi-biographical character had been contributed by Mrs. Clare Black, a sister of the composer, and Mr. Eric Fenby. The former contains a wealth of detail expended on the Delius family life in Bradford during her brother's childhood days, and the latter is a poignant and sometimes painful narrative by a highly sensitive youth of the last few years of an elderly man, blind and paralysed. But of attempt to trace the passage of his career in full there has been none up to the present moment. Some biographical matter—necessarily fragmentary—has indeed made its appearance, but much of it is unfortunately vitiated by factual inaccuracies and erroneous conclusions. For no small amount of this Delius may be held responsible. His memory was frequently unreliable, and in his lighter moments he easily descended to the commission of those two venial offences, tergiversation and mystification.

It is only fair to add that these little lapses were limited to encounters

9

with the Press and other agencies of publicity. Fundamentally he was one of the most honest creatures that ever lived and was in the habit of expressing himself in private with an outspoken manner of speech that now and then proved disconcerting to some of those who might be present at the moment. With outsiders he probably shared the view of Charles Lamb that 'Truth is precious and not to be wasted on everybody'.

Before embarking on the task proposed to me by Jelka, I first attempted to find out what was in her mind about the sort of book she wanted me to write. In short, how much was to go into it and how much was to be left out. It appeared that she had been recently reading a fairly popular piece of autobiography, which to me could serve as an almost perfect model of urbanity and complacency, and that something after this fashion was to her taste. I felt it a friendly duty to point out that between autobiography and biography there was a wide and unbridgable gulf of difference. A man writing his own life story can say very much what he likes. So long as he is judicious enough to outlive his contemporaries, or at least most of them, he has little to fear from contradiction, criticism or controversy. If his narrative halts for a while here and there, or betrays occasional signs of languor and weariness, he can always embellish cold fact with a touch of warm fancy, and no one will be found likely to quarrel with him. Indeed, this class of work, as some of us know, is read (if at all) less for edification than entertainment. Biography, on the contrary, is generally a severe and often gloomy affair, with unassailable veracity as its watchword. Be it the whole truth, or only a wise portion of it, it must be free from the suspicion of a single misleading statement. Not even a tiny and seemingly innocent fib can be permitted; for some pernickety fellow will be sure to pounce upon it sooner or later, raise a storm of protest, and cast a doubt upon the validity of everything else in the story. Above all, the temptation to burden Frederick with a load of wholly undesirable virtues must be sternly resisted. That would be entirely fatal to the success of the book.

During the first half of the last century there flourished the delightful superstition that a musician who wrote a beautiful melody must have been blessed by the gods with an equally beautiful soul. To this pious belief we owe all those romantic lives by sentimental admirers, adorned invariably with idealized portraits of their subjects, whose handsome features irradiated majesty, refinement, poetry and charm.

Thrilling were the accounts of their struggles and reverses; their ill-treatment at the hands of social superiors and dignified resistance to high official tyranny. Briefly, if one-half of all this had been true, the noble creatures would have been well on the way to candidacy for canonization. I have often wondered what might have happened if some misguided and malicious sceptic had dared to foretell that the day might come when most of these idolized figures would be discovered to have been scrubby little fellows, ill-favoured (with one exception), coarse of speech, disorderly of habit, and, in one notorious instance, distressingly boorish in manners. There would have been, I am sure, a mighty howl of execration followed by the kind of treatment meted out to hecklers at our admirable present-day political party demonstrations.

Alas, those happy days of simple faith were soon to be threatened by the advent of agnosticism, whose angel, unwittingly sponsored by Charles Darwin, was spreading his Saturnian wing over half the Western World, and deriding the beliefs of a thousand years and the aspirations of poor mankind to attain a state of perfectibility. Novelists, notably in France and Russia, lost no time in absorbing the changing atmosphere of society, and realism began to advance its claim to serious attention. Godlike heroes declined perceptibly from favour and even blameless heroines became exposed to the impartial scepticism of an unchivalrous scrutiny. The inevitable result of this spiritual and intellectual revolution was a return to an earlier and robuster era of thought and feeling, with some loss on its way of moral as well as aesthetic sensibility. It is a melancholy truth that in most works of fiction produced during the past two millennia, the unobtrusive nobility of the saint has generally failed to compete with the uninhibited roistering of the sinner. I trust that I shall not be accused of discourtesy if I attribute much of this seemingly unaccountable preference to the ladies, but for this there is a completely reasonable explanation. At no time have they manifested genuine esteem for excessive virtue in the male animal; undoubtedly for the reason that there is a superfluity of it in themselves, and I am tolerably sure that at the court of King Arthur they unaffectedly preferred the company of Sir Lancelot and Sir Gawain to that of Sir Galahad and Sir Bedivere.

Jelka, who had been slightly intimidated by this rather pessimistic exordium, regained tranquillity upon my assuring her that she had really little to fear on Frederick's account. He seemed on the whole to have lived, in comparison with the majority of his fellow-men, a decent and orderly sort of life; and, so far as I could report, the record of his earlier years disclosed nothing dangerously flagitious. As for his married life I considered that I could safely take the risk (with Jelka's consent) of citing him as an orthodox type of the model husband. Upon this understanding she promised to write down for me all she could remember of her association with Frederick from the day of their first meeting onwards, while I undertook to look after the rest of the life on the condition that I was given full access to the large store of letters (over six hundred of them) and documents hidden away in the cupboards of their house in Grez-sur-Loing.

The work went forward slowly mainly because of the letters just mentioned. In many of them the characters were almost faded: some were often half-illegible and others were without date or even signature. Only a protracted investigation in several countries eventually decided who had written them, when and why. Then came the Great War and while it lasted there was little talk of books (this sort especially) and music. Even after its conclusion there was a minimum of public interest in any form of literature save reminiscences of politicians and soldiers, relieved only by the interminable wrangles in print of rival economists and a torrential issue of mystery thrillers. But during the past few years there has been a growing reaction, more pronouncedly evident in all areas outside Great Britain, against the continuous flow of stories about 'old unhappy far off things and battles long ago'. Correspondingly the interest in our composer, which had never quite expired, has not only revived but increased. A small accumulation of legendary lore has always clung to his name, and there is a widening desire to find out how much truth there may be in it. To satisfy that desire is the modest aim of the present work.

I acknowledge with gratitude the help I have received from Herr Erwin Delius of Bielefeld, Mr. Gerald Tetley of Danville, Virginia, Professor and Madame Merle D'Aubigné of Grez-sur-Loing, Mr. Edmond X. Kapp of Monte Carlo, Sir Thomas Armstrong, and Mr. Norman Millar, ex-Administrator of the Royal Philharmonic Orchestra, who together with its present manager, Miss Shirley Hudson, have given me unfailing co-operation. My sincere thanks are also due to the Cultural departments of the French, German, Norwegian and Russian Embassies for their invariably courteous responses to my numerous enquiries.

I

ABOUT two-thirds of the way along the highroad that runs from Cologne to Hanover is the ancient town of Bielefeld. It is a pleasantly situated spot, sheltered on the south by the Sparenberg Hill with its top crowned by a twelfth-century castle, and bordered a little farther on towards the east by the Teutoburg Forest, where stands that proud symbol of early Germanic might the giant statue of Arminius. While making no claim to rival in historical interest such near neighbours as Münster, Paderborn or Minden, it has in its own way played a prominent part in the life of Westphalia as the centre of its linen industry for over seven hundred years. In 1270 it joined the Hanseatic League.

It was towards the close of the seventeenth or the beginning of the eighteenth century that there came to it from Berenkämpen, an insignificant townlet in the vicinity, one Johann Kaspar Delius. His father Johann Daniel was the grandson of that Johannes Delius who, born in 1554 at Kleinenbremen near Minden, was the earliest of the name from whom his descendants can trace an unbroken pedigree. But even the cautious custodians of the family archives in Bielefeld are not unwilling to admit the possibility of their lineage boasting an even remoter date, although there is no documentary evidence to confirm it. That there was at least one, and probably more than one, of the same name living and flourishing during a slightly anterior period we do have adequate testimony; for during the first half of the sixteenth century we encounter the interesting and impressive figure of Matthaeus Delius. It may be advisable, in view of a consideration to be advanced presently, to give some account of this worthy.

It was in 1528 that Johannes Bugenhagen, professor in the University of Wittenberg and pastor of its Schloss Kirche, arrived in Hamburg to preach the doctrines of the Reformed Church. In connection with this enterprise he founded, with the backing of the City Council, a school situated in the St. John's Cloister and lately occupied by a chapter of Black Dominicans. He appointed Gottfried Hermelates Theophilus rector of the school and Matthaeus Delius co-rector. Inspired by the teaching innovations of Philip Melanchthon ('Praeceptor Germaniae') the institution was devoted to studies of a humanistic pattern. A complete knowledge of Latin was the prime essential of the curriculum, pursued to the slightly bigoted extent of excluding the use of German in the higher classes. Greek at the beginning was of less consequence, being limited to an acquaintance with the New Testament version in that tongue: but later on some attention was given to Homer, Hesiod and Lucian, and eventually Ancient History and Mathematics came into their own.

Theophilus remained in active control for a few years only and upon his retirement, due to ill-health, Delius succeeded to the Senior Rectorship, a post he occupied for more than three decades until his demise in 1565. On the occasion of the 400th anniversary of the foundation of the Johanneum, as the school was named, Hamburg christened nine new streets in commemoration of its most distinguished citizens, one of them being the Delius Strasse. Was there any relationship between this gentleman and the Johannes Delius of Kleinenbremen? At that time the name appears to have been far from common, and although the entire family of Matthaeus is reputed to have perished with him in the plague epidemic raging around the period of his death, it is not impossible that one of the children or some other younger relative of his may have survived.

It cannot be over-emphasized that the public records of such events are far from being complete in any country of that century, so that most statements based on oral tradition have to be examined in a spirit of reasonable doubt. Assuredly many of the accounts of his ancestry supplied by the subject of this biography fail to be taken seriously. On one occasion he informed the present writer that a certain forbear was attached to the private chapel of Edward the Sixth of England. But a painstaking search at the Public Record Office in London has failed to discover the presence upon the scene, during that reign, of anyone bearing the name of Delius, or, indeed, any other possessing a cognomen that has the slightest resemblance to it in any language. Again, every previous biography makes reference to a mysterious Gualter Delius who is alleged to have come to England in company with Melanchthon about that time. More credence might be given to this legend if it were not that the great German scholar never came here at all. It is true that he was pressed by the University of Cambridge to pay it a visit, just as he received a similar request from Francis the First to travel to Paris: but he declined both invitations.

His tenacious belief in the Dutch origin of his clan may command greater respect, and the repeated asseveration that no one of that name is to be found in Holland is hardly correct. There were several of them discoverable there as late as the end of the eighteenth and even the beginning of the nineteenth century, mainly in Rotterdam and Nijmegen, although the spelling of their patronymic had deteriorated to Dellius and even Dillius. Also it might be remembered that during the first half of the sixteenth century, the Dutch surpassed every other nation north of the Alps as much in scholarship as in most utilitarian crafts. The name is obviously a Latinized form of something cruder and less easily pronounceable,[1] and Holland was also the leader of a fashion that spread over the Empire and penetrated even France. Such examples as Erasmus, Lipsius and Vossius speak for themselves, and need excite no comment; but it does come as a mild shock to find the owner of such an attractive family inheritance as De Saumais exchanging it for the unengaging pretentiousness of Salmasius. The possibility therefore cannot be wholly eliminated that the remoter ancestors of the Delian tribe had their original home somewhere in the Low Countries, and what we do know of a certainty is that there was quite an invasion from that quarter into Westphalia and other adjacent German lands, during the closing years of the fifteenth century and the first quarter of the sixteenth.

The removal of Johann Kaspar to Bielefeld was followed at intervals during the eighteenth century by a large number of immigrant relatives from surrounding places of lesser consequence, in particular Valdorf, Versmold and Heepen. During the course of this mass movement it is interesting to note a gradual change of occupation in the major portion of it. For the best part of two centuries the name of Delius had been associated almost entirely with the professions; the Church, the Law, the Army and Government services of every kind absorbed their lives and energies, and hardly ever is one of them to be found associated with commerce or finance. But from the middle of the eighteenth century onward, as if possessed by an inwardly common impulse, they gravitated towards trade with avidity and industry.

[1] Delicq or Deligh.

15

While Bielefeld became the principal headquarters of this new field of activity, with Bremen a good auxiliary, a strong centrifugal influence took many of them to every quarter of Germany. North, south, east and west alike, saw each one of them enrolled under the banner of barter and dedicated to the ungenteel pursuit of riches. Nor were they content to remain in their own territory. France and Spain, South America and Mexico and, above all, the United States, received and made them their own. In the last-named country there are no less than fifteen separate branches of this adventurous family, and they are as widespread in their new home as in their old.

The particular group with which we are concerned had its location in Heepen, and its most prominent member was Karl Ludwig, who, born in 1760, became headmaster of its leading school and a high dignitary in the Lutheran Church. He had three sons, the youngest of whom, Ernst Friedrich, fought as an officer against the French in the later Napoleonic wars, serving under Blücher at both Ligny and Waterloo. He settled in Bielefeld and in recognition of his contribution to the cause of national liberation was appointed for life to the position of Stadtdirektor. Of his six sons, three only reached manhood, the others dying in infancy; and sometime during the late forties of the nineteenth century the surviving brothers all removed themselves to England. Ernst Oswald Friedrich, the eldest, led the way, and settling in Manchester where there was already a growing German colony, started business as a middle-man in the wool trade. He was soon in a position to invite the second son, Julius Friedrich Wilhelm, to join him, and the youngest of the trio, Emil Theodor, followed a year or two later.

Neither Ernst nor Theodor ever married; but Julius in his thirty-fifth year[1] took to himself a wife, Elise Pauline Krönig, born in 1838 and also a native of Bielefeld. By this time he had succeeded partly with the help of Ernst in establishing a branch of the business in Bradford, whither he took his bride and lived for the rest of his life. On January 29th, 1862, was born to them a child who, baptized as Fritz Albert Theodor, was to become known to the world in after years as Frederick Delius.

[1] He was born in 1822.

2

FREDERICK, as from now on we shall know him, was a sickly and ill-favoured infant, like many other famous figures such as Richelieu, Victor Hugo and Swinburne. But he successfully surmounted this early stage and in the course of a short time grew into a vigorous and lively boy of distinctly attractive appearance. He was the fourth child of the union of Julius and Elise and their second son; and during the subsequent eighteen years ten more children made their appearance, a fruitful accomplishment on the part of the immigrant parents, even for those days of prodigious families. As the years went by, their home must have been increasingly an object of curiosity to the sober and conventional citizens of Bradford, for neither father nor mother bore the smallest resemblance to anything of the sort hitherto seen in that orderly northern town.

The piety of a daughter has sought dutifully to extenuate the faults of Julius and to present him in as agreeable a light as is humanly possible. But even she is obliged to admit that their dwelling-place was an abode of fear, and that all the children alike went in terror of a tyrant who ruled his little flock with a heavy rod of iron. Proud, unbending and intolerant, he was a characteristic product of Prussian rigidity; and while he may have inspired respect, he signally failed to stimulate affection. His spouse, if outwardly of milder demeanour, was equally dogmatic and incapable of comprehending any side to a question other than her own or that of her husband. Him she survived by twenty-eight years, dying at the age of ninety-three. If she ever experienced any satisfaction at the rise to international fame of her brilliant son, she contrived to conceal it with complete success, and it is upon attested record that during the period bounded by 1905 at the one end and 1921 at the other, when his name was upon many lips in more than one continent, she never bestirred herself on any occasion to hear a note of his music. Although this self-denying ordinance might be admired as a manifestation of conjugal veneration, it may be equally deplored as one of maternal singularity. But when all the imaginable good has been spoken on their behalf, they still remain revealed as portents, probably unique even in Victorian England, and types which it can earnestly be hoped are now extinct.

It was fortunate for Frederick that he was blessed with a nature both cheerful and resilient, and was thereby able to endure with a greater equanimity than his brothers and sisters the repressive environment in which they were being raised. He was the ringleader in every childish scrape and remained undaunted by any exercise of parental reprisal. There were, however, moments when the atmosphere of the household became a little too tense for endurance, and it was then that a recurrent urge to wander out of bounds overcame him, and he indulged in one or two unsuccessful attempts to run away from it all. But these moods quickly passed and he contrived to console himself effectively with his main boyish delight, the travelling circus; his favourites in it being the bare-back riders and the trapeze artists, whose hair-raising feats he longed ardently to emulate.

After some preliminary instruction at a private institution, he was sent to the Bradford Grammar School where John Coates,[1] slightly his senior, was also a pupil. An indifferent student, he obtained little benefit from these earlier teaching courses and spent as much time as was made available to him in reading stories of the Wild West and mystery thrillers, his favourite choice being that classic of crime fiction, Sweeney Todd, the demon barber. From an early age he was drawn to music and quickly learned to strum on the pianoforte and to handle a fiddle. The story that after a single hearing of a Chopin waltz he was able to play it from memory must be qualified by his own admission later on—'not, of course, very correctly'.

Bradford for those days was more adequately supplied with musical entertainment than most provincial towns, being visited regularly by the Hallé Orchestra from Manchester as well as touring chamber music parties. There was also a fair amount of private music-making in the Delius home where visiting artists, occasionally a celebrity such as Joachim and Piatti, were made welcome. Although music was young Frederick's main delight, he was by no means an indoors lad. He rode, walked and played cricket as well as most of his fellows, on one occasion narrowly escaping lasting injury while taking

[1] Between 1900 and 1920 the most admired tenor voice in England.

part in our national summer game. Although he acquired much more proficiency on the violin than the pianoforte, it was the latter instrument which held for him the greater attraction, and at which he was to be found during most leisure hours. But it was not so much to play set pieces whether by classical or romantic masters as to indulge in a species of improvisation, which even then surprised and interested competent musicians. Probably there was little form and even less melodic invention in these impromptus, but already the urge to explore harmonic potentialities which he had not yet found in the music with which he was acquainted, may not only have been born within him but was struggling feebly to emerge.

Frederick's elder brother, Ernst, the first-born of the surviving twelve children, and his senior by some six years, had by now turned his back on Bradford and the wool trade and had emigrated to New Zealand to take up sheep farming. To Julius it seemed obvious that the vacancy thus created should be filled by his second son, who so far had evinced no repugnance to commercial life. Upon leaving the grammar school Frederick was sent to the International College, Spring Grove, at Isleworth, to learn the rudiments and routine of office life, and here he spent three years, leaving at the end of 1880. During his residence there he continued his violin lessons, played, whenever invited, his improvisations upon the pianoforte, and took advantage of the proximity of London to attend any event of musical interest that was going on at the time. At the beginning of 1881 he entered the family business.

Towards the autumn a member of its staff, realizing that an individual of such ingratiating presence and social affability could be better employed in the company's interests than sitting on a high stool adding or subtracting figures in capacious ledgers, procured his transfer to the charming old town of Stroud in Gloucestershire which for centuries had been the headquarters of the woollen industry in the western part of England. Henceforward he was to be used as travelling agent, whose function it was to secure orders for the greater glory and profit of Delius and Company, Bradford. In Stroud he was accepted as a social acquisition to a comparatively unexciting community, and as heir-apparent to a flourishing commercial concern was made welcome everywhere. The place was quite to his liking. The country around was picturesque and offered chances for many a lovely walk to such an active pedestrian as Frederick. The softer character of the southern landscape with its little hills and valleys contrasted pleasingly for a time with the severer and more spacious vistas of the Yorkshire moors, while in the vicinage was a group of ancient cities and towns which, with their cathedrals, abbeys and other monuments of a bygone age, were a happy foil to the unromantic modernity of Bradford, Leeds and Sheffield. Stroud, too, was not so far from London as to hinder the embryo merchant from slipping away occasionally to hear concerts and even opera performances, without news of this harmless truancy reaching parental ears at home. His flattering progress along the straight and narrow path of business rectitude emboldened his superiors to transfer him to Germany and the busy commercial town of Chemnitz in Saxony, the first of the several perilous errors in tactics to be committed by Julius.

Here he was given an unsalaried post in the important manufacturing establishment of Wilhelm Fogel; but his duties appear to have been so undefined that he can hardly be blamed for making use of this, his only visit since boyhood to the land of his ancestors, to partake eagerly of the feast of music everywhere about him. Dresden, with its fine and historic Opera House, was near at hand, Leipzig round the corner, and even Berlin could be reached in a few hours. The great event of this sojourn was his introduction to *Die Meistersinger*, and it is not too much to say that the sound of the wonderful score was not only a revelation to him of what Opera in the grand manner could mean, but must have set in motion a spirit of revolt against Bradford and all it represented to him. This spirit henceforth was to harden gradually during the next three years, ultimately without hope of change or cure. He even took advantage of the presence in the town of an eminent teacher of the violin, Hans Sitt, to continue his studies on that instrument. Inevitably there came the moment when the good people of Chemnitz were obliged to report home that the *volontaire*, whom in all other respects they had found amiable and delightful, was hardly, if at all, devoting himself to the task for which he had been despatched there. The consequences were a swift recall from the agreeable region of Saxony and the first rift in the hitherto pleasant relations between father and son.

It was not long afterwards, however, that Julius was persuaded to give him an opportunity of repeating his stroke of success in the bagman line at Stroud, and June 1882 saw him despatched to Sweden and the town of Norköpping, also a centre of the cloth trade. Here, probably for the reason that there was nothing else to do, he demonstrated an unexpectedly surprising initiative in pushing the interests of his firm. Orders rolled in and the Bradford counting-house sang pæans of joy and congratulation. But, alas, the celebrations were a trifle premature. After a week or so spent in Stockholm, at its very best that time of year, he found so many opportunities of comparing life in this beautiful and civilized capital with that in his own mediocre and provincial birthplace, that he conveniently forgot all about his commercial mission, betook himself to the Swedish countryside and, later in the summer, to the Norwegian mountains and fjords. This was the second nail in the coffin of Julius's hopes. The influence of the scenic grandeur of the Scandinavian Peninsula, particularly the western extremity of it, was profound, mystical and indelible. For the first time he realized his own secret affinity with high and lonely places. There he could breathe freely, and there could his spirit gain that just balance and serenity which seemed to have been banished for ever from the crowded and noisy haunts of money-seeking men. He lingered in his newly found paradise until the early autumn and returned to face a really serious manifestation of parental wrath. But this time he could plead with fair justification that his services to the deities of profit and loss had amply set off his personal indiscretions, with the result that Julius, who was now beginning to feel distinctly uneasy about the wayward tendencies of his offspring, decided that his next assignment should be in some locality free from the distracting influences both of art and nature.

This time he should go to France to make the usual contacts with agents or associates of the Yorkshire house, and St. Etienne was the spot chosen for this infelicitous experiment. Apart from the tedium in a town where nothing went on of interest except the eternal, and by this time terrifying barter of wool, he was now subjected to a kind of surveillance and kept short of ready cash: all this to render him as immobile as was physically possible in a place whose social life was hardly less monotonous and dreary than that of Bradford. Frederick was now on the threshold of manhood, had always been high-spirited and adventurous, and to isolate, or even attempt to isolate, him from the art which was gradually representing to him almost the whole meaning of life, was even less hopeful of success than the ingenuous operations of King Canute and Mrs. Partington. Deprived of his main spiritual refreshment, together with the means of procuring it, he did the like of something that might have been expected of any other young person of enterprise.

He dashed down to Monte Carlo, staked the whole of the little he possessed on the uncertain motions of the roulette table and found himself to be favoured, as on a few subsequent occasions, by the capricious deal of fortune. After several weeks of indulgence in Riviera sunshine, concerts, operas and further violin studies he was hauled back to St. Etienne and shortly afterwards to England. It is some tribute to his tenacity of purpose that Julius, in spite of these repeated set-backs, remained undefeated, and mindful of his son's partial success in the Scandinavian zone, despatched him once again to what was now to Frederick the land of his dreams.

During his earlier visit he had gained some knowledge of the Norwegian and Swedish tongues: indeed, he had a decided linguistic knack, together with a good ear for retaining both the idiom and pronunciation of any language which it interested him to acquire. When the time came round for this second trip he had mastered enough Norwegian, not only to read whatever he liked of a new and comparatively unknown literature outside its own land, but to follow in the theatre the stimulating and provocative homilies of the greatest dramatist of the age. With what thrilling interest must he have listened to that bold defiance of every political creed of the day except anarchy, and which shortly culminated in the resounding proclamations:

'The greatest tyranny is the compact majority'

and

'The strongest man is he who stands alone.'

What a proud vindication of the oppressed or undervalued individual! The position of a young man almost bursting with the unanalysable afflatus of musical emotion in a place like Bradford must have been well-nigh unbearable, but he knew only too well that any drastic step he might take to achieve independence, such as bolting off to some faraway spot, would have been received with general condemnation by the kind of community which Carlyle, Ruskin and Arnold had all scourged on the score of materialism and stupidity. 'Just another Delius

22

'boy gone wrong,' would have been the inevitable verdict of the local compact majority'. Also Frederick was the sort of semi-aristocratic type in whom only a fit of desperation would have inspired the heroic step of snapping his fingers in his father's face and walking out of the house with nothing more to his credit than the clothes upon his back. Despite his love of and admiration for Norwegian simplicity, there was nothing in him of that robust peasant strain running through many great northern characters, which rendered them indifferent to those advantages and allurements of fine raiment, food, wine and other joys of the flesh which the well-to-do of those days regarded as an inalienable right conferred on them by a discerning Providence. His game, therefore, was to temporize and bow his head to the yoke in the hope that something would turn up to obviate a family quarrel that would not be easily accommodated. Julius, now beginning to realize that it was no longer in his power to control the recalcitrancy of his second son, played his last card, which, at the same time shifted some of the responsibility from his own shoulders to those of others. He called to his aid the successors of his elder brother, Ernst,[1] who consented to take Frederick into their own establishment in Manchester. But after some comical episodes, in one of which the resident managers and the visiting subordinate exchanged positions in the firm, rather after the fashion of the two Bultitudes in Anstey's *Brass Bottle*, and with a ludicrous disorganization of the steady routine of the office, this last effort ended even more ineffectually than all those preceding it. The unavoidable result was a declaration of war between father and son; the latter now announcing his fixed intention to renounce the family business for all time. The former stormed and threatened, but to no end. The rebel had within him a fair measure of the obstinacy of his parent where his own dearest ambitions were at stake, and there was no longer any question of surrender. Nor was he now wholly without allies.

In the north there were the powerful voices of the most vigorous thinkers in Europe; and towards the south he had found in Paris a kinsman of friendly understanding. On his return journey from St. Etienne he had stopped for a few days in the French capital to visit his Uncle Theodor, who was living there in a state of semi-retirement. Just as little as his nephew did he care for British provincial life, and he listened with sympathetic interest to the tale of distress

---

[1] Ernst had died in 1879 at Torquay.

poured out to him. He advised a removal from the hated centre of the now thrice-loathed wool trade to some congenial area where the sufferer would be at peace with himself for a while, free from restraint intimidation and daily recrimination. After a time anything might happen; perhaps even the very thought of sheep might ultimately lose the power to bring out the very worst in Frederick's over-strained and nervous condition. But whatever transpired he was to avoid a breach with his father that might prove impossible of healing. With this wise counsel in mind, the nephew dissembled to the extent of half-convincing his parent that the source of his discontent was a total incapacity for the family business rather than an unbridled inclination for music. How about allowing him to try his hand in some other field of legitimate trade?

There was at this time in Bradford another firm of merchants dyers by occupation, of larger scope and longer establishment than the Delius concern. Its proprietor, John Douglas, had two sons. The elder George, was already in the business, but the younger, Charles, had little fancy for it and, like Frederick's brother Ernst, was casting an eye on distant lands and an active outdoor life. For some years past there had been an influx of bold spirits into the north-eastern part of Florida most of them drawn there by the commercial prospects of orange growing. The two young men, Frederick and Charles, put their heads together, persuaded their respective parents to find the cash for a deposit payment on what seemed after enquiries to be a suitable purchase, and made all arrangements for a speedy departure. And so it happened that on a fine day in March 1884 the couple sailed in the good ship *Gallia* for New York, proceeded also by sea to Fernandina in Georgia and thence by train to Jacksonville. There they were met by the vendor of the property, one J. R. Pride, exchanged agreements and as the roadway at that time of year was impassable, set out in a boat on the St. Johns River for their new home, Solano Grove.

3

THERE they found a smallish property of about one hundred acres and upon it a well-built wooden shack containing a sitting-room, a dining-room, two bedrooms, and a kitchen, the latter separated from the main structure by a short passage. For some years it was concluded that this building had perished through neglect, leaving no trace behind. But in the late 'thirties of the present century an energetic Jacksonville citizen and Delius enthusiast, Mrs. Henry L. Richmond, succeeded in locating it, not without some difficulty. Its authenticity has been further established by another lady until lately a resident in St. Augustine, Mrs. Louis Pacetti, who in her girlhood lived on a plantation nearby, and remembers well the return of the composer there in 1897. As will be seen, it is in a partially ruined state, but the progress of decay has now been arrested and the cottage together with a portion of the original estate still known as Solano Grove has been acquired and converted into a Delius shrine by its public-spirited renovator. In the foreground rolled the wide St. Johns, one of the four rivers of the world to flow northward. Spanish moss abounded everywhere, adding much to the charm and mystery of its banks. A giant oak, with a limb-spread of over ninety feet, stood sentinel near the water's edge, and immediately in front of the house were palms, pines and immense magnolia trees. Around it were the various estates of the English colony of Picolata, some of considerable importance, with dwellings frequently large and elegant.

Frederick's first preoccupation was with the exotic beauty of his surroundings, and, just as the simple grandeur of the Norwegian mountain ranges appealed overpoweringly to one side of his nature, so did the heavy, lush and tropical profusion of this the most southern of the States of the great Union, strike another answering chord within him. Austerity and luxuriance like two originally opposite poles began from this moment to draw nearer to one another, although more than a decade was to pass before they became united in the indistinguishable amalgam revealed in the work of his maturity. For a short while he enjoyed a purely solitary and contemplative existence, but before long, his mind and spirit tranquillized by an aspect of Nature wholly

Map of the St. Johns River in North-East Florida showing approximate site of the Delius Estate at Solano Grove (marked ■)

novel to him, he took part in the social life created by the neighbours around him. The property adjoining the Grove was occupied by a family with whom he became on terms of close intimacy. The wife of the owner, Charles Edward Bell, and a member of the prominent Norwegian family Mordt, was a friend of Grieg and a devotee of music. As young Douglas had little love for the arts it was pleasant to enjoy the company of someone who shared his tastes and quickly recognized in him the signs of original talent.

Mrs. Bell became one of the three main influences at this time in aiding the restoration of his self-confidence and a belief in his mission. For years after his return to Europe he maintained a regular correspondence with her in which he more than once admits his obligation to her sympathy and percipience. The second and in many respects the most abiding impression made upon him was the Negro life with which he was in daily contact. When not fishing or alligator hunting, he passed most of his evenings listening to the unfamiliar sound of the music produced for his enjoyment by his unsophisticated coloured friends, and here he heard something he had failed to find in the so-called classical music which delighted the Teutonic taste of Bradford. This revelation helped partially to satisfy vague yearnings that had been intermittently aroused in him, and served to strengthen a suspicion that there did exist harmonic, as well as melodic worlds unsuspected by the traditionalists of Germany and England.

The joint occupation of the shack by the two young men was not destined to be of long duration and its termination coincided with another important, perhaps the most important single event in the Floridian episode of Frederick's career. Charles had a sharp attack of malarial fever and his companion hurried off to Jacksonville to secure medical aid. The doctor who had been recommended was not for the moment at home, and to pass the time he entered a music shop, retired to a room where there was a piano and sat down to improvise. A visitor to the store, struck by the uncommon sounds that were reaching him, insisted on introducing himself to their author, who was revelling in his first encounter with a keyboard since landing in the New World. To Frederick's surprise and pleasure the stranger proved to be a professional musician from New York who was visiting the south for his health. The pair were delighted with one another to such a degree that Frederick for the rest of the day forgot all about his errand of mercy, and remembered to call again upon the doctor too late for anything to be done in the way of returning to the Grove until the following day. It might have fared ill with Charles had not his nearest neighbour happened to look in and take control of the case. This indifference on Frederick's part to his friend's condition, in view of the habitual kindness and consideration he showed to everyone with whom he had any association, would be difficult of belief were it not

confirmed by the testimony of several credible persons on the spot
On the other hand a somewhat mitigating account has related that he
did really keep in touch with the secretary of the physician who was
temporarily absent, and that his messages failed to be passed on. Anyway, Charles lost no time in changing his quarters and seeking the
companionship of those upon whom he felt he could better rely for
timely aid in an uncertain climate.

Frederick remained for a few days in Jacksonville in the company
of his new friend, a certain Thomas F. Ward, organist of a Jesuit
Church in Brooklyn, procured a piano for the cottage, and finding
on his return there that Charles had left, invited Ward to stay in his
place. There the two musicians communed and worked together for
several months, the younger man benefiting incalculably from the
instruction of the elder (Ward was just over thirty) in the mechanic
of counterpoint and fugue. Indeed, he always declared that the only
teaching of any real value he ever received was that of the invalid
refugee from New York. Of special importance was the insight of his
mentor in recognizing that he had found a pupil of an uncommon
kind, bursting with enthusiasm and hungry for knowledge as well as
encouragement. The disciple tried his hand at a few songs, only one of
which—under the English title of 'Over the Mountains High'
(Björnsen)—has survived. There are also a few short piano pieces
among them 'Zum Carneval', a lively polka, which was published at
the beginning of 1885 in Jacksonville.

Towards the end of July there appeared at the Grove an emissary
from Bradford with instructions to take up the option contained in
the provisional agreement signed by Frederick and Charles on their
arrival and to complete the purchase of the estate. Accordingly on
August 13th a fresh contract was executed under which Julius became
its sole owner. This transfer of interests was facilitated by the retirement from the situation of Charles, who had now acquired another
property of which he was still in possession many years later. There
is nowhere any suggestion that the new deal was consummated without the full knowledge and consent of Frederick, and this casts some
doubt upon the authenticity of a statement made in another biography
that just prior to this event he had written home requesting parental
approval to his quitting Florida and proceeding to Leipzig to continue
his musical studies. Most persons, I fancy, would find it hard to believe
that Frederick, who had been no more than a few months in the region

of his own choice, who was for the first time in several years at peace with the world and who, in the company of Ward, was enjoying life as never before, should dream of presenting a request which he must have known quite well would be met with a blank refusal. Also, would he not be running the risk of provoking charges against himself of frivolity and irresponsibility that might not be wholly unjustified? On the other hand if any such request had been received by Julius, it was not out of keeping with his authoritarian tendencies to allow the option to lapse automatically, and afterwards to take control of the property, with a view to confining his son in a remote corner of the New World, from which escape to the dangerous area of Europe would be far from easy. As Frederick had always been financially dependent upon him, he may have convinced himself that the poor fellow would never have the courage and energy to strike out on his own. And so the pendulum of argument could be said to swing in fairly even motion with a slight bias in Frederick's favour, and against the probability that it was at this particular moment he had released such an untimely bombshell.

None the less, I have small doubt that the Leipzig project had been more than casually discussed between him and Ward. To the elder man, as to most musicians of his generation nearly everywhere, the great German centre of education stood for infallibility and commanded a veneration almost equal to that of the devout Moslem for Mecca. In the early autumn Ward returned to Jacksonville, where he had secured a permanent post, and Frederick remained alone in his cottage. But he was no longer the discouraged and debilitated creature who had arrived there six months earlier. He had recovered his former health and strength, was enriched with a novel fund of valuable instruction and was beginning to feel the need of some livelier and more widespread field of action. Florida was well enough in its way, but the tranquillity and isolation which at first had proved so beneficial were gradually becoming cloying and irksome. Clearly he must try to find some way of escape; but how was it to be accomplished? Through his acquiescence in the purchase of the Grove, he had placed himself under a definite obligation towards his father to remain there as both resident and overseer; obviously the place could hardly be left to run itself without some sort of supervision. From this tantalizing dilemma he was rescued by a surprising stroke of luck. This was the unexpected appearance in November of his elder brother, who was supposed by everyone including Frederick to be far away in New Zealand. Ernst had grown tired of the sheep farming experiment, was on the look-out for a new job, had heard of Frederick's adventure and was curious to see if there was anything in it for himself.

The descent of the newcomer upon the scene seemed hardly less than a dispensation of Providence. Ernst, after a decent interval, would step into his shoes and protect the family interest in the property, while he, Frederick, would disappear into the vast void of the States, to pursue the calling which he had now decided was the only one for which he had either inclination or aptitude. So, leaving his brother in possession, he removed himself to Jacksonville in the early part of 1885, where he set up as teacher of music, eking out a meagre and precarious living by singing in the choir of the local synagogue. From this scarcely auspicious commencement of a new career he was extricated by another romantic interposition of Fate. There appeared in the local Press an advertisement for the services of a teacher of music, competent to instruct the two daughters of a certain Professor Ruckert in the town of Danville, Virginia. Communication with this gentleman elicited that the help of the right sort of pedagogue was badly needed in the main educational centre of the place, and would be rewarded with a large following of pupils, all willing to pay handsomely for the genuine sort of enlightenment. He obtained glowing recommendations from Ward and the Rabbi of the Synagogue which had enjoyed for some weeks the benefit of his vocal endowment (he had a light baritone voice), scraped together enough money for the five-hundred-mile journey, and left Florida behind him.

He must have been a little surprised on arriving in Danville, to find himself heralded and advertised in advance as a celebrity who had deigned to honour the town with his presence, and very soon 'Professor Delius' became an unqualified success socially as well as musically. Danville, although of moderate size at that time, was a fairly important centre of the tobacco industry, wealth was on the increase and the unlooked-for arrival of a famous, talented and handsome young man acted as a galvanic shock upon the feminine portion of its population. Inside a few weeks he had more pupils than he could conscientiously handle and for the first time in his life tasted the sweets of financial independence. He was appointed music preceptor at the Roanoke Female College, a finishing school for young ladies of the Baptist denomination, and here he taught anything that anyone

30

wanted to learn about the mysteries of music-making. He demonstrated his capabilities as performer by playing at a concert the Mendelssohn Violin Concerto, a work for which in later years he always professed a particular regard, considering it to be in respect of style and craft a model of its kind, and also gave private lessons in French and German.

He found an enthusiastic admirer and loyal supporter in the most influential amateur of the town, Robert S. Phifer (originally Pfeiffer), who, impressed by the story of Frederick's difficulties with his family, took upon himself some months later to write to Julius in the warmest terms of his young friend's talent. Naturally this kindly act of appreciation failed to elicit any response, and Frederick remained at Danville, piling up the dollars until the spring of 1886. Having satisfied himself that he could make money out of his music one way or another, he had ceased to communicate with or trouble his mind any more about Bradford. It might even be possible to amass enough for the grand project of returning someday to Europe on his own account.

But Danville was only a milestone on his way; he needed a larger centre for his ambitions and this must be the commercial capital of the Republic. He bade goodbye to his large group of friends, bestowed a ring by way of troth upon the most attractive of his female pupils and set off for New York. How long he remained and precisely what he did there is far from clear. There is a faintly circumstantial story that, backed by introductions from Danville sponsors, he secured an organist's post in a Manhattan church; but industrious research has failed to discover any evidence of it. It might be that in a city where almost any building over twenty years old is rated as obsolete or derelict, the church in question has long since been demolished, leaving no trace behind. But against that supposition is the fact that ecclesiastical structures of all kinds have a stronger hold upon existence than those of a lay order, and for that reason, in default of some fresh testimony, the report had better be relegated like so many others to the realm of fancy. What we do know, however, is that he stayed some little while with a friend living on Long Island, whom he had met in Jacksonville. But wherever Frederick went or what he was doing had now become a disturbing problem to the family in Bradford, who had received no news of him for over half a year. Meanwhile the volatile Ernst, after a short occupation of the Grove, had also taken himself off to unknown parts, leaving the property untenanted and untended. It is little wonder that, faced with a situation which baffled his ability to handle from afar, Julius decided it might be wiser to make some effort to secure the return of his second son to Europe on certain conditions. He had been moved to write to Phifer for news, and a portion of the answer received had filled him with amazement. That his unmanageable offspring should have gone into the unknown to make music after his own limited fashion was sufficiently surprising: the staggering disclosure was the capacity of the incalculable fellow to coin money out of it, and easy money at that. Eventually, through the efforts of a private enquiry agent, Frederick's whereabouts were discovered and his father was enabled to get into touch with him.

It is with little relish that I find it necessary to confute some of the statements that have appeared in all other biographies touching the relations between Frederick and his parents; but there is rather less than a half-truth in the assertion that Julius considered the career of a musician to be unworthy of a gentleman. He had previously poured cold water upon the idea of a son of his taking up music professionally, for the simple reason that he saw therein no financial security for him. Neither he nor anyone else in his circle had the slightest idea that Frederick had in him a spark of original talent as a composer, and he was sufficiently well acquainted with the lives of even the greatest masters to know that many of them had led impecunious and troubled existences. He was aware, of course, that some of the giants of executive music, Liszt, Rubinstein and Joachim had done very well for themselves in a material way; but these spectacular figures were incomparable and their accomplishments entirely beyond the reach of a member of his own family. Around him everywhere he saw examples of the conditions in which the musician of mediocrity lived, and from these he honestly desired to save his son.

He was therefore more than a little bewildered that the refractory and obstinate youth, whom he was striving to rescue from committing a lifelong mistake, had been making over a period of several months a substantial name and subsistence in a comparatively unimportant provincial town. What might he not do in one of the great American cities, with the necessary credentials at his back? There seemed to be sense after all in the lad's ambition to go to Leipzig, as reported by Phifer, for a successful course at the great institution founded by Mendelssohn and Schumann might give a young man of promise

Claremont, the birthplace of Delius

Cow and Calf Rocks, Ilkley. A favourite walk

The cottage at Solano Grove

View from the verandah

just the extra touch of honourable dignity, an accolade in fact, weighty enough to carry him along the road anywhere to fame and fortune. Briefly, when Julius consented to bear the expense of an eighteen-months' course at Leipzig, he stipulated that his son upon the termination of his novitiate should return to the States and continue the career so unexpectedly and propitiously begun.

Full evidence of this bargain is to be found in correspondence passing a few years later between Frederick and other members of the family. For instance, his mother when writing to him on one occasion about his complicated financial affairs, insists

'that you went to Virginia was your blessing as that was the only time that you made a living for yourself. Then you were sent to Leipzig, which again cost hundreds [of pounds] with the object of obtaining a diploma and returning to America to do even better.... Even Theodor told us you ought to go back to America. You will have to do something, for on your future fame you cannot live. Go back to America as we have told you over and over again; there you have a future as other musicians have discovered.'

Having seen Frederick safely embarked on his return voyage to England which took place shortly after midsummer on the S.S. *Aurania*, let us consider for a brief moment the significance of this adventure in the New World, particularly that part of it spent in Florida. He had arrived there, to use his own words, in a 'state of complete mental demoralization'. The long struggle at home extending over three years had worked havoc with any capacity for ordered thought or mental concentration. Gradually regaining that equilibrium of mind which hitherto he had known only during his stolen escapades in Scandinavia, he had begun to think of music imaginatively, and there slowly grew within him not only the conviction that there was something he had to say on his own account, but a glimmering of how he would say it. The help and companionship of Ward, the third and decisive agency in moulding his future, was not only guiding but provocative. Others about him in Danville had a dim idea that the odd sounds produced by his improvisations on the piano were novel or intriguing. It was Ward alone who sensed how these impromptus might be translated into written forms of interest and validity. The impressions created within him by an exotic landscape and the simple Negro life with its songs and dances lingered for long years in his memory. If his spirit was attuned to hyperborean regions, snow-clad mountains where no birds sang, and mighty fjords, his senses were captured by and remained in willing bondage to the antithetical opulence of the tropical South.

4

Leipzig in the fourth quarter of the last century could make some claim to be the cultural capital of the Germanic world. Its Opera House, hitherto outrivalled by those of Vienna, Munich and Dresden, had acquired a new prestige due largely to the proselytizing activities of Angelo Naumann, that arch-propagandist of the Wagnerian creed. Its orchestra was at least highly efficient, its Conservatoire the recognized national centre of musical education and its annual fair attracted, just as it had done since the Middle Ages, all the book traders and half the students of Central Europe.

Although Frederick's later attitude towards the instructional opportunities provided by the Conservatoire may have been casual or even contemptuous, the preservation of notebooks crammed with fugal and other contrapuntal devices testifies that during the rest of the year and the early part of 1887 he attended his classes with some regularity. The teaching staff, while unable to compete in glamour with that of the preceding generation, boasted a respectable professorial group in Reinecke, Jadassohn and Sitt, and perhaps a more potent influence than any other of a permanent kind was the presence of Adolf Brodsky, who with his quartet not only gave regular performances of the bulk of the classical repertoire, but with refreshing goodwill gave a trial to any novelty of merit, whether it came from a tried or untried quarter. Brahms and Tschaikowsky occasionally came to conduct their own works and the visits of Nikisch to direct Wagner at the Opera House, especially in performances of *Tristan und Isolde*, were genuinely red-letter days.

No traces of authorship during the autumn months of 1886 have survived, but there are some modest efforts dating from the beginning of 1887. These are a group of part-songs for mixed voices and include a version of Heine's 'Lorelei', an Ave Maria with German words, and four settings of Björnsterne Björnsen poems entitled:

'Sonnenscheinlied'   'Frühlingsanbruch'
'Durch den Wald'   'Oh! Sonnenschein'.

They are all pleasing trifles, and while sufficiently well written, reveal little of the harmonic originality that began to make its appearance two years later. During the summer vacation he betook himself to Norway, visiting mainly the central area around Vik and Stalheim; and here, inspired by his surroundings, made a considerable number of instrumental sketches, all distinctly Scandinavian in style, with now and then a hint of unorthodoxy in the part-writing. Whether it was the trip to his beloved north or some other and unknown influence, he plunged upon his return to Leipzig into a steady course of creative activity which marks the start of his career as a composer of promise. The pieces that have come down to us are:

A Tone Poem—*Hiawatha* (begun at this time and completed in the early part of 1888).

Two short orchestral works:
   Ein Schlitten fahrt.
   Marche Caprice.

A Suite—*Florida*,

and a conventional setting of Heine's famous poem:

'Ein Fichtenbaum Steht Einsam'.

Although the four instrumental compositions, with the exception of a few passages of *Florida*, reveal little of the comparative maturity of manner that we shall encounter in the songs of 1889 and his first opera *Irmelin*, they are none the less all of them free from Teutonic influence, either in ideas or style; an achievement, having regard to his environment, distinctly creditable for a young man still in his apprentice stage. *Hiawatha*, a budding and not wholly unsuccessful attempt to capture the atmosphere of wild woodland life, is a

36

longish piece with two main sections of a serious and flowing character divided by a sprightly dance movement. Like nearly everything else that its author ever wrote, it ends quietly; in this instance with a passage illustrating the departure of the hero:

> In the glory of the sunset
> In the purple mists of evening.

Its chief weakness is an unequal and sketchy scheme of instrumentation, suggesting that Frederick was as yet only experimenting with that grand vehicle of sound, the full orchestra. Both *Florida* and the little *Marche* owe their superiority over it to the careful revision of them eighteen months later.

There existed during the early part of the present century a marked tendency to ignore or neglect the earlier works of those composers who later on had produced a string of acknowledged masterpieces. In the case of Mozart, the only pieces with which the public had been made really familiar were the four last symphonies, two operas, three piano concertos, a handful of sonatas, together with a few masses and motets. Of the remaining six hundred compositions a vast ignorance prevailed. It is only in the last few years that a sustained attempt has been made to rescue from oblivion the first six symphonies of Schubert, anything in that line prior to the *Unfinished* having been thought unworthy of serious notice. Only now is it being realized that these Cinderellas not only have a wealth of beautiful music, but are often in part, if not in whole, truly characteristic of one of the world's greatest masters. During the second half of the nineteenth century the heavens positively rained down marvels of inspiration upon us, and as the facilities for performance were meagre compared with those of today, it became perhaps inevitable that interest should be aroused by and concentrated upon those of instant appeal. But those golden days are over. We are now in the leaden age of music, and are fortunate if any year brings forth one new piece of moderate attraction. And yet by the irony of circumstance the opportunities for hearing music of all sorts have increased tenfold. If the present approved and hackneyed repertoire both in the theatre and concert-hall is not to run out in staleness and exhaustion, recourse must be had to that ample supply of superior merit that languishes unheard.

That the necessity of such a revival is at last being recognized is indicated by the renewed interest in the lesser-known operas of the Italian masters and in Handel, Haydn, Gluck and Berlioz, not to mention half a dozen of the smaller men. It is hoped then that the attention both of musicians and the Public may turn towards our composer and the considerable quantity of work he turned out between 1889 and 1900, hardly any of which has yet reached recognition or even audition. That Delius himself is partly responsible for this neglect may be freely admitted. He viewed with indifference the publication of virtually all the output of the period above-mentioned; an indifference due to the realization of a steadily growing development within himself, which rejected the accomplishment of each succeeding lustrum as unrepresentative. Even after the all but total ripeness of *A Village Romeo and Juliet* and the absolute fulfilment of *A Mass of Life* he was minded to talk about the new turn his work was about to take; and his *Fennimore and Gerda*, completed about 1910, is an experiment in operatic form that signalizes a deliberate severance from that of all its predecessors.

Returning to 1888 and the *Florida Suite* in particular, we have here a composition more than competently laid out for orchestra, and there is little in it for hardly any composer under thirty years of age to be ashamed of. The Suite contains four movements:

Day Break	Sunset
On the River	Night

The first opens with the theme to be used six years afterwards as the prelude to his opera *The Magic Fountain* and includes an extended version of the La Calinda Dance incorporated in the second act of *Koanga*. 'On the River' is an effective and well-made little piece typical of the earliest Delian manner. 'Sunset' after a quiet opening drifts into another lively dance, inspired by the kindly remembrance of his Negro friends on the plantations and the vesperal entertainment provided by them for his amusement. 'Night' recalls briefly the opening passages of 'Day Break' and then passes on to a quiet and lengthy episode in which horns play a charming and prominent part. The two short pieces are both concise and spirited, and the second of them, which now has been both published and recorded, is altogether satisfactory, notably in the free and effective use of the orchestra.

With the turn of the year came the hard necessity for Frederick to consider what his position was likely to be at the conclusion of his final term in the coming April, when the eighteen months conceded by his family would come to an end. The prospect of an early return to America had become increasingly distasteful to him, as he was by no means certain of finding there anything like the kind of life he had been living in Leipzig. Although his powers of invention had been stimulated by association with musical minds of worth and accomplishment, he had not yet acquired enough confidence in his ability to choose for himself a career other than the one mapped out for him. He therefore first took the step of submitting some of his compositions to the scrutiny of a recognized master of the craft, who was then in Leipzig; and it must have been not only to his relief but profound satisfaction that he received an answer dated Feburary 28th:

'Dear Sir,

Your manuscripts have given me a pleasant surprise, in fact they really excited me, and I recognize in them a very great talent of vast resource, indeed one aiming at the highest goal. Whether you will achieve your end depends solely on how your material circumstances shape themselves. If in the interest of your career you will allow me to offer you some advice it would be that, instead of taking a regular position, you should devote yourself entirely to the study of your art and follow your own true nature and the call of your ideals. For that purpose it is essential that you should choose the environment which your genius demands.

It is my sincerest wish that you should find in your own country the recognition that you deserve, and also the means to achieve your noble purpose which I don't doubt for a moment you will.

Assuring you of my warmest sympathy,

Yours faithfully,

EDWARD GRIEG.'

Two conclusions at least may reasonably be drawn from the style and contents of this letter. The relations between the older and younger musician are still on a formal basis, thus discounting the authenticity of statements which have suggested some degree of an earlier intimacy. Also Frederick must have taken Grieg a little into his confidence over the position of affairs in England, and have sought his opinion as to the desirability of obtaining some appointment, possibly a professorship that would free him from dependence upon his family. But with an insight into the character of the pieces in question, which cannot be too highly extolled, the great Norwegian had recognized the presence of gifts which needed for their full and fortunate development not only time, but sympathetic surroundings. Unfortunately the attainment of this end might necessitate the continuance over an indefinite period of those slender financial resources supplied somewhat grudgingly by the old folks at home, and the chances of procuring any such benefit appeared decidedly remote.

It was no wonder then, in spite of the gratifying recognition of his abilities on the part of an admitted expert, that his uneasiness as to what the immmediate future might yield grew apace as the day of his departure drew near. But he had determined before leaving to strike another blow for his cause, which was to discover how the music that on paper had been lauded so highly would really sound when submitted to the test of actual performance. Some reference can be found in nearly every piece of Delian literature to the amusing circumstances under which *Florida* obtained its first hearing. How in place of the usual cash remuneration the members of the orchestra, conducted by Hans Sitt himself, received a liberal supply of good German beer. Evidently the rigid and occasionally repressive code imposed by the trade union regulations of a later day were not in force at that time. The result was a distinct success for the young composer, and his satisfaction was unreservedly shared by his new friend and protector.

Easter came round and it must have been with some regret that he had to say goodbye to a place where, if he had added little to his store of academic knowledge, he had spent many happy hours, heard any amount of good music, viewed and even talked with artists of the highest rank, and had formed friendships, many of which continued while life lasted in undiminished cordiality. It was therefore in a slightly more hopeful mood that, fortified by the goodwill and approbation of his associates and the expectation of a certificate which would bear witness that he had passed his examinations with honours, he returned to his native land. Proceeding at once to Bradford, he arrived there on April 11th and the following day wrote to Grieg who was still in Leipzig.

'I do not think I shall be able to remain here very long. I miss you all a great deal, and this sudden transition to conditions so totally different from those I have left is depressing in the extreme. If you feel like spending a couple of days with me here I should be very happy to make you and your wife welcome. If not, I hope we shall meet in London before I leave for Paris. Do write me a few lines when you have the time and feel like it.'

To this Grieg replied on April 16th:

'You ask me to write when I have the inclination and time. The first I have in a high degree but hardly a moment to spare of the second. I can well see that you are breathing an air which is different in more than one sense, and as you know, work thrives only in a congenial climate. We cannot unfortunately accept your kind invitation to come to Bradford, and as for seeing you in London, it will not be more than a mere handshake there. . . .
Yours in friendship,
Most devotedly,
EDWARD GRIEG.'

The purpose of Grieg's forthcoming visit was a concert of his works to be given at St. James's Hall, and the composer, accompanied by his wife, journeyed as planned on April 24th, finding quarters at No. 3, The Cedars, Clapham Common, the residence of Mr. John Augener, the head of the publishing firm of that name. Awaiting him was another communication from Frederick:

'Many thanks for your letter which gave me much pleasure. You will by now have arrived in London and I hope you had a pleasant trip. Our fine times in Leipzig have now faded into the past, days of good fellowship such as I have never known elsewhere. On Monday I am coming to London and shall stay at the Hotel Metropole. Will you and your dear wife have supper with me on the 4th or 5th, when we can have one of our pleasant evenings?'

To this he received an answer dated the 26th from Nina Grieg:

'Many thanks for your letter from Bradford which we have just received. Please do not mind if I reply, but Grieg is terribly busy now and has no time for writing. Unfortunately he is quite out of sorts with everything and everybody, and wishes he hadn't come to London. Let us hope he will feel better after the concert. The weather is foul, windy and cold, almost like winter and we long for those lovely days in Leipzig. We should be happy if we could see you again and be together for a little while: in any case we accept with pleasure your kind invitation for May 4th.'

When a few days later Frederick came to London, the weather had changed for the better, and Grieg, once more his naturally amiable self, was delighted to see him again. Although of a warm and affectionate nature, he did not easily form new associations, and his rapidly grown attachment to his young friend was a highly unusual event in his life, as may be gathered from a passage in another letter of his written about this time, where he says, 'I must tell you that very rarely have I met anyone who has given me so much pleasure.' Accordingly, his restored tranquillity of mind, coupled with a sincere interest in the difficulties of a much-harassed fellow musician, were propitious to the execution of a plan, by which a very lame dog might be helped over an exceedingly awkward stile. Delius senior would also be visiting London at the beginning of May, and the storming of the citadel of resistance might be attempted at the same time.

We have been led to believe by all previous historians of this period in our story, that, until the eventful moment when a dogmatic father was brought into the presence of a famous musician who over the dinner-table completely talked him round, the former had no intention of aiding and abetting his son in the pursuit of a career which, so we are told, he considered unfit for any gentleman. There is no substance, as I have already related, in this unconvincing piece of fiction. The new plan placed before Julius involved a continued residence in Europe for a period of time over which Frederick's manifest talent as a composer would flower and flourish. The recognition of it would not only confer on him a higher distinction, but almost certainly guarantee richer financial rewards than if he became known to the public only as a pedagogue. If Julius two years earlier had been surprised to hear that any child of his could make good money out of music, he was positively astounded by the suggestion that he had brought into the world a man of genius. Frankly he did not credit it, either then or at any later date. The thing was too fantastic for belief. But confronted with the honest opinion of a world-renowned and highly successful musician, he compromised for the moment with his own convictions. Frederick should have a further chance even if he, Julius, thought that nothing of consequence would ever come of it. After all, America was still in the background and if everything else failed, there remained at the end of a long and winding road Bradford and the safe haven of the wool and noil trade. Reluctantly he gave his consent, but to make certain that Frederick would have no outlet for his tastes and energies other than hard work at his chosen calling, he declined to raise the allowance he was willing to contribute towards the experiment beyond the sum of two pounds weekly.

The prospect might have appeared daunting if he were to be dependent entirely on this none too princely provision; but Frederick had already sounded his uncle in Paris with a view to the latter giving him a helping hand in the event of Julius doing no more than furnish what most persons would judge to be a minimum allowance for mere living expenses. Theodor responded as anticipated, and for the time being it seemed as if the four years' struggle of Art against Commerce had terminated in Frederick's favour. It now remained with the victor to decide what his next move should be.

5

IT MIGHT have been expected that his eyes would be turned to Germany, where music was more actively cultivated than anywhere else, and whose prestige was paramount in more than one continent. This is certainly what ninety per cent of non-Teutonic musicians would have planned, and what would have seemed the obvious thing for Frederick to do. But to a few watchers of the skies it was becoming convincingly evident that the sceptre of sovereignty in the creative sphere of Europe's music held by the Fatherland for nearly two hundred years was slipping rapidly from its grasp, and that he whose need was a fresher and truer fount of inspiration must seek it in another land. Such a development would hardly be observed or even suspected in England, always the last member of the European family to learn what was really happening outside its island limits. And a further quarter of a century, if indeed not longer in certain circles, had to run its course before our musicians could bring themselves to believe that German supremacy in the one field of art where it had for so long been pre-eminent had now vanished, and possibly for ever. But to one young Englishman at least not only was this sufficiently clear, but much more besides concerning the community among which he had been living for a year and a half.

It has been said, as if it were an adequate explanation or cause of his outlook upon life generally, that Delius was a rebel. This is true, but only to the extent of being but one out of thousands of the ripening minds of his day, who were in revolt against that formidable mass of mental and spiritual inertia in which they were imprisoned. For more than a generation our own sages had raged and inveighed against all classes of the British nation in respect of their low standard of culture, complacency and inaccessibility to ideas, especially if they happened to proceed from any foreign source. In that case they could not be other than pernicious and must be instantly rejected. Frederick was doubly unfortunate inasmuch as, in addition to the oppressive weight of an antipathetic public environment, he had to endure, as I have already written, all the repression of a typically Teutonic home where parental authority was almost as absolute as that of the Roman Republic during its earlier days.

Pleasant as had been his brief residence in Leipzig, with its quasi-university atmosphere, he had small taste for German life and thought in general. That which he required above all else for his inward content and the orderly development of his talent, was less a purely musical society—*per se*—than one in which men spoke their minds without fear of ostracism on the part of their neighbours, wrote down their honest convictions without the interdiction of censorship and, best of all, enjoyed immunity from the sinister influence of narrow prejudice and petty tyranny. This being his ultimate desideratum, it was inevitable that Frederick's instinct and experience should lead him to share the view of Germany's brighter spirits that the mind of that nation, so far from refining and expanding during its eighteen years' rise to political and commercial greatness, had coarsened and contracted. Material success had gone dangerously to the head of a people unaccustomed to it, and who were indulging lavishly in the pathetic belief that an increase of wealth and power must automatically generate a sudden elevation of spirit and access of wisdom.

It was therefore to an area of wider social freedom and livelier interchange of thought that his inclination was directed, and to its capital city in particular, which for the past two hundred years had been the undisputed intellectual centre of Europe. A factor of a more practical nature was the presence there of a fairly wealthy relative, his father's brother, who had always looked upon his nephew with a kindly eye. A man of cosmopolitan outlook and discernment, with an agreeable contrast in social philosophy to his kinsman in Yorkshire, he had been both interested in and amused by the appearance in the family of one who combined in himself much charm of manner and a stubborn capacity for getting his own way over an issue that seemed to the little circle way north hardly short of a catastrophe. Accordingly he had demonstrated his approval of the step Frederick was taking, by supplementing the modest provision which Julius was finding for his son's maintenance with a contribution from his own pocket, which he continued for the next seven years.

These material arrangements for his immediate future now

accomplished, the happy object of them lost no time in transferring himself to Paris, where he took up a temporary residence in his uncle's apartment in the Rue Cambon, until such time as he could find suitable quarters of his own. For a few weeks after his arrival he did little but frequent the opera houses and concert-rooms, and renew acquaintance with a few writers and painters whom he had met on their visits to Germany. Early in May he takes his pen to let Grieg, this time back in Norway, know how he is getting on:

'I am now more settled down and must say that so far I find everything most pleasing. There is in the air something quite different to anything in England or Germany. Life and work here are noteworthy, and one can imagine that the very streets enjoy living. . . . I heard the last Lamoureux concert yesterday and must say that for ensemble and finesse the orchestra is much better than that of Leipzig.'

A few weeks later we find him again writing to Grieg, who has quitted Bergen without leaving another address, and it is not without interest to note an impression already forming in his mind, which he never subsequently saw reason to modify.

'The last eighteen days I have been quite alone here: my uncle has been in London and returned only today. The whole time I have worked and have written a lot, several songs and *Paa Vidderne* of Ibsen, a piece for tenor voice and orchestra. For you I have written two songs for remembrance which I should like to send to you when I know your exact address. . . . It is very beautiful in Paris, but I shouldn't like to live here always. The French are very artistic, but it is always a slightly empty art. The great strength of nature is lacking and it is generally too refined and artificial. But one can learn a great deal here. The people are free, have power, and everyone does as he likes, quite different to Germany. . . .'

A projected trip to Spain failing to materialize, he returned to Bradford for a week or two in August and then set off to St. Malo for September, where he began but never completed a set of variations in rhapsody form for full orchestra. From here he explored the whole coastline of Brittany, increasingly to be a favourite resort of his.

Shortly before this he had sent a batch of songs to Grieg for approval. These were (including the two songs of 'remembrance'):

'Slumber Song'	(Björnsen)
'The Nightingale'	(Welhaven)
'Summer Eve'	(Paulsen)
'Longing'	(Kjerulf, Th.)
'Sunset'	(Munck, A.)
'Now Sinks the Summer Evening'	(Ibsen)
'Dream Roses'	(Heinitz-Marie)
'Quicker, my horse'	(Geibel)

The last-named has had a curious history. It was highly praised by Grieg, was translated into French under the title of 'Plus vite, mon cheval', was sung in more countries than one, and for some reason known only to the composer, was arbitrarily withdrawn by him from circulation eight or nine years later.

On his return to Paris he found a letter dated September 23rd from Grieg, who gives his opinion of the songs sent to him:

'You have given us great joy with your songs and my wife thanks you very much for the dedication. . . . There are so many deeply felt things in them . . . and one day I shall show you that I can steal after all. Yet there are other things which don't appeal to me—I don't mean in the ideas themselves, for nowhere do you lack invention, but in the handling of the voice. A Norwegian tune and a Wagnerian vocal line—these are dangerous things to bring together: but we shall talk about it.'

We do not know if Frederick completed his *Paa Vidderne* scene for tenor voice and orchestra: probably not, for there is no extant trace of it. But he continued to be fascinated enough by the subject to plunge into a more ambitious and hazardous experiment with it. This was a melodrama, the music accompanying a recitation of the entire poem and covering over one hundred and twenty pages of orchestral score. He worked on it assiduously throughout the later summer and, towards the latter part of October, forwarded the piece together with a fresh handful of songs to Grieg, who replies on November 6th:

'This letter I have written to tell you that after closer acquaintance with your songs I look at them with different eyes. As little flattering to me, it is all the more so for you and your songs. They are so beautifully felt and I shall never become so stupid as not to recognize that this is what matters.'

About this time he removed from the Rue Cambon to Ville d'Avray, a charming village some six miles out of Paris and on the main road to Versailles. On the banks of a small lake was and still is an old-established and famous inn, Les Chaumières de Cabassud, founded in 1845. Corot for many years owned a studio and apartment in its grounds which also contained on the opposite side a few small cottages, which have now been replaced by larger buildings used when custom is more than usually high. One of these cottages was Le Chalet de Lilas, deriving its name from the numerous lilac trees which surrounded and screened it from the road in the rear. Frederick, who during the previous summer had made acquaintance with this popular but unspoilt retreat, settled in the Chalet soon after his return from Brittany. It was a modest and unpretentious establishment of a few rooms, but ample accommodation for a man who passed most of his time out of doors, either on the lake or in the three surrounding forests, all of them within easy walking distance.

On December 9th Grieg writes interestingly on the subject of melodrama in general, but with an especial eye to Frederick's experiment in that line:

'This in my view is the trouble with a Melodrama: you must not compose absolute music. In it the imagination is being constantly stretched upon a Procrustean bed. It is only by making such allowance that one can achieve a good effect, and not otherwise. . . . What would you think if those beautiful and impassioned passages were to be played softly in order to hear the Narrator? You will not hear what you intended to be heard. I think that the music being as it is, you would have done better to use a singing voice. . . . The first thing to be understood is that the whole poem must be heard with ease; if not, the listener is dissatisfied. The struggle between voice and music is terribly awkward, and how incredibly little is needed to drown the voice. How much I wish that we could hear a rehearsal together! Some things would come off very nicely; it is only about the work as a whole that I have any qualms.'

Delius, aged about
twenty-three

Ten years later

The house at Croissy

Rue Ducoüedic

The poem, professedly allegorical, seems to contain a personal significance which supports the theory that it had coincided with a turning-point in Ibsen's own attitude to life and its problems. No longer a warm and comfortable existence in the sheltered valley with ties of home and love! Up into the high mountains where, although the way be hard and the wind blow cold, the poet and thinker untrammelled by human associations can look Fate calmly and fearlessly in the face! It required the courage, or perhaps the presumption of youth, to attempt the handling of such a piece of verse, running as it does into something like four hundred lines; and while endorsing generally what Grieg has to say about the unsatisfactory nature of the Melodrama as an art form, my own judgment is that for a comparatively inexperienced composer Frederick made a reasonably good job of this particular specimen. Even under the conditions of normal performance, most of the words would easily break through the barrier of orchestral sound; and if heard on the radio, where most inequalities of balance can be successfully adjusted, the whole text should be heard without difficulty. By way of relief from his labours on the Melodrama he wrote about this time his first string quartet which he sent off to his friend and ex-fellow pupil, Christian Sinding (who was still in Leipzig), for critical comment.

Opera next began to occupy his mind. He came across Bulwer Lytton's mystical romance *Zanoni* and thought seriously of extracting from it material for a libretto. He got so far as to sketch out some fragments of the music, of which only a portion of the prelude and opening scene remain. They do not read invitingly and it is evident that the composer soon lost interest in and discontinued his work upon the piece. A little later he was fascinated by Ibsen's splendid historical drama *Emperor and Galilean*, but was more than a little intimidated by its vast and diffused geographical plan. He communicated his doubts and reservations to Sinding, who advised him not to rush hastily into an undertaking of such magnitude, but to wait until he found the right sort of subject. He went on to suggest that he (Delius) might find it more satisfying to invent his own libretto.

Here is perhaps the place to draw attention to a phase of Frederick's personality, which to the best of my knowledge has next to no parallel in the history of genius or even talent. This was the capacity to command and hold not only the admiration for and confidence in his artistic integrity on the part of those nearest to him and best qualified to appraise it, but an affection and respect inspired by a knowledge of his character and disposition. That a young man of half his attainments should be the idol or spoilt child of any ordinary domestic establishment is explicable and generally inevitable. The dull goose of most average families is too often magnified into a radiant swan, whose capacities, unhappily, are seldom recognized by the larger world or acknowledged by his intimate associates in it.

In Frederick's case we may view the exact reverse of this. At home his ability, judgment and instinct were not only questioned but derided, while outside, where he might have expected criticism founded upon technical knowledge, as much as scepticism based on experience of human nature, we find ready acceptance and approval. Indeed, it may be questioned whether any other creative artist, poet, painter, or musician enjoyed, over a long period of years, the same unswerving esteem and devotion of so many gifted and intelligent men and women. Of the nature of Grieg's attachment to his young friend, a sentiment which endured until the death of the elder of the two men, we have had some indication. Another instance at this time and one which continued for over forty years was that of Sinding. Within a few weeks of Frederick's departure from Leipzig we find him writing in this strain:

'You cannot imagine how much I miss you. I have hardly ever before met a human being whom I could trust so completely. . . .'

We come across a similar respect for and confidence in him as the years go on, expressed by such men as Ravel, Schmitt, Messager and Gauguin in France; Strauss, Humperdinck, Max Schillings and Felix Mottl in Germany; and Elgar, Vaughan-Williams, Granville Bantock, Norman O'Neill and others in England. The soundest tribute that could be paid to him is that once having gained a friend he, to my personal knowledge, never wholly lost him.

At the close of the year he could look back with satisfaction upon his activities of the last six months. He had become more spiritually acclimatized to his Gallic environment and, as a token of outward conformity, grew a handsome beard.

6

THE Paris that he came to inhabit in 1888 was at the height of its splendour and charm. The vast schemes initiated thirty years previously by the Baron Haussman under which a good part of the capital took on a new face and shape had now matured and mellowed. The spectator standing in the middle of the Place de la Concorde enjoyed a panorama of beauty both ancient and modern unapproachable in any other great city of the day. Eastward he could read the story of the past from the Louvre, the Palais de Justice and Notre Dame de Paris: and westward his eye could travel up the gradual acclivity of a Champs Elysées as yet uninvaded by the taint of commerce.

Prosperity and elegance abounded, and the very air seemed to vibrate with life and excitement. In the world of music there were Massenet, Gounod, Franck, Fauré, with Debussy just appearing on the horizon; in that of letters were Anatole France, Zola, Verlaine and Maupassant; while painting was entering upon the noonday period of Impressionism led by Manet, Monet, Renoir and Degas. Around these last-named great personalities were grouped small circles of lesser effulgence and it was to these rather than to the haunts of musicians that Frederick was drawn from the first. While at all times willing to allow French composers the desirable merits of clarity and style, he never experienced much kinship in either spirit or sentiment with any one of them, old or new, except Bizet. He would often declare: 'What they have to say, they succeed in presenting better than the composers of any other nation, but I find it lacking in warmth and depth.' In contrast he was much more at home with some Italian music, notably the later operas of Verdi, and envied a little, I think, several of the rousing effects and unerringly dramatic strokes of *Aïda*.

Throughout the first two years of his residence in and around Paris he was obsessed with the ambition to write an opera on some grand historical subject, involving the employment of large resources such as processions, pageants and dancers. He had already decided that apart from every other objection there was too much talk of religion to please his taste in *Emperor and Galilean*, and turned his attention to the two dissimilar possibilities of Tiberius and Cleopatra. I have always regretted that he did not adapt the story of the Egyptian queen to the measure of his talent of that time, which might easily have produced a tuneful, singable and not unpicturesque sidelight on a theme of 'infinite variety', without resorting too much for inspiration to Shakespeare, Fletcher and Gautier.

He had a slight set-back in health at the beginning of 1889 that extorted anxious letters of enquiry from Grieg and Sinding, but which passed off satisfactorily by the early spring. On March 14th a letter from August Manns brought him his first experience of the uncertainties or difficulties in the way of securing performance of his works. Through the intervention of Grieg he had been encouraged to believe that his *Florida Suite* would find its way into one of the Crystal Palace concerts of that spring, but now he is informed that there will be no time available for preparing it, owing to the Concert Society's heavy preoccupation with Handel, Haydn and Beethoven. We do not hear of Manns again until ten years later, when he writes in the same strain about the difficulty as well as ultra-modernity of *Lebens Tanz* which, if adequately rehearsed, would displace in the programme several indispensable favourites. Frederick soon recovered from this temporary rebuff and applied himself to the composition of another string quartet and an orchestral suite, which (in addition to containing the rewritten *Marche Caprice*) consists of:

'La Quadroone' (Rapsodie Floridienne)
'Berceuse'
'Scherzo'
'Theme et Variations'.

He also made the extensive changes in the instrumentation of the *Florida Suite* to which allusion has been already made and for his own amusement transcribed Grieg's *Wedding March* in E Major for orchestra.

A good part of the early summer was given up to taking friends around an exhibition almost certainly the most splendid and artistic of its kind ever devised. The Opera and Concert-hall, after his first indulgence in an orgy of attendance during the previous year, had lost much of their attraction through his lack of sympathy with most of the unfamiliar pieces brought out there; and with the classics, thanks to Leipzig, he was almost too well acquainted. Before his removal to Ville d'Avray the sights and varied life of the great city were a constant source of interest and delight to him, and in one of his letters to Grieg he claims that there are five distinctly separate communities to be found there, all of which he is diligently investigating. He evinced a decided preference for low life, and it is hard to resist the impression that he had been digging into *Les Mystères de Paris* as much for enlightenment as amusement. Dressed in his oldest and shabbiest clothes he frequented all sorts of dubious quarters, where he would have been less welcome or secure if venturing in his costlier habiliments, and for a time his curiosity led him to a weekly inspection of the Morgue where he appeared to derive a macabre interest from gazing upon the unfortunate anonymities exposed there. Opportunities of a more frivolous kind for relaxation from his severer hours of work were in abundance. Outdoor entertainments were then enjoying high favour in every part of the city, and of these the most popular as well as reputable was the Café Concert. Superior to all its competitors for distinction and elegance was the Jardin des Fleurs in Les Champs Elysées, where occasionally singers and dancers from the opera houses could be heard and seen. Every section of Paris society could be observed there, from the *grande dame* to the *grisette*, and the ditties sung penetrated the respectable walls of bourgeois establishments, just as the gay lilting strains of the Christmas pantomime were repeated on the lips of every young man and woman in the middle-class homes of England.

It was only a full year after his departure from Leipzig that, with the assistance of Sinding, he succeeded in extracting from the none too willing authorities of the Leipzig Conservatoire his diploma. Their objection to handing it over was that, although Frederick was a 'nice kind gentleman' he had hardly ever attended classes during the latter part of his residence, and therefore could not have profited much by his association with their venerated institution. They were eventually won over by the undeniable proofs of industry revealed in his capacity to turn out a prodigious mass of composition since his departure, and were obliged to admit that there could be no better evidence of the beneficial influence they had exercised upon him! The precious document arrived and after dwelling briefly upon his academic activities, extolled at some length his agreeable disposition and high moral character. In all probability he felt that to possess such a certificate of good conduct might be of use, should he ever be obliged to accept a professorial post of some kind in Europe, or to yield to family pressure and return to America. All sorts of musicians now seemed to be migrating there and perhaps that might be his fate also.

During the autumn and early winter he wrote a fresh batch of songs:

'Chanson Fortunio' (De Musset)

and the Norwegian cycle of seven:

'The Minstrel' (Ibsen)   'Cradle Song' (Ibsen)
'Secret Love' (Björnsen)   'The Homeward Journey' (Vinje)
'The Birds Story' (Ibsen)   'Evening Voices' (Björnsen)
                'Veneril' (Björnsen)

Quite as important in its way as any of these was his setting with orchestral accompaniment of the charming poem 'Sakuntala' by Holger Drachmann. This is notable for the simplicity and breadth of the melodic line and its absolute fitness to the words of the text. The composer's refusal to permit its publication may be due to a feeling on his part that it was less typical of his manner at that time, than some of the other songs already mentioned. Should this be so, I am inclined to think that his judgment here was over-scrupulous, as it is in no way less characteristic than at least three of the Norwegian cycle.

July came round and with it the long-anticipated visit to Norway in company with Grieg and Sinding. There he was taken into a region with which he was so far unacquainted, the Jotunheim. He climbed Galdhöpiggen, scrambled over the Josterdalsbrae and explored the country around. This he declared to be the most memorable of all his frequent visits to these parts: fine weather prevailed throughout and his companions were two highly cultivated Norwegians who revelled as much as he did in grandeur of scenery. One result of this latest Scandinavian trip was the determination of a problem that had been troubling him for twelve months, namely, the choice of subject for his first opera. It should be emphasized that whether or no his dramatic works are successful as operas in the conventional sense, the theatre during the period extending from 1890 to 1910 played a large part in his life and was rarely absent from his thoughts. By 1902 he had written four full-scale operas and another of smaller dimensions, and when it is remembered that the only important works he wrote for orchestra alone were:

On the Heights (1892)   *Life's Dance* (1898)
Over the Hills and Far Away (1896–7)   *Paris* (1899)

it will be better understood where his real inclinations lay. In other words the four operas with over eight hours of playing time to their credit, and more than a thousand pages of full scoring, outweigh easily the rest of his output until the beginning of his full maturity. Norway and the influence of the Norwegian way of life, simple and unspoilt by over-urbanization, cleansed his mind of the perilous stuff which had for too long been haunting it, and brought it back again into the enchanted work of folk-lore and fairyland.

In October after a year's residence at Ville d'Avray he moved to Croissy, a few miles away on the right bank of the Seine, and adjoining the popular resort of Bougival. There he found accommodation in a wing of a picturesque Louis Treize house, 8 Boulevard de la Mairie.

7

FREDERICK must have spent a good deal of 1890 in getting the libretto for his first opera well in order. His preoccupation was to choose a subject suitable both to his lately purified taste and his musical capacity of that time. To accomplish this end he united two old legends *The Princess and the Swineherd* and *Irmelin*, an early mediaeval heroine of fastidious disposition, who bears a certain likeness to her Chinese sister Turandot in her continued rejection of the numerous suitors for her hand. She did not share, however, the sanguinary inclinations of her oriental counterpart, but preferred to spend her idle moments dreaming of an ideal lover and listening to voices from the air that promised his coming. The Swineherd story takes on a new slant, remoulded by the composer himself, to bring in more effectively the influence of an element of nature. Nils, the hero, is a young man whose brain is haunted by the vision of a Silver Stream that flows on to an unknown region, where he shall attain the fulfilment of his heart's most secret desires. While looking for its source in the woods he is captured by a band of robbers who are ruled by Rolf, a rebellious noble, who lives a life of banditry in a castle upon a mountain-top, from which he defies the authority of his king, Irmelin's father. Nils, however, has a privileged position in Rolf's wild establishment, thanks to a gift of minstrelsy welcome both to his rude followers and the company of young women who soften the savagery of the outlaw's stronghold.

As the piece has obtained no more than a few performances in a university town, whose alumni marked the honour conferred on them by an almost total disregard of its existence, I make no apology for dealing at some length with both the subject and the music of it. After a short prelude the curtain rises and a Voice in the Air is heard singing reassuringly to the dreaming Princess. Her attendant reproaches her for her constant indifference to the various nobles who pay their regular visits to the castle; but Irmelin replies, 'I am waiting for him, the one I see in my dreams.' Presently her father the King enters, to announce the arrival of three more knights, but each one of them is repulsed courteously by her. The King, angered by her obduracy, gives her six months in which to take a suitable husband, and if by that time she has not chosen one, he will himself do so. Up to this moment the music has gone along in a tranquilly idyllic mood, but upon the retirement of the Maid, leaving Irmelin alone, we get frequent orchestral touches until the end of the act of a genuine Delian character, amongst them his favourite device of distant horns off-stage. A merry chorus of villagers passing by under her window leads to a moment of exalted emotion and the scene closes with the sound of the Voice in the Air.

The second act opens with a somewhat lengthy prelude, after which we see Nils reclining despondently under a pine tree—'The lost Prince herding obscurely among the swine.' He laments his misfortune in being lured from the quest of the Silver Stream by fatal flowers of enchantment and longs for freedom from his servitude under Rolf. Night begins to descend and following a call from the castle he makes his way through a thunderstorm to the summit of the height. As the scene changes to a Banqueting Hall we hear the voices of Rolf and his men drinking and singing. But while the music given to Nils when down in the valley is both poetic and characteristic, that of Rolf and his followers is less successful and we feel that the composer lacks some fellow-feeling with the merry-making of a rude and vigorous band of outlaws. The noise subsides as he enters and a song is demanded of him. In reply he declares his intention of singing no more to them until he has been given freedom to find his Silver Stream. Rolf summons his company of maidens in the hope that they may influence Nils to remain, but in spite of a charming episode in which they use their blandishments in a manner reminiscent of the Flower Girls in *Parsifal*, he repulses their efforts and, to the dismay of everyone, rushes suddenly off into the night. The scene changes once more, this time to a mountainous and rocky country down which a rivulet is seen flowing. Dawn begins to break, and at the end of an animated interlude the sun emerges to disclose Nils making his way down a cliff. This interlude and the section which follows, during which he discovers that it is at last the Stream, to which he has now been miraculously led, is one of the most effective portions of the work.

At the beginning of the third act we have the King's Palace again, where a bridal ceremony is taking place. The six months of probation are over and the King has carried out his threat of choosing a husband for his daughter. But the occasion lacks any customary air of gaiety, for the bride is plunged in depression and the rest of the gathering is obviously affected by her melancholy mood. Suddenly there appears a stranger and the King upon learning that he is a minstrel, orders him to strike up in honour of the event. But Nils prefers to sing about his life in Rolf's service and his loneliness in the valley while tending his herds. His noble bearing strikes the beholders, who conclude that he must be a prince in disguise, Irmelin most of all being startled by his beauty and distinction. Presently the King takes everyone off, except Nils and Irmelin, to a hunting party and the couple, left alone, lose no time falling in love. They agree to meet after sundown in the garden, where they join in a lengthy and passionate duet. After this, with a truly operatic disregard for the materialities of life, they wander off hand in hand over the hills and far away.

These two scenes taken as a whole constitute the culminating point of achievement attained, in what may fairly be defined as Frederick's earliest period. All his previous endeavours and experiments find fulfilment here, all is carried out with a sure and steady touch and the melodic inspiration is of a high order. The long passages between Nils and Irmelin have a poetical and lyrical quality which, with the exception of the last scene in *The Magic Fountain*, we encounter nowhere else until similar episodes in *A Village Romeo and Juliet*. Much of the music, too, has an impetus and swing that makes its appearance less frequently in later compositions; at least they are more rarely sustained in them. Indeed, the final section of the concluding Love Duet arises to a noble height of ecstasy which diminishes only on the concluding page, when the orchestra makes a characteristic diminuendo as Irmelin and Nils disappear from sight. Taking the work as a whole I have little hesitation in claiming for it the distinction of being the best first opera written by any composer known to me. Its main and obvious feature is the consistently sustained level of a lyrical style that, with the exception of the short Rolf bacchanalian scene, is marked by romance and dignity throughout. There are surprisingly few weak moments; some have real power and many exude charm and allurement.

The task of completing *Irmelin*, both libretto and music, occupied the best part of two years, that is until sometime in 1892, and he obtained some relief from it by planning a 'Legende' for Pianoforte and Orchestra which he left unfinished and a return to smaller forms, both vocal and instrumental. Deserting for a while his favourite Scandinavian poets, he turned his attention to Shelley and Tennyson. Of the former he wrote three lyrics, of which two are among the most popular of all that he has achieved in this line: 'The Indian Love Song' and 'To the Queen of My Heart'. The third, 'Love's Philosophy', is on a clearly lower level of melodic invention. The cycle of songs from *Maud* consists of:

> 'Birds in the High-Hall Garden'
> 'I was Walking a Mile'
> 'Go Not Happy Day'
> 'The Rivulet Crossing My Ground'
> 'Come Into the Garden Maud'.

All the five have orchestral accompaniment.

Tennyson's order of the poems has been slightly altered, so as to make a good beginning with 'Birds in the High-Hall Garden', which runs to more than one hundred bars in length. We then have three intervening numbers, none of which has more than fifty bars, while 'Come Into the Garden Maud', the *pièce-de-résistance* of the group, exceeds two hundred and makes, as intended, a stirring climax to the whole. It is fairly obvious why he chose these particular poems. They are admirably designed for song-writing by a poet, the most musical of his century in England, and the vocal line of them is invariably clear and singable. As an effective background to each of them we have the voice of nature speaking of birds, flowers, the sun, the clouds and the sea, and all this secondary element is illustrated, as it is in *Irmelin*, by the orchestra, which serves the composer well and faithfully in his devotion to the supreme influence in his life. Only two points of criticism occur to me, and of course they are purely personal. One is the length of the final lyric, which does not appear to warrant such extension, and the other is the approach to the climax beginning with the words 'There has fallen a splendid tear From the passion flower at the gate', which might have been handled with more deliberate preparation. There is just a suggestion here that Frederick thought it time to bring the piece to a speedy conclusion and betrays a little impatience in accomplishing it.

As I have said, the orchestra functions as the interpreter of nature and here Frederick ventured upon an experiment, novel at the time, and in my view wholly successful in his manipulation of it. In the first four of the series he has refrained from bringing in the heavy-weight members of the orchestral family, reserving its full power and majesty for the final number. In this there will be little room for carping on the side of want of energy and passion.

In addition to these we have four poems of Heine:

'Hör ich das Liedchen Klingen'
'Mit deinen blauen Augen'
'Ein schöner Stern'
'Aus deinen Augen fliessen meine Lieder'.

None of them is unmistakably Delian and all fail to rise to the level of his Scandinavian songs. There is also a solitary setting of a poem of Holger Drachmann—translated by the composer himself under the title 'On Shore how still, All Nature seems asleep'. A curious feature of this little song is the interpolation towards the close of a few bars of semi-recitative, not to be observed again until used some years later in Verlaine's 'Le ciel est pardessus le toit'.

Immediately succeeding these comes a short suite in two move-ments for small orchestra. It is tuneful, unaffected, and not without a mild charm, while its scoring is beyond cavil. Its chief failing is a curious lack of individuality, and touches of the real Delius are too infrequent.

Lastly there are two little tone poems:

'Summer Eve'
'Spring Morning'.

These were played for the first time at the Delius Festival of 1946, when it was appreciated that the first of them was in every way the more attractive. Slight as it is if compared with later pieces of its kind, it is none the less entirely authentic, and the leading melody haunts the ear in the way as does the popular 'Serenade' from *Hassan*, written thirty years later.

In the summer of 1891 he left Croissy for Paris and installed himself in a small flat at 33 Rue Ducoüedic, Montrouge.

8

NO ACCOUNT faithfully recording the events of the two years
that followed Frederick's return to the capital, can make
wholly satisfactory reading. Not only did the pace of his
creative impulse ease off perceptibly, but its quality suggests that it
had come to a temporary point of standstill. It may be not unnatural
that after the unceasing activity of the three preceding years, some reaction may have set in prompting him to relax for a time, look into
his inner self and examine critically the value of his work up to date.
If this be so, one is obliged to admit that his self-communion could
not have been very rewarding, for taking the period between the
completion of *Irmelin* and the beginning of his next opera, we see little
sign of forward development in either style or invention. It may be that
he devoted some part of these comparatively barren years to a series
of experiments, for we know that sometime hereabouts he composed,
according to his own statement, a considerable amount of music all
of which was ruthlessly destroyed.

What is of greater certainty is that he now made a total change
in his social habits. He renounced his taste for what cannot be described as other than 'low life', and obtained access to the seats of the
mighty as represented by the salons of the Faubourg St. Germain. For
this introduction to aristocratic 'high life' he was mainly indebted to
his acquaintance with Isidore de Lara, who combined happily the
careers of an occasionally successful operatic composer of the second
rank and an indefatigable *coureur de femmes*. He speedily became a
success in these lofty circles, especially with the feminine portion of
them: less on account of his music or even his agreeable personality,
than his professed leanings towards occultism. His speciality was the
somewhat esoteric craft of astrology, and his gift as a maker of
horoscopes was in great demand among those who did not shrink
from giving approximately truthful accounts of their days and hours

of birth. A keen admirer of his proficiency was the famous prima donna Emma Calvé, greatest of all the interpreters of Carmen, who after a slightly reticent opening correspondence, supplied the information essential to his task, adding, however, in her final letter, 'Pardonnez à ma coquetterie feminine de ne pas la répèter.'

Other diversions of this time were alchemy and metallurgy, into the mysteries of which he was inducted by August Strindberg, with whom he became on terms of intermittent cordiality. One of Strindberg's most spectacular performances was the alleged discovery of gold in the unlikely quarter of Montparnasse, and Frederick submitted some of the specimens collected for examination to the Laboratoire de la Bourse de Commerce. Although to the great excitement of the two friends the report received from it confirmed the presence of the precious metal in minute quantities, the prospects of a worthwhile find proved too dim for a sustained continuance of their investigations. During the period of his troubled residence in Paris, the great Swedish author was frequently to be found dabbling in sideshows having small connection with his own art, but which entertained him innocuously until the end of the century, when he recovered the normal use of his splendid faculties and returned to his own country.

When able to turn aside from his new-found social distractions and quasi-scientific tangents, Frederick produced a Sonata for Violin and Pianoforte, another String Quartet and a little Legend for Violin and Orchestra. Of these only the last named has been published, and was played for the first time at his London concert in 1899. A few fragments of the String Quartet remain in manuscript, and these in their lightness and easy movement have an odd kinship with Mozart. The Sonata is a solid and vigorous affair of some merit; is strictly orthodox in construction, and contains three movements. The second is a Romance and the pianoforte leads off with the kind of chordal passages which in the case of Delius so frequently seem to call for the substitution of strings or woodwind. But it has a genuinely warm and pleasing flavour and the violin part is both well and attractively contrived. In the finale we return to the spirit of the opening section, noting, by the way, that the pianoforte part is somewhat overweighted and none too easy to play. But in the present dearth of such works for the two instruments, a performance of the piece might prove to be worth while. It is true that it bears little or no resemblance to his later ventures of the kind, but as twelve years separate it from its successor that should be not a matter for wonder or reproach. The Legend is genuinely Delius in his earliest style, both melodically and structurally, and only an unreasoning attitude towards youthful efforts would hinder its more frequent hearing. On a more ambitious scale was a tone poem inspired like his melodrama by Ibsen's *Paa Vidderne*. Breadth and vigour are the main characteristics of a work which, rather surprisingly, is a little lacking in the serenity and lyrical charm discoverable in all the other earlier pieces. But there is no fault to be found with its architecture and its downright force makes it an effective show-piece. It obtained its first audition at a concert given at Monte Carlo on February 25th, 1893, thanks to his friendship with de Lara and a modest subvention from the amiable Theodor. It appears to have had a substantial success, for the following day Alice, Princess of Monaco, writes an enthusiastic letter of congratulation, inviting him to send her any other composition of his that he would like to have performed. This was sufficiently encouraging, but *Paa Vidderne* does not seem to have been played anywhere else, and remained forgotten until its revival also at the London Festival of 1946. By this time with the sound of such masterpieces in its ears as *Sea Drift*, *A Mass of Life* and *A Village Romeo and Juliet*, the English Public not unnaturally failed to discover in it much that it had grown to look upon as typical of the composer.

In the autumn occurred an incident which is worth mentioning as throwing some light upon his changing fortunes during the next six years. This was a letter from Bradford dated November 29th and was written by a certain William Shaw, the secretary of his father's business. This worthy man, while completely loyal to his employer, had more than a little regard for all of the three sons, and was given to constant regret that circumstances had arisen to prevent any one of them occupying a responsible position in the firm. He writes in a way to give Frederick some cause for reflection.

'Latterly business affairs have tended towards an utter collapse. Your brother Max having no financial interest in the concern, appears to have no control or say as to how business should be conducted. During his absence on the Continent to settle several differences with customers, offensive and defiant letters had been despatched in advance from here which made it quite impossible for him to approach these friends in an amicable way and to arrange matters satisfactorily. It is the general opinion of all employees that your father is not abreast of the times, and unless he ceases to manage, not a customer worth a straw will be left in six months' time. As a close observer of your brother's business abilities it appears to me a sin and a shame that he is not allowed full say. There is money to be made if he were permitted to control all affairs, but no good can ever result from a continuance of the present state of things. Seeing that you know the different temperaments of your father and brother is my reason for writing you in the anticipation that you might suggest a remedy which I could have the opportunity to advocate for settling the present state of affairs.'

We do not know if Frederick ever made any move of intervention, but we may be tolerably sure that nothing he might have said or done would have had the slightest effect upon the mind of Julius. It is within our knowledge that after a while Max left the business, set up on his own account, and with unhappy results.

During all this time Frederick had maintained an active correspondence with both Edward and Nina Grieg. These simple and kindly people had already been a little worried by ominous signs in some of his music, the Shelley songs especially, of excessive eroticism. In this Edward affects to discern an undesirable indulgence, and prays for a speedy return to a more restrained conception of amorous expression. Nina on her part is hopelessly bewildered by his sudden conversion to vegetarianism, and writes:

'For Heaven's sake, why have you done it? How terribly dull! I hope you will have had enough of it when we meet again.'

Equally sincere are their regrets that for the past two summers he has discontinued his annual visit to Norway and the Jotunheim. But from a few sly hints conveyed in some of the letters, it would seem that they are quite alive to the possibility that he may be finding diversions of a more intimate kind in Paris.

9

URING the summer of 1893 his thoughts turned again to Opera, and after much vacillation over the choice of a subject he decided, as in the case of *Irmelin*, to write his own libretto. He chose for the background of his story another locality with which he was intimately familiar and one which would provide opportunities for picturesque scenery and incidents calling for a rich choice of instrumental tone. The period was to be the early part of the sixteenth century, when the enmity between the native Indian and the buccaneering Spaniard who had descended upon the Florida peninsula was at its height. The destiny of the new work was to be almost unique in the history of the lyric stage. No one today knows what it is about, no one knows the names of the characters in it and no one living has heard a note of the music. If it had been any other composer it would not be hard to discover the causes of this complete ignorance of an opera covering three acts and a whole evening's entertainment. Because it was set down in one biography written over thirty years ago, and repeated parrot-like in every other since that time—not forgetting a stream of articles, monographs and lectures—we have been led to believe that *The Magic Fountain* was accepted for performance at the Weimar Theatre, but withdrawn by the composer, who within a few months after its completion repented having written it. His recovery of the score from the theatre, as well as all other material, including scenic designs, has been lauded as an act of supreme self-criticism.

Unfortunately for the validity of this pretty tale the archives of the Weimar Theatre contain nothing to suggest that it has ever heard of the work either at that or any other time. Both before and after the Second World War enquiries were made and full co-operation was lent to discover the truth about this unusual transaction: but the result was a total blank. Are we confronted with just another legend or have all the parties once concerned with it conspired to suppress all available information? Anyway, the year 1893 in which all this is alleged to have taken place is painfully inaccurate, as not a note of the music was written until 1894. It is a fact, however, that two years later there was a serious proposal to give the work at the German Opera House in Prague, and, as will be seen, the affair had reached a definite stage, for sundry persons, including Grieg and Sinding, had full knowledge of it. But this did not take place until the close of 1895, or even the beginning of 1896.

The Magic Fountain, both musically and dramatically, is a work of unusual interest and merit, and I feel that it is due both to the memory and reputation of Frederick Delius, to let my readers know something about it. The curtain rises upon the picture of a ship hopelessly becalmed at sea. In the prow is a group of sailors lamenting that their leader Solano is always reading and dreaming, but never thinking of their needs. They despair of ever seeing a shore again. Solano occupies the stern portion of the craft and is poring over charts and books. He recites a passage from one of the volumes before him:

'Far away in the Western Isles lies the fountain of eternal youth
A fountain ready for those prepared to drink it in wisdom and truth.'

This is his quest and he has become indifferent to the interests of his followers who are concerned only with the discovery of gold on the mainland. Aroused by their repeated complaints Solano, in a burst of excitement, calls upon the winds to dispel the dead calm and drive them shoreward. His prayers are only too well answered; a storm of the utmost violence strikes the ship, which founders. The scene changes to the coast of Florida where we see a long sandy beach with Solano lying insensible upon it. The wreck of the vessel is visible far out to sea. From an adjoining grove emerges a female figure; it is Watawa our heroine and the princess of an Indian tribe, who regard all Spaniards as mortal enemies. On seeing that Solano is about to revive she retires to the grove, but presently reappears accompanied by a group of Indian warriors, who raise and bear him away. The most noticeable feature in this opening scene is the effectiveness and solidity of the male voice choral writing which shows a considerable advance upon that in *Irmelin*. The theme which introduces Watawa, or rather the first two bars of it, were afterwards used by Delius by way of reminiscence at the beginning of the final section of *Sea Drift*, where the voice sings of lost, happy, days.

The second act opens upon an Indian village in a forest by the borders of a great swamp. In the foreground a few Indian warriors, with Solano in their midst, are sitting and smoking. A larger group intones a monotonously wordless chant. Their chief Wapanacki asks Solano what has brought him to their land, and the latter replies that he has come with no hostile intent and is unarmed. He is seeking nothing but the fountain from whose waters flow both wisdom and truth. Wapanacki reveals that one man alone can help him. This is a seer of great age whose knowledge is boundless, and who lives in solitude on the bank of a far distant river. Solano asks for a guide and the Indian chief undertakes to find him one. Watawa, who has over-heard this conversation, takes Wapanacki aside and asks if he has forgotten the sorrow which the white man has brought upon them all. Wapanacki assures her that he has not forgotten their people's wrongs, but insists that no Indian is permitted to harm a man like Solano who is entirely defenceless. He counsels her to wait upon events. Presently the scouts return, who have been investigating the country in the vicinity, and the warriors begin a war dance which becomes increasingly animated as the squaws join in. As the men rush off into the forest on a foray Wapanacki, pointing to Watawa, says to Solano, 'There is thy guide.' Wapanacki follows his warriors and Watawa retires into her wigwam. The moon rises over the tree-tops and all is still.

Now follows a gradual transformation of scene and we discover Solano and Watawa working their way through the thick under-growth of a luxurious swamp. Solano's eyes are frequently turned upon Watawa in admiring astonishment, but her attitude towards him is one of calm unconcern. We pass on and arrive at a small hut, the home of the ancient sage, Talum Hadjo. The venerable mystic is soliloquizing and looking intently into the running water. Presently Watawa appears alone and on making herself known to him Talum Hadjo hails her as the last of her race. Watawa answers: ' 'Tis even as thou sayest, my kin are all gone. Death they suffered at the hands of the hated paleface. But I have now within my power one of that cursed race, and as his guide I brought him hither only to revenge our disgrace. Hidden close within my belt lies a poisoned knife. Holy father, now advise me—shall I take his life?'

Talum Hadjo asks why Solano has come and Watawa replies, 'Only in search of wisdom and to find the spring of life eternal.' The sage comments on the vanity of the quest in so young a man and asks, 'Tell me, dost thou truly wish to kill him?' She begins to answer agitatedly, 'I hate his people——,' but the ancient man interrupts her, saying: 'Hate, always hate! Hate means death and strife—Love means hope and life.' He then advises Watawa what to do. 'This limpid stream here gliding past us flows from where the fountain plays. If his death thou truly wishest, guide him to the spring, for to all the unprepared, its waters death will bring. The wild Jessamine needs the knife not if by my counsel she will abide: the white man's life lies in her keeping, but let in this her heart decide.'

He finishes speaking and the scene once more changes to a soft and dreamy woodland where Solano is waiting for Watawa. She is seen by him far off in the trees and as she advances Solano says to himself: 'How strangely fair she is. What form and subtle grace. How beautiful the proud expression on her soft and noble face,' and calls out passionately, 'Watawa!' She starts at the sound of his voice, but at once recovers herself and regarding him coldly says, 'There lies thy path.' They go on their way into the depths of the glade, and finally disappear into the almost impenetrable bush. Night gradually falls, stars are twinkling above the tree-tops and fireflies glimmer by hundreds in the heavy fragrant air. This whole episode, beginning with the appearance of Talum Hadjo and continuing to the end of the second act, the point at which we have arrived, is one of sustained beauty; and played before the background of the lush and heavy swamp yields an impression of high mystery and charm.

Beginning with a fairly lengthy introduction, by turns tranquil and impassioned, the third act discloses a landscape entitled 'The Everglades'. It is night and the moonlight casts sinister shadows upon the waters of the lake by which Watawa is standing. In an overlong soliloquy she analyses her emotions which are now painfully contending. The desire for revenge still lingers within her, but it is rapidly giving way to the influence of an irresistible passion. Solano's voice is heard in the distance calling, 'Watawa, Watawa! Where art thou hiding?' and Watawa says to herself, 'Love, what anguish, Love, what pain, more intense because in vain.' Solano now approaches and cries: 'Why this torment? Why this sorrow? Why should our love be in vain?' But Watawa, her heart still divided, answers: 'Turn and go, love between us is a treason that should strike Watawa dead. Speak not, plead not, list to reason—go ere my strength has fled.' But Solano refuses to depart and she falls into his arms. Watawa now confides in him her fel' intentions on their first meeting and how hate has been driven out b/ love. A highly emotional duet follows and as it terminates there arise from the lake vapoury forms of beautiful women that glide gracefully around the sleeping lovers, who gradually become invisible. This ghostly ballet represents the rising of the mists of night from the lake and foreshadows the discovery of the fountain of Eternal Youth. The fountain begins to reveal itself slowly and the haze which obscured it gradually dissolves. The ethereal forms also fade away slowly, singing: 'Play fountain, play, two lovers are come to drink in thy waters. Say fountain, say, is it night they shall win or day? If not prepared, beware, beware.'

A cold green light now floods the whole scene and Unktahé the God of Wisdom appears in an attitude of complete repose, bearing some likeness to the traditional images of Buddha. He is immovable and does no more than cast a shadow over the recumbent pair. As he too vanishes, the fountain bubbles higher than ever, and Solano, awaking, hails it ecstatically. But Watawa, seized with terror, starts to her feet, crying: 'No, Solano! Touch not those waters. Poison lurks in that sparkling spring!' and as its colour turns to red, points to it in horror and gasps, 'Look, to blood it is changing. Death and destruction those waters will bring.' But Solano pays no heed to her wild exhortation and answers: 'Awake, sweet love, thou surely art dreaming. What is this fancy that haunts thus thy brain? Trust to thy lover, come, trust to Solano, and life everlasting we two shall regain.' Watawa again adjures him solemnly: 'Nay, not life but death awaits thee there, for all the unprepared its waters poison bear. Talum Hadjo the all-wise the truth to me disclosed.' But Solano will not listen. 'Trust them not, those Indian legends, ne'er believed by my white race. Dost thou think in such pure waters Death could ever find a place?' Watawa in great anguish falls imploringly upon her knees and makes her last appeal, 'I know nothing but I feel that those waters Death conceal.' Her lover, who has now quite lost control of himself sings wildly, 'Come then, Watawa, if thou lov'st me, follow me unto death,' and she responds with exaltation, 'Not afraid is Watawa, she will follow unto death, and while drinking of the waters bless our love with her last breath.' Then rushing to the fountain she stoops over it and drinks. She arises, and then as if in mortal pain, stumbles to her knees. Solano, in spellbound astonishment, receives her fainting in his arms. She murmurs: 'Farewell, sweet love, I am dying; see how the moonbeams flood the fair magnolia grove. Listen, the mocking-bird is warbling songs of love—there I will wait for you, in the fair magnolia grove.' Solano, half-frantic with grief, ejaculates, 'I have killed thee, Watawa, my beloved.' Then with face transfigured he too approaches the fountain and drinks, totters back to where Watawa is lying, and falls dead upon her breast. The sunlight of dawn floods the scene as the curtain descends.

The whole of the third act is replete with romance and melodic invention of a high order and the two principal characters are drawn with all clarity and contrast. The climax of the love scene like that in *Irmelin* lacks nothing of strength and impulse, and the final catastrophe is heightened by the splendour of orchestral sound that sheds lustre on it. Thus ends a truly remarkable work of which, as I have said, no one living knows either a word or a note.

10

THE score of *The Magic Fountain* was completed in the early
summer of 1895, and we find Sinding on June 25th sending a
letter of congratulation. On September 1st Sinding writes
again, a little anxiously, 'You don't seem to be very gay.' If Frederick
was feeling any depression about this time there was ample reason
for it. He had definitely quarrelled with his friend and protector,
Uncle Theodor. For months past this excellent man had been seriously
worried about his protégé. Seven years had gone by since the tri-
partite arrangement had been concluded in London under which both
Julius and he were to support Frederick, until the latter had established
a clear reputation as a composer of distinction. Acording to his lights
that happy consummation seemed even farther off than it had done
in 1888; and although it might be true that Frederick had written a
good deal of meritorious music, no one so far as he could judge seemed
to want it. What good purpose could be served by continuing a
course of patronage that was yielding such a disappointing return?
The time had come for the original plan of returning to America to
be put into force, as it was there only that he, Theodor, saw any
definite future for his nephew. If his advice were not taken, he would
cut off his share of the supplies.

It was a decidedly awkward moment for Frederick, who had just
completed a new opera, with favourable negotiations for its production
at Prague well in train. He certainly was not going to leave Europe
at short notice to please his uncle or anyone else, especially as there
might have come at last the chance for which he had been waiting so
long. Theodor saw the matter in another light. Frederick had already
written one full-scale opera and nothing had come of it. Instead of
settling down to compose something which had a fair chance of obtaining performance and winning a little popular favour, he had
followed only his own erratic inclination, and here was another

71

operatic undertaking which, even if carried out, would probably fail to please. Attached as he was to his young relative he had begun latterly to find him a more serious responsibility than at first anticipated. He had got into the habit of assisting him in more ways than one over and above the allowance he was providing, and on occasions had even helped some of his friends, such as Sinding, out of tight corners. Then there was the easy and pointless kind of life that he seemed to have drifted into leading in Paris. Surely by this time he should be making his own way without further assistance from anyone. It may be that more than once there came into his mind the familiar line of La Fontaine:

'Dans beaucoup de plaisir je mêle un peu de gloire,'

with the thought that it might not be inapplicable to Frederick's ways. Anyway, in his eyes, the position seemed nearly hopeless, and to make matters worse Julius, whose business was seriously declining, had cut his son's allowance in half, acting very possibly in collusion with Theodor to effect a common purpose. But the stubborn fellow was not to be beaten. He threw himself upon the sympathies of a female relative in Berlin, Frau Krönig, a sister of his father and known in the family as Aunt Albertine. Fortunately he had a friend in her son Arthur, who, both liking him and admiring his music, was helpful in persuading the kindly lady to make good the deficiency created by her brother's defection. Accordingly he remained in Paris, defying the world in general and his family in particular.

For a time all appeared to be going well for we learn from a letter of Sinding dated December 24th that the music had arrived at Prague. On January 10th, 1896, we have another letter from the same source: 'Do you know exactly when the opera is to be performed? Hennings [Director of the theatre] wrote to me that it would probably be in February,' and further on he adds: 'Novàček[1] told me the day before yesterday that he had cabled you. What is happening—can't you make some money now on your opera? . . . Aren't you going to Prague?'

This is the last we hear of the work, for certainly Frederick did not go to Prague, nor was it ever produced. It is, of course, conceivable that at the last moment he may have called the whole thing

---

[1] A Hungarian violinist and composer of merit. His works, which include three string quartets and a concerto for pianoforte and orchestra, enjoyed some popularity during the eighties and nineties of the last century. The concerto was frequently played by Busoni.

off, but taking into account how far the matter had gone and that so many of his friends were keenly interested in the coming event, such a supposition seems hardly probable. But whatever may have been the reasons for its non-appearance, these are unknown to us, and there is no scrap of information anywhere to help solve the mystery. The whole affair is inexplicable, and to add to our bewilderment Frederick starts the New Year with the sketch of yet another opera libretto up his sleeve.

In the meantime he had diverted himself with two songs of Verlaine: 'Il pleure dans mon cœur' and 'Le ciel est pardessus le toit', and towards the close of the year he had began his first version of *Appalachia*, to be completed in the early part of 1896. It is quite a modest effort if compared with the splendid achievement of 1902, from which it differs widely in thematic material. Some features there are in common, notably the use of the cow-horn in the Introduction and the tune upon which the variations in the later version are founded, and which here is taken along occasionally at a very spirited tempo.[1] We have also liberal doses of both 'Dixie' and 'Yankee-Doodle', so that the general effect is one of light-hearted gaiety. But compared with the eventual *Appalachia* it is of slight dimensions, the score consisting of less than thirty pages. If the later version were not so well known and remarkable, it might be just possible to give the earlier one a hearing; but on the whole it may be more judicious to forget that it was ever written.

An unexpected ray of sunshine came about this time from the New World. He had made the acquaintance of a certain Victor Thrane, a concert agent in New York, who was interesting himself in the performance of Frederick's works in that quarter. His travels took him to most parts of the States, and learning about the property in Florida, he paid it a visit. For some years the orange-growing industry had been deteriorating and was shortly about to suffer a blow of near-extinction in 1896 through the great climatic changes that swept through the entire peninsula. In its place was springing up an incipient tobacco-growing enterprise and Thrane professed to see a promising opportunity for it on Frederick's plantation. If efficiently worked, and the initial cost would be small, it might bring in a steady income for its owner in the not too distant future. But the first thing to do

[1] This tune he had heard Negroes singing in the tobacco factories, known as 'stemmeries' in Danville.

was to find someone who would join him in a workable kind of partnership, reside on the estate and run it for their mutual benefit. This was not altogether an easy task, as it meant relying upon Solano Grove for a living pending such time as the tobacco seeds to be planted would produce results that could be marketed speedily. But the idea in itself seemed not only feasible but welcome, and Frederick seized upon it as a drowning man might clutch at the proverbial straw. It would help matters, Thrane went on to say, if Frederick could see his way to revisit his property and view the situation for himself. During the ten years since his departure it had been managed by a Negro, Anderson by name, who existed by farming a small portion only of the hundred acres. The house was in good order and, save for the expenses of transport, the stay there would cost very little. It remained only for Frederick to determine how this could be accomplished. He could not, however, leave for some months at least since he would be absorbed in a new operatic venture, this time with a librettist other than himself, who had made arrangements for close collaboration with him during the early part of the forthcoming year.

II

THE composers of nearly every period would seem to be divided roughly into two classes. There are those whose earlier works are separated from their later by a comparatively narrow gulf of difference or none at all. The increase of years may bring with it the fuller capacity to plan and execute on a larger scale; in short, a higher command of the tangible resources of the art such as form, construction, the expansion of ideas and so on. But in respect of the intangible elements of style or originality of theme, the possessors of them are seen to be fully endowed almost from the very start.

In the case of Mozart we may observe in dozens of the pieces he wrote before his twentieth year all the essential characteristics present in those written ten and fifteen years later, and it is quite certain that Mendelssohn never succeeded in producing anything more novel or typical than his Overture to *A Midsummer Night's Dream*, that amazing achievement of a lad of eighteen. The later works of Berlioz show little, if any, fuller maturity than some of his earlier; and although more than thirty years passed between the appearance of the *Symphonie Fantastique* and *Les Troyens*, the two pieces could have been written at the same time, for all the contrast they reveal in manner or invention.

But it would have needed powers more prophetic than any yet possessed by mortal man, to have foretold that the author of *Rienzi* or *The Flying Dutchman* would one day enrich the world with *Tristan* or *Parsifal*. To what strange spiritual alchemy we may attribute this virtual metamorphosis of the creative faculty may not be beyond all conjecture, as Sir Thomas Browne opined when brooding over what song the sirens may have sung. But when all speculation and wonder have had their say, we remain confronted with a phenomenon verging on the miraculous. Almost as unaccountable is the passage of Sibelius from his First Symphony to the Fourth where, if it were not known beyond doubt that they came from the same pen, we might be forgiven for insisting upon the presence of two obviously independent and irreconcilable personalities. But I am inclined to think that of all those rare spirits, who sooner or later have found a true understanding of themselves as well as the range and potentiality of their gifts, and who, after much zigzagging to and fro of mind and intention, have fashioned for themselves the one inevitable medium for the embodiment of the spirit moving within them, the most singular and baffling is Frederick Delius.

After all, both *The Flying Dutchman* and *Tannhäuser* are indisputable works of art, wrought by a steady and skilled hand. Yet Wagner was less than thirty when the earlier opera was written, and barely beyond it when its successor was first heard. Sibelius, still in his twenties, had greeted his generation with an unquestioned masterpiece, *En Saga*, whose architectural splendour and brilliant sonorities still have the power after more than half a century to hold us in willing thrall. But at an age when every other composer known to us, Gluck excepted, had achieved either excellence or renown, Frederick remained unknown, unplayed, and unpublished save for a handful of songs, and seemingly content to wait for the day when the coil of notions and fancies haunting his brain could be unravelled and imprisoned in forms fitting to receive them. And it is permissible to doubt whether he would ever have approached the heights which he eventually scaled, had it not been for a chain of events which began to be forged about this time. Many years ago I read somewhere a suggestive comment that although the *Ring* might have been written in Germany, had Wagner not been driven from it into exile, it would not have been the towering monument he has left us, had he not been forced to spend so many years in the midst of the rugged magnificence of the Swiss mountains. Similarly if Frederick had prolonged his ten-year residence in Paris indefinitely, and without the choice of an outlet elsewhere, the creation of *Sea Drift*, *A Mass of Life* or *A Village Romeo and Juliet* might not have been wholly thwarted, but I question if we should have had these absolute expressions of his individuality in quite the shape they took, and with the quality of workmanship bestowed upon them. Happily for its salvation the High Gods took his affairs in hand just as with Richard Wagner, and worked out his future for him, though with less stress and antagonism than for the great German master. They chose the more agreeable agency of feminine influence, and gradually guided it to ends which the gentle instrument of their design could never have foreseen.

76

A year or two before this time, 1896, a young woman had come to Paris to study painting. The French capital was basking in the reflected glory of that school of artists, which less than a generation earlier it had refused to honour. But the long battle over Impressionism had been fought and won, and Manet, Monet, Renoir, Degas and Cezanne were the gods of the hour. Jelka Rosen, although born in Belgrade, was a member of an old Schleswig-Holstein family, well known and distinguished in diplomatic and legal circles. Strikingly fair and a true child of the north, her appearance, although without pretensions to orthodox beauty, was fresh and winsome, and her manners were habitually gracious and amiable. She had an undeniable gift for painting, impressionistic naturally, was well read, fond of music, and like every other young female of that pre-recording-cum-broadcasting age, could sing a little, her favourite composer being Grieg.

One of her friends whom she frequently visited had often spoken of a young Englishman who also loved Grieg and was by way of being a composer himself. And so it came about that on a momentous evening in January 1896 the painter and the musician were brought together for the first time. Several years before her death in 1935, as I have already related, Mrs. Delius wrote down at my request an account of her early acquaintanceship with the man who afterwards became her husband, and I venture to draw upon much of her own version of what passed between them, as it is far more vivid and subjective than any narration of mine could be. Speaking of a dinner-party arranged by a friend, Jelka tells us:

'He was there too, a tall thin man of aristocratic bearing, with dark curly hair slightly tinged with auburn, and an auburn moustache which he was perpetually twisting upwards. He wore a red tie, a memorial of earlier association with Russian revolutionaries. At that time I was full of enthusiasm for Nietzsche's *Zarathustra* which I was reading, and I was greatly surprised when this young Englishman said that he also knew and admired the book. It was out of my copy of it that years later he selected the text for *A Mass of Life*.'

After dinner there followed the customary hour of music-making, and Jelka 'obliged' with two songs of Grieg.

77

'In after years [she goes on to say], I often marvelled at my naïveté in doing such a thing, as my voice was a very small soprano and I had received only a few singing and breathing lessons. But Delius seemed to like it, for he offered to come to my studio with a book of his own songs.'

The visit took place a couple of days later; the promised songs, twelve in number, were played by the composer, and the effect on the listener was instantaneous and unforgettable.

'What a glorious revelation,' she writes, 'the harmonies, the "Stimmung" were so fresh and delightful, more so than anything I had ever known before.' The group selected by Frederick included four songs familiar to our public through their English titles:

'The Cradle Song'   'Venevil'
'Homeward Journey'   'Twilight Fancies'.

Of the last named she tells us:

'Even now, when this song is popular and hackneyed, I cannot think of it without a pang of my old passionate anxiety. For after a while it began to symbolize my fear that such a poet could not find enough in me to interest him seriously, that his friendship would soon come to an end and that the world then would be a blank—"*und die Sonne sank*"—the sun gone down for ever.'

The romantic reader would be hasty in jumping to the conclusion that here was a charming instance of that rare occasion, love at first sight on both sides. The experiences of the hero and heroine in the immortal tale of Musaeus and Marlowe are not so common as might be popularly imagined. But so far as the lady was concerned, it took her next to no time to decide that here was the one man in the world for her, and never would there be another. For Jelka Rosen was by no means an ordinary young woman. Although the studios of Paris had not yet been crammed to overflowing by the crowd of dilettante daubers, mainly Anglo-Saxon, whose preoccupation was less painting than a good easy time, after the style of *La Vie de Bohème*, there were already too many of those who without definite talent had mistaken their occupation, as well as others of wandering aim and fragmentary effort. But Jelka was a creature of a different stamp.

She worked in her studio ten hours a day, took little pleasure in the company of her acquaintances of either sex, especially the men of her own age, whom she found uninteresting and ill-read, and possessed even then a disposition inclined to gravity of thought and a quiet intensity of emotion which never deserted her.

As for Frederick, I do not think that at that moment he had travelled any farther in his thoughts of this new friend than a natural gratification at having aroused the interest of an attractive and gifted young woman, who clearly adored his music, probably failed to conceal her lively admiration for himself, and whose tranquil and reflective nature formed a fitting foil to his own volatility and discursiveness. But that the couple soon became fairly close friends is evident from the reminiscences of Jelka, and it is not straining probability to surmise that the relationship may have inclined on occasion towards the agreeable direction of an *amitié amoureuse*.

Spring had now come and with it the universal longing to get out of Paris into the country. Thus Jelka:

'Delius loved going for long walks and often took me with him. We went by train to some outlying place and then rambled about in woods and unfrequented lanes, talking the while, but often quite silent. On our return to the city we dropped sometimes into his flat, a part of a small old house in the Rue Ducoüedic on Montrouge. He had persuaded the proprietor to knock two little rooms into one, and this made a pleasant two-windowed apartment containing a grand piano, a red carpet and a square table. Next it was a tiny bedroom and an equally tiny kitchen. He would rush out, buy a large beefsteak, some eggs and a bunch of watercress. We then put the kettle on the sitting-room fire and lit the oven, a charcoal affair in the kitchen where, as always, he did his own cooking, something he had learnt during his Florida days. While all this was getting ready, he would play for me bits of compositions, new and old, and I can remember clearly one afternoon listening to a lovely fragment about the sun rising on a stream, from an opera *Irmelin* of which he seemed very fond. After the meal he would clear away and I then felt it was time for me to leave as he seemed to be wanting to return to his music. It was my salvation, I think, that I well understood this, as it always angered him if people kept hanging about when the fit was upon him to be alone with his task. He hardly ever wrote in the daytime, as noise of any kind he found destructive to concentration, and at this particular time it was more than usually impossible owing to the constant hammering of someone in the vicinity who was making or repairing copper utensils.'

The nocturnal habits of Frederick seem from the beginning to have caused anxiety to the maternal instinct in his young companion.

'The picture of Delius coming along the Avenue de Maine where I had my studio stands out most vividly. An old grey hat, his blue vivacious eyes, pale face, and a red tie accentuating the pallor. He wore a McFarlane coat of greyish tweed, a cherished garment that lasted many winters in Grez, the flaps of which he used always to throw back over his shoulders. I remember well too the pang of apprehension I felt at the almost entire lack of colour in his face. He worked most of the night, smoking and drinking red wine, stayed in bed late well into the next morning, debarred from work by the various noises in that populous and busy courtyard.'

With the coming of May painters sent off their newest works to the annual show at the Salon, and Jelka was among those exhibiting. She had just finished a large canvas called *Le Dernier Accord*, which represented a nude female sitting in a landscape enveloped by the dying golden sun of early evening and striking a chord on a harp. Of a certainty Frederick will have repaid the young painter for her unqualified devotion to his music, by some candid and useful advice on an art of which he had more than average knowledge. He was a personal friend of some of the masters of the craft of which as yet Jelka was but a promising apprentice, and his gift of criticism, pungent but kindly, seems to have been gratefully acknowledged.

'Having then known [she says] only men who either unduly flattered or decried me, it was wonderful to find a friend who not only took me seriously, but was always sincere. This sincerity Frederick preserved throughout his whole life, and it carried him through some highly difficult situations where I would not have dared to be so completely truthful.'

Jelka, having packed off her potential masterpiece to the hall of pictorial judgment, sought a few days' rest and relief in her regular

The house at Grez

retreat, the village of Grez-sur-Loing, some forty miles out of Paris. In the adjacent hamlet, Bourron, was staying an Englishman and an author, C. F. Keary by name. It was to him that Frederick had given the somewhat unenviable job of writing an opera libretto based on a tragical story of the American novelist Cable, and depicting Negro life on a plantation in one of the Southern States of North America during the early part of the nineteenth century. Keary's share in the transaction was to embellish the outline of the tale with suitable verbiage, which he at first found some difficulty in hitting upon. His natural style took small stock of the need for easily singable words, and both his lyrical and tragical periods had a high-flown redundancy wholly obnoxious to the taste of his musical partner. Apart from the thought contained in any literary work, poetry or prose, Frederick valued above all else the virtues of clarity and simplicity. This is evident in his choice of subjects where the use of English words is involved, as in *Sea Drift*, the *Idyll*, *Songs of Sunset* and the lyrics of Jonson, Herrick and Shelley. The rich and ornamental utterance of Swinburne, for example, fatigued his ear, in seeming to hinder that easy and instant perception of the point of a lyric allied to music, which for him was essential to its rapid comprehension on the listener's part.

Milton has told us that poetry should be primarily simple, sensuous, and passionate, although it may with deep respect be hinted that he was not always faithful to this excellent precept. So much of the best English verse likely to come a composer's way in the 'eighties and 'nineties of the last century was elaborate, rhetorical and narrative; and a preponderant leaning to heroic metres rendered it unwieldy for musical purposes. The revival of interest in Elizabethan and Jacobean literature, dramatic and lyrical, had not yet passed beyond the circles of scholars and connoisseurs to the larger public, in spite of the devoted proselytizing of men like A. H. Bullen and Havelock Ellis. Of that golden age when nearly every poet, great or small, brought forth with bewildering facility a store of matchless song greater and lovelier than any known before or since, and of which half at least should be on the ready lips of everyone in any really cultured community, Frederick was probably unaware. It is significant that it was not until 1915 and after his several visits to England which, excepting the isolated excursion in 1899, began in 1907, that he began to realize how adaptable to his own touch for epigram were the three examples chosen for musical treatment of Jonson, Herrick and Nashe.

12

THE necessity to exercise a moderating control over the exuberances of Keary, joined possibly to the attraction in the near neighbourhood of a highly sympathetic female companion, soon brought him down to Bourron. He lost no time in persuading his colleague, who luckily was a man of good sense and perfect amiability, in spite of his previous conviction that operatic language should emulate such expansive and luxuriant models as *Hesperia*, or even *Lucile*, to adopt a plainer type of diction for the requirements both of the subject and the music for which it was being designed. For recreation, author and composer took walks in the adjoining forest, where they were often accompanied by Jelka, who was living barely a mile away. After lunch one day Frederick, to the delight of his two friends, brought out a fiddle on which he played many Negro melodies, some of which he was minded to introduce into the work under way. His method of execution on this instrument was similar to that of the Norwegian peasant upon the Hardanger Fela (a species of violin), on which the performer fills in as many of the harmonies to the tune he is playing as he can conveniently manipulate. On one of his return visits to Jelka at Grez, they hired a boat and rowed along the little river Loing, a tributary of the Marne. With some effort they passed under the old stone bridge just outside the village, for the river was running unusually high that day, and gained the landing-place of an ancient and deserted garden, the property of a certain Marquis de Carzeaux. Concerning this adventure, worthy of note in the light of events yet hidden behind the veil of futurity, I will draw again upon Jelka's own account.

'For several summers I had obtained permission to paint in this grand old garden. I used to take there my nude models and work away undisturbed by anyone, except now and then the Curé who, living next door in the "Presbytère", would climb up to a little terrace high upon the tower of the church, a part of which dated back to the days of Charlemagne. Sometimes he was joined by a few other priests who had been lunching with him, and they made a point of ascending to view our activities, appreciating especially the sight of the loveliest of my models, Marcelle. Delius was enchanted with it all on this beautiful spring day of blue sky and fleeting clouds, the grey pile of the big solid church, opposite to it the ruin of an early mediaeval castle, "La Tour de Gal", also grey in tone, and at the far end of the garden the outline of a rambling but cosy-looking dwelling whose front door opened to the village street. Surrounding the buildings forming this picture were the numerous little houses all wearing the colour of antiquity and breathing forth an atmosphere of tranquillity and content. At a very still moment Fred whispered to me "A place like this one could really work in; everything is quiet and unspoilt." Prophetic words, but neither of us knew how much so at that time. What made this garden so perfect was that it ran right down to the river with no path or public right of way to divide it. And on the opposite side there were meadows bordered by French poplars, a terrain on which no houses could be built as it was so often completely flooded in spring-time.'

During the early part of the summer, Frederick settled down to work on the music of *Koanga* and in all probability finished the sketches of the first two acts. There is a recognizable consistency both in the style as well as the management of all the scenes in these sections of the work, just as it is equally obvious that some interval of time separates them from the final act, where we can unmistakably hear a richer and deeper note. But one hint we have already had, small though it be, of his growing power to give utterance to moments of dramatic intensity in the second of the two Verlaine songs 'Le ciel est pardessus le toit' with its powerful and unexpected climax in the setting of the words 'Qu'as-tu fait de ta jeunesse'. Rarely I think can a lament over lost happiness in youth have been sung more poignantly. In August he paid his almost annual visit to Norway, staying on a farm in the Valdres district. The peaceful regularity of his holiday was uninterrupted save for the death of the very aged grandmother of the family. Such an occasion was even more ceremonial than in Ireland, and as everyone in Norway seems to be related to someone else within a radius of a hundred miles, it was traditional to procure the presence on the scene of a vast assembly. This took about a week to ensure, during which the huge operations of killing, baking and cooking went on without pause. The chief problem during these seven days of preparation was the corpse and what to do with it. This was happily solved by stowing it away in a freezingly cold cellar, where it remained in perfect condition until the arrival of all the clans. Shortly after this he varied the monotony of a long rural vacation by embarking on an extensive concert tour in company with a violinist, Halfdan Jebe by name, and Knut Hamsun[1] the author. Frederick accompanied Jebe on the piano and even gave solos on his own account. I once asked him what he had played, and he answered, 'All Chopin.' As at that time I had heard him occasionally strumming on the keyboard in a way that in no wise suggested overfamiliarity with the character and capacities of that instrument, I gazed at him incredulously for several moments. But he smiled somewhat mysteriously, and assured me that in very truth he had essayed this courageous task. I remained for quite a while undecided as to which of two possible explanations of the mystery could satisfy my curiosity: his own unbounded assurance, or the undeveloped state of musical culture in Norwegian provincial audiences. What part Knut Hamsun played on this remarkable tour I never could learn, but he could not have been the most accommodating of companions on such an expedition, penetrating as it did into remote mountain villages, some of which did not contain more than a hundred inhabitants. He was a man of imposing appearance and never went anywhere without wearing a top hat and frock-coat, to the delight and astonishment of the smaller communities included in the wanderings of the trio. One apparently authentic, although unpublished, story of the eminent writer has come down to us, and it tells of a highly important occasion when he was to appear in some function at one of the principal hotels in the capital. He ascended the steps leading to the verandah on which was gathered a large number of guests waiting to welcome him, and it was observed that he had taken more than ordinary care to adorn his person and enhance the majesty of his demeanour. Suddenly he fell down full length, half-way up the steps, resolutely declined to move or be moved; and although it was

[1] One of the greatest of Norwegian poets and novelists. His most famous work *The Growth of the Soil* won the Nobel prize for literature in 1920.

84

a beautiful bright day with a fresh breeze blowing across the town, ingeminated more than ten times in a stentorian voice, 'Bring me air, bring me air.' One cannot help being reminded, though grimly, of the last lines in *Ghosts* where the unhappy victim of an immeasurably greater disaster asks for the sun.

It cannot be stated with absolute certainty what tasks Frederick was engaged upon during the autumn months, but from calculations backwards and forwards, and also from the very definite knowledge of what he was doing through the succeeding years 1897–8, it may be fairly assumed that he was proceeding with the score of *Koanga*, making the first sketches for the Piano Concerto and planning, if only in a fragmentary and tentative way, the layout of *Paris*. Among the numerous manuscript fragments brought to light after the composer's death were three sketches of material for the great nocturne entitled

'Scènes Parisiennes'
'L'heure d'absinthe'
'Heureuse rencontre',

which would seem to date from this period. Towards the close of the year occurred an event which brought dismay and apprehension to one of the principal personages in this narration. I will let Jelka speak for herself.

'About Christmas I went to supper with Fred at the Rue Ducoüedic. His Norwegian friend, Jebe the violinist,[1] was with him, and I learnt that they were intending to make a trip to the orange grove in Florida and would be away several months. I was miserable and a terrible fear clutched my heart that all might be over and that by the time he returned he would have forgotten our happy association. I knew that he had many women friends, French, English, Scandinavian, and some of exceeding beauty, while I was only too conscious how plain I must look with my hair tightly twisted and pulled into a figure eight on the top of my head. My clothes too, were all totally unbecoming, ordered by

---

[1] This extraordinary person, like his famous countryman Ole Bull, spent most of his life wandering with his fiddle, up and down the world. He was a brilliant player whose style reflected a disposition of the liveliest ebullience. While on his travels he wrote occasionally to Frederick and his letters are among the most outrageously Rabelaisian I have ever read. He was about the only Delian intimate whose appearance, speech and habits Jelka signally failed to appreciate

my dear mother from inferior dressmakers. I never had leisure to think about such things, for I worked nearly all day in my studio and in the evenings had to amuse my mother, either by taking her to concerts, or going with her to dine at some friend's house. One of her intimates was a Mme Danke whose husband had been a composer and whose songs, quite commonplace and tedious, I was always being asked to sing. When I became acquainted with the Delius songs and brought them forward one by one in that household, the old lady began to be suspicious that something had happened to cause a change in me. She knew Fred's uncle who had often spoken to her of his gifted nephew, and one day said to my mother, "*Ah, méfiez-vous, madame, la musique a perdu tant de filles.*" '

It is probable that poor Jelka would have been even more worried had she known at the time of the comically romantic conditions under which her hero began his second voyage to the New World.

The avowed purpose of the trip was to inspect the plantation he had abandoned ten years ago, and to satisfy himself that the optimistic expectations of Thrane would sufficiently justify him in carrying out a scheme that might prove advantageous to himself. If the estate were in the good condition as reported, he would make an offer to his father, under which the latter would hand over the title deeds and be released from all obligation to pay him any further moneys by way of allowance. I might here anticipate events by several months and disclose that the offer was made and accepted upon Frederick's return to France, when Julius executed an assignment to that effect on August 14th, 1897. At the same time I cannot resist the impression that Frederick was finding life in Paris a trifle too complicated for his comfort and peace of mind and, like many a wise man before him, had considered the best thing to do was to get as far away from the scene of the imbroglio as was possible. The possession of a piece of property about five thousand miles away, that needed some sort of attention, was a heaven-sent excuse and apology for withdrawing for a brief while from the dangerous charms of Lutetian society. If there be anything in this interpretation of one of the reasons for his departure for the land of the free, it will be the easier to imagine his consternation on discovering that his beautifully planned scheme had been mined and blown sky-high by the ingenuity and resource of one of that fascinating crowd of lovely sirens who tortured the dreams of poor Jelka. There she was, a distinguished and high-born dame disguised as a young man, smiling and triumphant, her purpose accomplished; which had been that under no circumstances was she minded to endure separation from Frederick, and now—what was he going to do about it? The answer, if he ever gave one, was obviously—nothing. Four hundred miles out at sea, and six full days to run before reaching the haven of New York. I am tolerably sure that Frederick, who was an eminently rational creature in many respects, soon bowed his head to the compelling force of circumstances which he was powerless to control, and made the best of the situation.

At least three or four famous men, I think the latest of them was Mr. Somerset Maugham, have professed to find something slightly ridiculous in the attitude of Joseph to Potiphar's wife. Into the ethics of this opinion I am not competent to enter. But looked at from the angle of view of an aesthete or philosopher, I am not ashamed to admit that the spectacle of a willing lady *versus* an unwilling gentleman is one that rarely fails to plague me with a touch of discomfort and embarrassment. There are, of course, plenty of stoical and impassive souls who can suffer such minor emotional disturbances with either indifference or fortitude, but Frederick, I have reason to suspect, was of a different mould. For we find by one of those roundabout methods which appeal irresistibly to the industrious historian, that our travellers not only passed the rest of the time on board in perfect amity, but journeyed through Danville down to Florida together, where they happily united their talents in attending (exclusively it may be hoped) to the task of placing the affairs of Solano Grove on a sound and proper basis.

There we can comfortably leave them for the rest of their trip, and return to Paris to see how the real heroine of the story is bearing the sorrows of separation. Again her own words:

'I struggled through this winter of 1896–7, very unsettled, uncertain and unhappy. Paris life and the people I knew, most of all the men, I was growing to dislike actively, and the insistent thought of Delius never left me. In the spring I was informed that Le Marquis de Carzeaux was trying to sell his estate at Grez, as he was in urgent need of ready money.'

He had invested, it is related, a million francs in the famous

87

'Coffre Fort' of Mme Humbert, one of the astutest swindlers of the age, and it had all vanished, together with the financial contributions of a hundred others of similar credulity.

'The proposed sale was a heavy blow for me. Deprived of my garden, where could I find anywhere another at all like it in which to paint? And just at the moment too when more than ever I felt that I should live more at Grez and less in Paris. Although the property was being offered for a comparatively moderate sum, the money I had inherited from my father would barely cover half the purchase price. But a voice within me kept on saying that I *must* buy the place, and that I must do all within my power to accomplish this end. Perhaps my mother would agree to loan me the balance of the sum I needed. The struggle, anxieties, set-backs, hopes and fears of this time are beyond description; yet through it all I knew that I simply had to have my way, live in the house there, forget Paris, start again leading my own life and no longer wait for Fred who surely did not care for me at all. At last I got my poor mother to acquiesce, and we journeyed down to Grez the day before completion of the purchase with the money in cash, for the Marquis had stipulated that it must be deposited on the table upon the signing of the contract.'

His unhappy experience over the Humbert safe must have made him highly suspicious of any kind of payment less tangible than the picturesque green notes of the Bank of France.

'My mother could not sleep a wink that night, mortally afraid of being murdered with all that money in her charge; but when we were on our way next morning in a little pony cart to the château of the Marquis, we found that bewildered by fear and excitement she had forgotten to take her precious hoard from beneath the pillow of her bed.'

To furnish the residence Jelka had only the few pieces in her Paris studio. These she removed to Grez, and entered into actual possession of her new domain on May 17th. The first night of occupation she slept alone in a house as nearly bare as an empty shell. But what did that matter? The garden, so overgrown with nettles that the flagstones

88

in the courtyard were quite invisible, was flooded by moonlight; owls flew to and from the church and the castle, and the Gloire de Dijon roses, now grown as high as the first floor, were scenting her bedroom. Here she would find peace and forgetfulness, and gradually recover that tranquillity of mind and soul which had departed from her on the day she first looked upon the stranger, whose personal charm and mysterious music had so unhappily diverted the even course of her life. Yes, unhappily; for how could there longer be any doubt that the dream she had cherished for nearly eighteen months had never any real chance of fulfilment, and the time had come for it to return through that ivory gate whence it never should have issued. For no man who really cares one rap for a woman stays from her for the period Frederick had been absent, without any intimation of when he would be returning: and surely the purpose of his Florida trip could have been accomplished satisfactorily long before this. Again, was not the air full of rumour about the disappearance from Paris, on the opening day of his voyage, and the prolonged absence of one of that fascinating bevy of Delian admirers, whose beauty, elegance and sophistication had harassed the waking and sleeping thoughts of a simple servant in the outer court of the temple of a great art!

Yes, from this heavenly sanctuary in which she would resume her former untroubled existence, all vain desires would be expelled and the vision of fame dethrone that of love.

13

ALMOST immediately Jelka was joined by her oldest and greatest friend, Ida Gerhardi, also a painter of some merit. The new-comer, who had a slight advantage over Jelka in age and experience, brought along some of her own furniture so that the house quickly became habitable and fairly comfortable. They repainted the inside walls and transformed that part of the building which had been a tiny tobacconist's shop looking on to the street into a serviceable dining-room. They procured the permanent help of a middle-aged Bretonne who had formerly been employed by a Swedish-American family living in Grez, and this admirable person quickly took over the control of all domestic responsibilities, even found time to work in the garden, and best of all never allowed her young charges to be cheated of a sou. Thus began an idyllic existence for the fair dwellers in their little Arcadia, shut off from the outer world of clamour and bustle, as seemingly safe from the intrusion of the unsatisfactory male as the 'sweet girl graduates' who bound themselves 'not for three years to speak with any man', and self-dedicated to the austere cultivation of their art. But alas for their pious aspirations! Hardly six weeks of their cloistral happiness had gone by when, about the end of June or beginning of July, a card was dropped through an open window by the village postman, that set up a mighty perturbation in the breast of the younger of the two ladies in this miniature Academe.

The wanderer had returned to France, had learnt all about the chaste establishment in Grez and was proposing to visit it the very next day. 'Oh, was all the old anxiety to begin again?' sighed the palpitating recipient of this fateful communication, but adds 'and yet how heavenly it was'! And come he did, simply and naturally, we are told, as was his wont, with a little suitcase and said no more than, 'I suppose you can put me up.' The mental reaction of most ordinary individuals unacquainted with the respective characters of two highly unusual personalities to this decidedly unconventional request, would very likely be expressed in such resentful terms as, 'What colossal impudence!' or 'Any self-respecting woman would slam the door in his face.' But in the case of Frederick there was nothing at all out of the way in this his own method of handling what was manifestly a delicate situation; and as for Jelka, an inner voice counselled that it might be unwise at this critical juncture to exhibit too much interest in her friend's adventures of the past half-year. Doubtless before long, and in one way and another, the true story would be told; and as the main stake in the game was her own happiness, she would play her cards with patience and care.

But although her emotional response to the apparition that had turned up so unexpectedly was one of overwhelming relief and pleasure, her native good sense and strict training under a vilgilant maternal eye recoiled instinctively from admitting it at once, in this unconventional fashion, to the intimacy of her little circle. Much as she might have liked the idea of installing the visitor safely under her own roof, there were the good neighbours to think of, not forgetting the Curé who lived next door. Besides, friend Ida had gone away on a brief visit, so that, save for the excellent and pious treasure from Britanny, she was alone in the house. The conflict between heart and head was satisfactorily adjusted by moving her piano into a yet unfurnished room, adding a table and a chair so that Frederick could come whenever he liked during the day to work there, and procuring for him sleeping accommodation near at hand. As it gradually became known where the voluntary exiles from Paris had retired, friends, mostly painters and writers who were spending the summer months in one of the adjoining villages of Barbizon and Marlotte, began to make their appearance, dropping in usually at the end of day. If the callers were many and the evenings fine, the party went out of doors and sat in a circle round a table bearing refreshments, either in the little paved courtyard under the shadow of the house, or at the bottom of the garden by the river bank. And should there be present a few lively souls blessed like Frederick with an aptitude for animated argument on any subject touching the Arts, conversation rarely failed to become violently controversial. A dozen years later when I was sometimes privileged to take part in these dialectical orgies, his polemical powers were as vigorous as ever, and on one occasion, as hour after hour went by and the twilight began to merge into nightfall, I found myself recalling the similar experience of those two famous characters in Cory's poem 'Heraclitus'.

A permanent neighbour was his countryman, Alfred Sisley, who for eighteen years had been living in the old walled town of Moret, to which Thomas à Becket, six hundred and fifty years earlier, had fled from the anger of a vengeful monarch. A strain of similarity runs through the two lives of Delius and the great Impressionist.[1] Both were of English origin and the sons of well-to-do industrialists. Both had turned their backs upon Commerce in favour of Art, and both had chosen to pass their mature years in a foreign land. But although the closing days of each were in their own different ways almost equally painful and frustrated, there is no parallel between the musician and painter in the quest of worldly success. For while the fame and popularity of the former steadily lifted him to the status of a national figure, the latter, one of the greater artists of his generation, was harassed throughout a long public career by total neglect and unrelieved hardship.

It has always seemed to me that there is a distinct affinity between the minds and methods of this remarkable pair. The power and scope of the elder of the two in his own art cannot approach that of the younger, who has comprehended, captured and transcribed into sound nearly every mood of nature. But in the depiction of her gentler and softer aspects, the poet of colour fairly rivals the poet of tone. Less bold, startling and experimental than most of his companions of the Impressionistic school, Sisley excels where a simple delicacy and one may even say restraint of advance to the subject under his hand are needed. This moderation or temperance of touch was regarded by some of his contemporaries as timidity or lack of initiative. But I attribute it to the streak of Britannic reticence in him, to be observed also in Delius, who shrank instinctively from even the suspicion of strident excess in any form of artistic expression. When hearing 'A Song Before Sunrise', 'A Summer Garden', or 'Summer Night on the River', it is a pleasing indulgence and one in no way disrespectful to the composer, to permit the mind's eye to wander away to the contemplation of some of Sisley's lovely scenes of the Seine and the Loing. And conversely it is

[1] The distinguished Modern Art critic Monsieur Raymond Cognait has written about him: 'Sisley est, avec Monet et Pisarro, et peut-être plus encore ceux-ci, celui qui a su rester un Impressionniste a l'état pur, et qui ne s'est jamais lassé de dire la poésie toujours renouveler des paysages de l'Ile-de-France, ses sous-bois, ses ciels cerises et rues charmantes—même sans pittoresque—dans les petites villes de banlieue.'

equally agreeable, when we view them in the life, to fancy that we are listening to Delius's counterparts of them in sound.

It was during these pleasant summer months that Frederick completed the third act of *Koanga* and the tone poem *Over the Hills and Far Away*, an actively and at times a vigorously happy sort of piece. Its combination of serene content and lively impulse is none too frequent in him, for while there are copious examples in his music of one or the other of these two contrasting moods, they rarely contrive to come together. As in the case of *Eventyr*, written nearly twenty years after, we meet a general style together with a choice of phrase that give it something of the ring and lilt of a fairy-tale; and the opening passages of both works seldom fail to lead the imaginative listener back to childhood days, and those eagerly awaited words that ushered him or her into so many a land of magic and mystery, 'Once upon a time'.

As the year moved onward towards autumn, Frederick was invited to leave his lodgings over the way and take up his residence where, hitherto, he had been only a daily visitor. The author of this migration somewhat surprisingly was neither Jelka nor her friend, who was still living with her, but the admirable auxiliary from Brittany. More efficiently perhaps than any other specimen of human kind does the French peasant contrive to harmonize or reconcile the duties, so often warring with one another, to God and Mammon. At least twenty years older than either of the two ladies of the house and a zealous churchwoman, she was as protective of the good name of her two youthful employers as any scrupulous parent could be. But to her solidly practical intelligence there was an incongruity of a material kind in the inter-relations of the three charming persons who, living and working the whole day under the same roof, separated at nightfall. Here was a fairly capacious house with several rooms as yet untenanted, and a dozen yards away was an estimable young man, in whose affairs she took almost as much interest as Jelka and Ida, who occupied unattractive quarters, and, worse still, was paying rent for them when he might be made far more comfortable in the free and unoccupied section of the establishment under her care. As Jelka, we may be sure, offered no serious objection to this proposition, coming as it did from a quarter of such unimpeachable propriety, Frederick found himself the virtual master of a spacious wing where he could work any hour of the day or night, and even strum on the piano during the small hours of the morning, without disturbing the labours or rest of the other occupants of the building.

He still continued, if not so methodically, his old Paris habit of composing mostly at night, and it was not for another few years that Jelka finally succeeded in converting him to a more normal scheme of work. From that happy moment onward we may discern a growing metamorphosis of spirit in nearly all the productions of the succeeding decade. Sunshine and fresh air began to penetrate more freely into the brain and nerves of one accustomed to labour too habitually by lamp-light for the good of his genius. With the exception of a portion of the third act of *Koanga*—and that is a peep into a scene heavy and almost overladen with the luxuriance of the Deep South—we have not yet felt the full healing influence upon the composer of his closer daily communion with the sounds and sights of a sober and yet stimulating landscape. And with this lightening and brightening of the spirit, there were to come a tighter grip upon the raw material the worker had to mould, an easier and broader style of utterance, and enlarging resources of device and colour. But it is only by slow-moving degrees that we shall trace with pleasure the processes of this changing course of development; for bright, fresh and picturesque as is *Over the Hills and Far Away*, the essence of the Delius that is to be is not easily discernible there. Truly and indisputably magnificent is the picture of Paris by night, that Song of a Great City, with its startlingly contrasted episodes of boisterous revelry and tender romance. Yet, when the stars have faded from the sky, when a sudden silence falls upon the emptied streets and 'the dawn comes up like thunder', we hardly feel upon our cheeks, as we should assuredly have done a few years later, a touch of the reviving breath of the new-born day.

This happy period was one of continuous activity for Frederick and unbounded gratification for Jelka, who witnessed with delight the appearance of some fresh piece of creation almost every week, and all happening under her roof. It was now that, after a break of two years, he turned again to song-writing, choosing six lyrics of I. P. Jacobsen and one of Holgar Drachmann. The English titles of them are:

> 'On the Sea Shore' (Drachmann)
> 'Through the Long, Long Years' (Jacobsen)
> 'Wine Roses' (Jacobsen)
> 'Let Springtime Come' (Jacobsen)

'Irmelin Rose' (Jacobsen)
'In the Seraglio Garden' (Jacobsen)
'Silken Shoes' (Jacobsen).

The first three of these remain unpublished. Of the other four 'Irmelin Rose' is, perhaps, the most attractive, although the charming refrain is borrowed from the earliest of his operas. 'In the Seraglio Garden' is not only an excellent song in itself, but in contradistinction to 'Irmelin Rose' which looks back to the past, anticipates the future by presenting us with the theme which opens the third number of *A Mass of Life*.

What the composer's reasons were for withholding publication of the two other Jacobsen lyrics I do not know, for they are, 'Wine Roses' especially, both more interesting and typical than any of the four Nietzsche songs written a year later. It may be that his judgment of the poetical quality of the philosopher's verse was influenced by his admiration for a prose style, which he always ranked above that of every other German writer, with the possible exception of Heine. Although he periodically reverted to it, song-writing was never something vitally essential to him. Unlike men such as Grieg, Wolf and Fauré with whom it was largely and, in one instance, the almost exclusive preoccupation of a career, he seems to have regarded it as a species of relaxation from what was to him the serious interest of his life, the orchestra and any class of composition in which it played a leading part. It is true that, during the few years following his return to Europe from America, he produced four sets of songs numbering twenty-one in all, six still unpublished; but these were incidental to the several larger designs on which he was then working, including a dozen instrumental pieces and two operas. It is significant that during the forty-four years of life remaining to him after these youthful efforts he brought forth no more than twenty-five, of which nine were never sent to the printer: and if we take the period 1900–1920, there remain hardly a dozen, two of them ditties for children and one other still reposing in manuscript. But of more interest in every way than these casual fragments, or indeed anything else he was labouring upon at this moment, was the fortunate discovery of a melody which was to serve years later as the central theme or 'Motto' in the most important of all his creations outside the Theatre.

Jelka recalls how late one evening she and Ida were called down from the side of the house they occupied together, to hear this fresh piece of musical coinage from Frederick's inventive mint, and how they sat upon the floor (there was as yet only one chair in the room), watching him play by the faint light of a single candle the first sketch of Zarathustra's Nightsong. I should like to think that the composer made a point of including in his little audience the kindly agent of his presence there, for we know that more than one eminent author or musician has set some store by the opinion of his housekeeper or cook, as being likely to be blessedly free of all prepossessions or prejudices of an academical order. Ethel Smyth once told me how while staying with her elder sister, Mrs. Charles Hunter, at her house in Epping Forest, she played a newly written piece of hers to the entire domestic staff. Shortly afterwards I had an opportunity of asking the butler what was the impression made upon him and his associates by this performance, executed as usual by Ethel with all imaginable vocal and manual vigour. His reply was, 'Well, sir, we all fell agaping.' I felt then that I had pushed my curiosity to the furthest point this side of indiscretion, and disrespect to the principal figure involved, and refrained from any attempt to elucidate the meaning of this slightly cryptic judgment.

As seen by Riccardi,
aged about fifty-four

With Henry Clews at Grez

View from the garden at Grez

The garden seen from the river

14

ABOUT the beginning of September there arrived at Grez, Gunnar Heiberg,[1] bringing with him the script of his new comedy *Folkeraadet*. For this highly diverting satire on Norwegian political life Frederick had consented to write incidental music. The task was neither complicated nor arduous for the character of the play provided small opportunity for lyricism and romance. Although some of the music had been sketched out in piano score, no orchestration had yet been attempted, owing to the difficulty in discovering what instrumental resources would be available in the none too wealthy Christiania theatre. The four main movements of the work bear the marks of hasty composition which prompts the conjecture that its author may not have found the subject wholly congenial. It is also probable that he was giving more attention to the Piano Concerto on which he had been working earlier in the year, and putting finishing touches to *Over the Hills and Far Away*, which had been accepted for performance by Dr. Hans Haym in Elberfeld at the beginning of November. There are, however, a few characteristic features here and there of his good earlier style, notably in the contrapuntal handling of themes, intended (presumably) to match the ironical nature of the text, and at least one pretty tune of decidedly Scandinavian lilt associated with the heroine of the piece.

It was not until September 29th that he heard from Heiberg, now back at home, that there would be available for him in addition to strings and a wind octet, no more than 2 horns, 2 trumpets and 1 trombone, and that it was intended to put on the play about the middle of October. But as frequently happens in theatrical affairs there must have been some postponement of the opening date, for the composer did not set out for Norway until the end of the first week in October,

[1] Playwright and essayist of importance in the history of Norwegian literature. For some years director of the National Theatre of Bergen. His best-known works were satirical in tone, mostly at the expense of his countrymen.

with the score barely finished and the orchestral parts as yet uncopied.

A great deal of public interest had been aroused over the forth-coming event; information had been circulated as to the character of the new piece, and Heiberg informed Delius that he was looking forward to a lively reception. His expectations were realized to the full. The play was a riot with an audience largely consisting of students from the University, who demonstrated their disapproval every fifteen minutes by catcalling and hissing. The crowning moment came towards the later part of the evening when it was discovered that Frederick, who was conducting, had conceived the injudicious notion of introducing into the score a parodied version of the Norwegian National Hymn. The undergraduates of Norway's chief seat of learning arose in wrath as if to storm the stage, and one bright spark fired a blank cartridge from a pistol at the offending composer-conductor, who promptly vacated his place in the orchestral pit, fled the building and took refuge in the neighbouring Grand Hotel. There he found the venerable Ibsen, brooding over his habitual evening refreshment; overtly indignant about the affront offered to a distinguished visitor, but covertly amused and slightly gratified. For it has been credibly related that he remarked later on to a friend: 'I didn't think the young devils had such spirit in them.' All the same, the play proved to be a great draw and the malcontents soon thinking better of it passed a vote of censure on themselves for their unseemly conduct.

On the way back to France, Frederick halted the journey at Elber-feld to hear the performance of *Over the Hills and Far Away*. It was to Ida Gerhardi that he owed his introduction to the man who before long was to become the chief apostle of his music in the Fatherland. Dr. Hans Haym was an uncommon personality. A talented musician with an enquiring mind and a strong and tenacious disposition, he possessed an insight into unfamiliar works of merit well in advance of most German conductors of that day. Although he had taken some trouble over the piece and gave a tolerably good rendering of it, the Public was indifferent, the management of the concert hostile, and Haym was severely criticized for having inflicted upon the town such an outrageous specimen of musical modernity. After this second experience of unfriendly behaviour within a few weeks, the composer must have been more than a little relieved to regain the tranquillity of Grez, where he remained for a few weeks before returning to Paris. He had not yet abandoned his apartment in the Rue Ducoüedic, although he was gradually growing to look upon Grez as his main residence. Old habits are not easy to discard quickly, and some years had to go by before he irrevocably terminated his connection with the life of the brilliant metropolis.

His immediate task was the completion of his Piano Concerto and this was first played from a four-handed arrangement at a private house in Paris. The first part was taken by a friend of Jelka, a Franco-German pianist, Henry Falke and a Premier Prix du Conservatoire and the second by the composer himself. I do not imagine that the fashionable audience who had been invited to what was a French musical 'at home' made very much of the piece. Falke's share of the performance, according to the evidence of two or three present, including Jelka who had some knowledge of the work, appears to have been dry and unimpassioned; while that of Frederick, through technical limitations, could have done little to counter any deficiencies. This, the original version of the piece, remained unchanged for eight years and was that which was played frequently in Germany between 1904 and 1907. Next came the completion of the third and last act of *Koanga* which had been lying untouched since the late summer. I have already referred to the palpable disjunction between this act and those preceding it, and what is perhaps of some interest is a partial return to the spirit of his previous work *The Magic Fountain*. This I have little doubt was inspired by his recent Florida trip: for in the introduction to it we find about a hundred bars lifted bodily from the earlier opera. What is more noteworthy is that *Koanga* differs from all his other stage enterprises, except the one-act thriller *Margot la Rouge*, in being frankly and unashamedly 'operatic'.

If compared with its two predecessors we feel the absence of an underlying basis of emotional sincerity. Also unlike the principal characters in both *Irmelin* and *The Magic Fountain*, those in *Koanga* are drawn in obscurer outlines and have an odd unreality that fails to command our complete sympathy and interest, as is the case with Solano and Watawa, and Sali and Vreli.

It is not until the final act that Delius, forced to fall back upon nature, or in other words his better self for guidance and inspiration, gives us threequarters of an hour's music that we can hear with full satisfaction. At the beginning of its second scene we have a curious little tune which is quite Russian in sound and sentiment, although it is improbable that Frederick was acquainted with any of the operatic scores of Moussorgsky or Borodin at the time. While the lament of Palmyra over the dead body of her lover is rhetorical rather than poetical, it is fortunately not overlong, and the intermezzo which brings us back to the scene of the prologue together with the finale of the whole opera, are characteristic of the best work of his middle period. These two major compositions behind him, Frederick now felt free not only to conceive but to realize far more ambitious experiments in the purely orchestral line than anything he had hitherto attempted, so that it may be confidently said of 1898 that it was his critical year of advance and self-development. By the close of it he had completed *La Danse se Déroule*, the Nightsong of Zarathustra, the general line of the *Paris* that we know today and the re-planning of the *Appalachia* of 1896.

In the early part of the year the quarrel between himself and his uncle Theodor was patched up to the satisfaction of both parties, and the relief of our composer's best friends, to whom the drifting apart of two fastidious creatures who had so much in common in all things touching the external side of life, seemed a wanton blunder. The reconciliation if viewed from a worldly angle was accomplished almost in the nick of time, for a few months later in October the old gentleman died unexpectedly at the age of seventy-nine, bequeathing his nephew the modest legacy of 25,000 francs. Although the latter did not come into legal possession of this bequest until the end of the following March in 1899, he was able to anticipate its payment in expanding 500 francs over the purchase of a Gauguin picture 'Nevermore', which the painter on leaving Paris had left in the custody of his friend and representative Guy de Montfried. Montfried acknowledged the receipt of the payment on November 11th; the picture was despatched to Grez, was hung in the main sitting-room of the house and, except for its temporary removal during the First World War, remained there for twenty-four years.

His next venture was to lay the plans for an orchestral concert to be given during the late spring of 1899 in London. The business arrangements were entrusted to the Concorde Concert Control of 186 Wardour Street, regarded by many amateurs as the most progressive and active agency in London. To these people he had made himself known earlier in the year through his friends C. F. Keary and G. H. Clutsam, over one of those grandiose and visionary projects that occupied his mind from time to time. This was the creation of a permanent Opera in London, to be controlled by musicians, who would bring forward works of distinguished or meritorious composers unfamiliar to the public. It was perhaps natural that Frederick who had now three unperformed operas up his sleeve should have formed the view that having so far failed to secure a hearing for any one of them on the Continent, he might have better luck in his native country. It was also to be expected that those many other composers who were suffering from the same disability should look upon the scheme with full favour, and the Concorde firm realizing that there was attractive publicity value in the idea took it up with enthusiasm. Sir Augustus Harris, under whose firm and able control Covent Garden had flourished for over a decade, had died two years previously; and the Syndicate formed to take his place was, for the time being, pursuing a policy of caution and conventionality. It was therefore hardly to be expected that it would endanger or complicate the early period of its career with a wildly speculative flight into the unknown.

Norman Concorde, the senior of the two directors of the firm (the other was his wife) fired off his first gun in the form of a circular, which to the present writer has a ring of familiarity that is almost nostalgic.

'A certain number of persons recognizing that Opera as it has been given in England within recent years has not been an artistic success, have decided to found a permanent Opera in London upon the only system calculated to improve the condition of this art. The intention of the Company is to give not only the fine existing operas, but to introduce to the public unknown works of originality and genuine merit, altogether independent of the nationality of the composer. Whilst excluding entirely the present abominable 'star' system, their chief endeavour will be to establish the highest level of artistic expression. The operas will be produced in English; and English artists both vocal and instrumental, will receive every encouragement.'

The first effects of this announcement were a storm of enquiries at the Concorde offices and some highly sceptical and even cynical comments in the Press. This evoked from headquarters another pronouncement, full of fair promise, but carrying the matter little further. The energetic Norman, feeling that he was getting out of his depth, wrote on January 26th to his principal:

'The Press notices still continue to pour in, and as we have no one to consult, we do not like to make any move. We wish that you were here in order that you might formulate a strong plan of action. . . . All the Press notices seem to indicate that the scheme is simply visionary, and the sooner we can put it on a practical basis, the better. . . . We think that before issuing the prospectus to the public another strong circular should be sent out criticizing the Press and the position that they have taken. The question is: Is the Press influenced by artistic merit, or is it only dazzled by moneyed names?'

On the 31st he wrote again somewhat more insistently:

'I was glad to get your letter, but was extremely sorry that there is no chance of your coming over just yet. People will begin to think that I have been playing a practical joke on them, if something is not shortly issued. It would be both illegal and fatal to appeal to the public for money until we have formulated a scheme and something tangible to work on. It would be necessary first to form a syndicate before you can apply either to the public to sell shares or issue a prospectus. What we must do first of all is to send out another circular to the Press, criticising *their* criticisms and showing how they have misread or misinterpreted the first circular. You should be on the spot as soon as possible, as a scheme like this wants a man to devote a great deal of time to it, which we cannot afford to do.'

This seems to have stirred Frederick to suggest that an appeal for funds should be made forthwith, to which the prudent Norman replies:

'If we were to approach the public for money at the present time, we should be doing an absolutely illegal act, besides provoking damning criticism. We must form a syndicate before we take any such steps and then float the company properly. In the meantime we think that the circular we enclose as originally drawn would serve the purpose well. Please let us have a reply by return.'

But by February 24th he has begun to be acutely anxious about his own position in the affair and he writes very pointedly to say so:

'It seems that we are to be put in a most awkward position—we have committed ourselves by issuing the circular as a genuine scheme and now you appear to take no more interest in it; and as we depended entirely on you and were only carrying out your wishes we are at a loss what move to make next. We are daily being asked if it is a "game of spoof" and when the Press and public find it *is*, our position will not be enviable—in fact it would be our ruin. No one can say we are mercenary or that self comes first in any of our undertakings but those who are jealous of us would be only too glad to condemn us and hold us up to ridicule, and we cannot allow that to be. We don't want you to educate the people but simply to go through with what has been begun. We will wait till Monday for a letter or telegram saying if we are to issue the circular. As you say you are not a business man, a great deal could be arranged without you, but not minus your consent. Thousands of people and a large section of the Press are already interested and we have little fear of ultimate success if it is worked energetically and truthfully.'

Frederick appears to have poured a little soothing balm on the troubled spirit of his business associate, for we find Concorde writing on February 28th:

'I was very glad to get your letter this morning and to hear that you still take as much interest in the L.P.O. as ever. . . . Undoubtedly the best course for you to take is to give your concert and after that we can form the syndicate and apply to the public. We shall then have something to work upon, as we shall be able to say truthfully that we have an unusual man at the head of affairs. I have plenty of courage, only I do not want people to say that I have rushed in where angels fear to tread! . . . As soon as I hear from you I will book the Hall. Let me also know the number and description of the orchestral players you require.'

With the great operatic project put aside for the moment, the essential thing now to do was to divert Press and Public attention from it to the forthcoming concert of the works of an entirely unknown English composer.

15

THIS enterprise was vastly easier to bring off in 1899 than it would be today. Orchestral concerts of any kind in central London were a rarity, there was only one orchestra playing together with fair regularity, and a one-man affair was almost as startling an event as a visitation from another planet. Everyone relegated the opera project to a discreet background and awaited May 30th at St. James Hall. Practical difficulties had appeared from the beginning of preparations. Delius had written to his old friend Percy Pitt asking him to persuade Henry Wood to conduct, without first giving notification that he had nominated as managers the Concorde firm. On March 3rd Pitt writes:

'Pleased to hear from you again and I should have answered sooner but for a beastly lot of work. With regard to your concert, I had already sounded Wood re conducting when your letter and that of Concorde Agency arrived. I fear that the fact of your having placed the arrangements in Co's hands will prevent Wood from doing your thing as Newman[1] will step in and refuse permission. You see, Wood is retained solely by Newman and cannot accept outside engagements. Had you waited, I was going to write you—in fact I had done so but happening to call on Wood before posting same, found the two letters. I had advised you to write Wood personally, applying for him and the Queen's Hall Orchestra. This would have been placed before Newman and I believe that between Wood and myself, a favourable result would have been arrived at. As it stands, however, I don't believe you will be able to do much, for it will not be possible for you to have our men, and all the other good players will be required for Covent Garden. I

[1] Robert Newman, for over ten years lessee of Queen's Hall and sole sponsor and manager of the Promenade Concerts.

would advise you to put off the concert for the present, take it out of Concorde's hands and wait until the Autumn. If you will then write Wood, I daresay we can arrange with Newman for the orchestra *and* the Male Voices of our Chorus. This is a thing you did not bear in mind—it is most difficult to pick up a Choir off-hand! Let me know what you intend to do!'

By the middle of March it seems to have become certain that Henry Wood would be either unable or unwilling to conduct, but Frederick's fears about the engagement of good orchestral players were allayed by this report from Concorde:

'You misunderstood matters in thinking that the Queen's Hall orchestral players cannot be obtained except through the Queen's Hall. It stands to reason that the men could not live if they were under a contract only to play at such concerts as are given there. You will see by the enclosed circular that we ourselves have an orchestra that includes the pick of London. There are certain new young players, who have lately joined the Queen's Hall Orchestra, who, we believe, are under a contract to stay for a certain period, but even then we do not think they have bound themselves to play only in the Queen's Hall Orchestra. The same remarks apply to the Chorus. . . . We are well in with orchestral players and could we think obtain concessions from them with regard to rehearsals.'

Meanwhile Frederick had approached Alfred Hertz, conductor of the Elberfeld Opera, who accepted gladly the opportunity of making an appearance in London under conditions likely to draw a good deal of attention to himself, and it now remained to draw up a programme representative of the composer's achievement up to date, and to select singers and instrumentalists who could interpret it to his satisfaction. The bill of fare by today's reckoning was of formidable dimensions and consisted of:

PART I

1. Fantasia for orchestra, *Over the Hills and Far Away*.
2. *Legende*, for violin and orchestra.
   (Solo violin: John Dunne)

3. Third and fourth movements from Suite for orchestra, *Folkeraadet*.
4. Danish songs (with orchestral accompaniment):
     'Through long, long years'
     'Let springtime come'
     'Irmelin Rose'
     'On the Seashore'
     'Wine roses'.
           (Vocalist: Christianne Andray)
5. Symphonic poem for orchestra, *The Dance Goes On* (*La Danse se déroule*).
6. *Mitternachtslied* (from Nietzsche's *Zarathustra*) for baritone solo, men's chorus and orchestra.
           (Soloist: Douglas Powell)

PART 2

Excerpts from *Koanga* (Opera in 3 acts with a prologue and epilogue).
1. (*a*) Prelude to Act III.
     (*b*) Quintet and Finale of Act I.
2. Act II.
           (Soloists: Ella Russell, Tilly Koenen, G. A. Vanderbeek, William Llewellyn, and Andrew Black)

The concert had been well advertised and the hall judiciously papered so that there was a specious show of interest on the Public's part. The Press on the whole was not unfriendly. In spite of this fair show of acclamation, no individual promoter or organization made the slightest attempt to play for years to come another note of music that had been pronounced to be of undoubted individuality, with more than occasional signs of genius. So far as England was concerned the event might never have taken place. Frederick stayed for a few days only in London after the concert, but had time to discuss with one or two professional libretto-mongers subjects for his next opera. He already had in mind Gottfried Keller's novelette *Romeo und Julia auf dem Dorfe* but was hesitating over committing himself definitely, as most of those about him saw little incident in the story for dramatic treatment.[1] The general view, evidently influenced by the sound of the strains heard at his concert, was that something bright and cheerful, with heaps of dancing and happy endings to round off, was what would be best for both his talent and his prospects.

[1] From the series *Tales of Seldwyla*.

But for the next few weeks he was drawn into the troublesome business of settling the accounts of his adventure into the concert-room. On first launching it he had allowed himself to believe that the total cost would not exceed £200. He was now presented with a bill for something like £500. A lively exchange of letters passed between him and the Concorde Control which, although he inevitably had to pay up in the end, left him with the unpleasant impression that he had been either misled or victimized. Twenty years later he was still cherishing some resentment against his former agent, but a study of the numerous letters passing between the pair, as well as others from third parties, has left me unconvinced that he was even partially in the right. It is correct that Concorde's first estimate of expenses did not much exceed the amount fixed in the composer's mind; but this calculation represented an orchestra of no more than seventy-five musicians with the customary single rehearsal, a very moderate amount for printing and publicity, and no provision for Chorus, Conductor, Concert-Master or management. The demands of the programme increased the number of players to ninety; and upon the advice of Hertz contained in a letter dated March 20th two extra rehearsals were added, one of them occasioned by the necessity of reading through and correcting a mass of manuscript parts, most of them hitherto unplayed. It is, I think, worth recording that in spite of the extra expense incurred the fees of the orchestra amounted to no more than £233 and those of the choir to £11 1s. More was spent on advertising than planned at the outset and a new item of forty pounds for a booklet of analytical notes, written by the first critic of the *Daily Telegraph*, helped to swell the total. The orchestra led by the enthusiastic Halfdan Jebe was first class and included a handsome proportion of the best instrumentalists in the country. The cost of such a body of players engaged today for a concert and three rehearsals would hardly be less than £800, while the total expenses of the concert would probably exceed £1,500. But whatever may have been the measure of his dissatisfaction with the commercial side of music-making, he made preparations for a second concert to be given in the following autumn, though this time it would be someone else who would foot the bill.

In Bielefeld, the ancestral home of the clan Delius, it had been customary for some time past to hold family reunions at which gathered as many members of it as could find opportunity to attend. To cover partly the cost of these agreeable junketings there had been formed a financial pool, to which all concerned made contributions. There was usually some surplus discoverable at the conclusion of each occasion and this was deposited in a fund which dealt with applications for assistance from less fortunate but deserving members of the family. Frederick began to cast a covetous eye on this instrument of beneficence, for we find him writing towards the end of June to the most sympathetic of his cousins on the male side of the family, who was living at Calcombe in Sussex. Daniel Delius answered by approving the design of another concert and undertook to bring Frederick's call for financial aid before the Committee of the Bielefeld organization. He appealed to the most influential member of the family, Albrecht Delius who was resident in Bielefeld itself, and consequently in closest touch with the spring of operations. To Daniel's disappointment Albrecht responded in distinctly frigid terms, uncomfortably reminiscent of Julius himself. There could be no prospect of support for a project of this kind, there was very little money left in the till after the last three years' celebrations; and even if there were any surplus available, it would certainly be devoted to some worthier cause. Lastly he went on to hint that the application should have been more fittingly addressed to a quarter sufficiently blessed with this world's goods; namely the house of Delius in the north of England.

As the efforts of the Concorde Control to secure backing in London had by the early autumn failed to secure anything but a fraction of the amount required to justify the risk of another expensive musical treat, the plan was shelved indefinitely and Frederick returned to the easier and more agreeable labour of composition. He had still at his disposal a fair amount of his legacy and he could look forward to a spell of untroubled tranquillity for the next year or two.

16

IT MAY be remembered that since the transfer of the Florida property to himself, the annual remittance from Bradford had ceased. At the time this did not cause Frederick undue concern, for encouraged by his friend Thrane's cheerful prognostications for the future of tobacco growing in Florida, he had been looking forward to securing for himself, if not a fortune, at least a moderate competence. We shall now see how this new enterprise was working out. Between the time he had vacated the Grove in 1887 and his acquisition of it, the property, with the exception of some twenty acres devoted to simple farming, had been allowed to run wild. But during the last few years a drastic change for the worse had overtaken the whole neighbourhood. The first heavy blow at its prosperity came in 1896 with a startling climatic transformation. North Florida for the first time experienced a winter of extreme cold, which all but ruined the entire fruit industry. As this was not a transient phenomenon the district gradually lost its residential charm. One by one the numerous establishments that had arisen in the Picolata area were deserted and the fields and plantations surrounding them were abandoned to the care of Negroes, who worked no larger portion of them than would suffice for their own needs.

Mere living was on the whole easy and pleasant for those who could endure the extremes of weather now changing the character of the seasons. Apart from oranges and other fruit such as shaddock and mango, there was plenty of game, mostly partridge and wild duck, the river abounded in edible fish, and the supply of minor necessities was cheap, plentiful and easily obtainable from Jacksonville or St. Augustine. Frederick's preoccupation from the moment he entered into sole possession was to find some energetic person or persons who would settle there and run it largely for his own benefit as a tobacco plantation. He began to look out for the right sort of prospective manager or even partner as early as the summer of 1897, and shortly after his return from Florida he entered into negotiations with a certain Robert Starke who lived at Detmold in the little north German principality of Lippe, and who for some six years had been a practical farmer, as well as student of agriculture. By the end of the year the parties were sufficiently in accord on terms and conditions to enter into what was virtually a fifty-fifty contract, executed in the following January 1898, and Starke in a letter dated the 19th announced his intention of leaving for America before the end of the same month.

One of the more tiresome obstacles confronting any biographer of Delius is the occasional appearance of complete gaps in the orderly course of the story, for which there is no rational explanation except the disappearance or destruction of letters and other documents that should have bearing upon certain events, their causes and effects. For instance, from 1888 to 1896 inclusive we find in each year letters exchanged between Delius and Grieg or his wife Nina. Between 1897 and 1902 there is a total blank. Considering the unusually cordial relationship that existed between these three friends, it might be assumed that some event had taken place to interrupt or terminate it. But nothing at any time had occurred to vary the nature of this happy association, the participants in it seeing one another at fairly regular intervals, and yet there is not a scrap of epistolary information to tell us what any one of them was saying or doing. When the correspondence was renewed in 1903 it is clear, at least from the Grieg side of it, that there had been no break of any sort. Similarly, in the Robert Starke affair, so far as written records are concerned, the last we know of the man is that he signed an agreement to take over the management of Solano Grove, and thereafter, with the exception of one brief postcard, vanishes from our knowledge for ever. What he did there, and how many pounds of tobacco he shipped either to the American or European market we do not know. There is a tiny fragment of evidence that he may have gone so far as to arrive in the States, but that is all. Over the property and the activities thereon there is an impenetrable cloud of obscurity.

But whatever might have been the practical outcome of the agreement between the two partners, it is quite clear that it was no longer in existence by the beginning of 1899. Fully occupied at the moment with his London concert and the task of extricating himself with some degree of dignity from the abortive scheme for establishing a permanent

Opera in London, Frederick had invoked the services of Ida Gerhardi who was still living on and off with Jelka at Grez. This industrious lady, who made frequent visits to relatives and friends in Germany, undertook to spy out the land there for an eligible candidate, and pitched upon a certain Adolf Frolicke of Minden in Westphalia, who was cherishing the ardent desire, shared by several millions of his countrymen in the latter part of the nineteenth century, to quit the Fatherland and seek change and fortune in the New World. All seemed settled with the newcomer on the scene when at the last minute he, influenced by cautious members of his family, backed out. In the meantime Frederick had secured the services of two young Americans of the name of Peters who agreed to reside upon and manage his exotic estate. What they did in the way of extracting revenue from the Grove we do not know, but there is evidence that periodically they borrowed sums of money, fifty pounds at a time, from their employer, who must by now have begun to wonder whether his main material asset was not turning out to be in the nature of a white elephant. The elder Peters, after a while, departed from Florida for Wisconsin, leaving his younger brother in charge. But he too soon had the itch to move on elsewhere, so that the place became for a short while tenantless. Luckily for Frederick, by the close of 1900 young Frolicke, emancipating himself from family control, decided to take the chance offered him of getting away from home. He brought along with him a companion, Paul Nicholas, also of Minden, and another contract was drawn up and executed on January 12th, 1901. Under it the two adventurers put up two hundred and fifty pounds each and became owners of one-half of the property; the house and a small portion of the land being excluded from the deal. This seemed on the face of it to be an advantageous transaction in Frederick's interests. Here were two keen young fellows prepared to risk their own money, instil some energy into the tobacco industry and relieve him of the double burden of supporting the property and subsidizing incompetent or unsuccessful tenants. It really looked as if at last he had shifted the load on to someone else's shoulders, could sit back, relax and wait for profitable results.

The new combination began its career auspiciously. In answer to a letter of enquiry from Frederick, we find Paul Nicholas towards the end of March sending a fairly encouraging report. The house is in good condition, perfectly clean, and he and his partner have repainted all the rooms. They are thinking of investing in a motor launch for their private use on the river, as the steamers plying between Picolata and Jacksonville run too infrequently. They have secured an admirable cook, a Negress, seed-beds have been planted on the moistest corner of the land and tobacco shoots are already coming through. The seed merchant in Jacksonville is very kind and helpful and Anderson is a tower of strength. They have also begun to cultivate the overgrown land, although that is in such an unmanageable state that there is not much hope of clearing more than thirty acres in one year. Indeed what with the presumably novel diversions of hedging, ditching, fencing, digging and sowing, the young pair are blissfully and optimistically employed, except for one deficiency. Since the general exodus from the district of near neighbours, the place is very quiet and they are beginning to be a little irked by the solitude and lack of society, especially that of the opposite sex. They indulge in the hope that when Mr Delius comes out to visit them in the near future, he will bring with him the two ladies resident at Grez. Everything will be in perfect condition for their reception and stay.

This pleasant state of things did not continue long. In truth hardly anything connected with Frederick Delius of a mundane kind ever did or could. A few months later Nicholas announces that really terrible and unforeseen things have happened. A positive tempest has swept through the unhappy plantation, deluging beyond hope of drainage the carefully planted beds of tobacco seed and destroying in one night the work of months. The two young men on the advice of Anderson, have posted off to Jacksonville to obtain a fresh supply of seed from the merchant there and started over again. But this time nothing at all came up, and since in their view the wily vendor must have tricked them badly in providing poor material, they bought elsewhere and went on hopefully planting. But always without results. Advised now that in all probability the season was too advanced and the soil too hot for the success of this kind of operation, they are reluctantly resigning themselves to the unpleasant necessity of waiting six months, before anything further can be done. Meanwhile their labours will have to be limited to clearing a portion of the arable land and raising some crops; less in the hope of making money than finding some way of relieving an otherwise tedious spell of inactivity.

By the end of the year however their money has run out, and we find by January 1902 they are advising Frederick that the best thing to do is to sell the plantation to anyone prepared to pay a fair price for it. Of course there was bound to be a heavy loss on the original purchase as, owing to the severe winters and the stricken condition of most of the surrounding estates, land had become very cheap. The neighbouring farm of Charles Douglas could be bought for five hundred dollars, and the once handsome residence of Frederick's former friends, the Bells, was unoccupied and partly derelict. Unless he was prepared to sink more capital in a highly dubious commercial proposition, he had better get rid of it on the best terms obtainable. Nicholas had already given up and gone elsewhere to make a living, but Frolicke stayed on awaiting instructions and passing on the information that in the opinion of a local estate agent the property was no longer worth more than a thousand dollars. None of this was agreeable reading for the unlucky owner of the place, who had obtained the transference of its title deeds from his father in the hope that the tobacco venture on it would prove to be a source of regular income. Shortly after this he received an offer based upon the estate agent's valuation from Anderson himself which he unwisely declined, as subsequent events proved.

Frederick gave up nearly the whole of 1900 to settling the form of the libretto of *A Village Romeo*, completing the music of the first and second acts, revising the tone-poem *La Ronde se Déroule*, which was now rechristened *Lebenstanz*, and writing three more songs:

> 'The Violet' (Holstein)
> 'Autumn' (Jacobsen)
> 'Black Roses' (Jacobsen).

Of these the most emotionally impressive is 'Autumn'; the most fanciful 'The Violet'. The latter has not found much favour with most Delian commentators, but for my part, I find it charming, poetical, of much harmonic interest and a genuinely characteristic example of the composer's style during this period. But both it and 'Autumn' should always be given with the orchestral rather than the piano accompaniments. The keyboard in both instances fails to support the vocal part adequately, or sustain the gently shifting harmonic sequences.

The concert of the previous year had been in the nature of a revelation to him. With the exception of the performance of his early tone-poem *On the heights* at Monte Carlo and that of *Over the Hills and Far Away* at Elberfeld in 1897 he had been unacquainted with the sound of his own music. The stimulus to both his imaginative and technical powers was immense. Just as years ago in Florida he had first realized what music could fully express, so now he saw the way expanding before him for the realization of much that had been haunting his brain for years past in terms of sounds and forms hitherto unexplored. During the period 1897–1901 he had divided his residential life between his apartment in the Rue Ducoüedic and Grez, frequenting the latter place mainly in the spring and summer months. The year 1901, a year of comparative seclusion and concentrated effort, saw the completion of *A Village Romeo and Juliet*, and the first performance in Germany of *Paris* under the directorship of Haym at Elberfeld. This occasion may be said to be the certifiable starting point of what was to become, within the next four or five years in Germany, a Delius vogue, second only to that of Richard Strauss.

17

IN OCTOBER 1901 occurred the death of Julius, unchanging to the end in his refusal to acknowledge the existence of Frederick, not as a man, but as a composer. The financial relations between father and son have been the subject of disagreement between some of the biographers of the latter. Philip Heseltine has accused Julius of downright meanness, a charge from which the devotion of a daughter who was also Frederick's favourite sister, has sought to exculpate him. Mrs. Clare Black (*née* Delius) has treated this difficult and delicate matter with a fair show of impartiality, laying emphasis upon the obligation placed upon Julius to deal with all his twelve children alike, and to display no sign of favouritism towards any particular one of them. She, I think, is satisfied that this is what her father not only intended but carried out; but while I find it wholly distasteful to adopt a partisan attitude in such a thorny affair, I cannot agree that she is even partly in the right. I am well acquainted with the adage that statistics can be used to prove anything either way, and even to make black resemble white. But figures when supported by plain statements of fact, as well as likely probabilities, must be taken a little seriously into account.

Although he is not specifically mentioned in Julius's will, we do know that Frederick received less than £600, as his share of the testator's estate. His father is alleged to have kept an account of all moneys expended on each member of his family since he, or she, came of age, and to have deducted such payment from the recipient's share in his property. It is also stated on the authority of Mrs. Black that her father spent the sum of £37,000 upon the education of his twelve surviving children. If equally divided among them this would mean that something over £3,000 could have been absorbed by Frederick, if we are to grant parity of treatment. What then do we find in his case? His earlier days of tuition, first at a Claremont preparatory institution and next at the Bradford Grammar School, lasted five years. Both were day schools and the annual fee for a boy at that time, at each of the two mentioned, was about £30 a year. Then came the three years at Isleworth where he lived as a boarder. Here the fees were in the neighbourhood of £70–£80 a year. This is all the scholastic training that he ever received and the total cost of it could not have exceeded £400. After that he entered the family business, in which he remained for nearly three and a half years, but it could hardly be advanced seriously that this term of commercial apprenticeship came under the heading of education. To the above moderate sum may be added the cost of his violin and piano lessons, covering a period of some thirteen years. As his masters during his residence at Bradford lived in other cities such as Manchester and Leeds, their visits were probably not more than one a week, or perhaps two at the outside.[1] Judging therefore by the scale of instructional charges at that time, the total covering eight years of school and college life would have been in the neighbourhood of £500 to £600. As I can find no record of his receiving any form of regular teaching except the foregoing, it is manifest that the cost of what might be called his education, so far from being £3,000, failed to exceed £1,000. Presumably the eleven other children, or some of them, benefited by the difference of £2,000.

The cost of his eighteen months' residence at Leipzig was borne by Julius and was in the neighbourhood of £300. During his Paris residence he received for seven years £104 annually and for a further short period £52. After the transfer to him of the Grove, he received nothing more. These various sums, excluding the initial cost of Solano Grove, amount approximately to £2,100.

On the occasions of his visits to England his travelling expenses were provided, and while in Yorkshire he stayed either with his parents or his sister Clare. But even if the trip to his home area was an annual event, which was certainly not the case from the evidence of letters containing mention of other excursions, the cost of travel was moderate in those days and would hardly have topped an aggregate of £100. We are further informed on the authority of Mrs. Black, that her brother indulged in the occasional practice of running up heavy bills at tailors and hosiers, which were sent to his father for payment. But this agreeable device for the renovation of his wardrobe was not the sort of thing to happen every month or indeed every year, and if Julius had seriously

---

[1] The writer, who lived as a child in a village between Liverpool and St. Helens, received two lessons weekly from teachers living in each of these centres.

objected to the frequency of this easy-handed kind of procedure, he could easily have taken effective steps to bring it to a stop at any time.

Let us examine the Florida episode. We know that Julius paid his son's outward passage (some twenty pounds) and contributed one half of the two hundred and fifty dollars paid on account of the purchase price of the Grove. He, in all probability, although I have no figures here to guide me, will have furnished funds sufficient to cover, let us say, one year's cost of living there. Considering the prolificacy of game, fish, fruit and vegetables that abounded at that time in the Picolata region, we can safely assume from what we know of the father's notions of personal expenses in the case of his second son, that this year's provision would not have exceeded £100. A few months after, as previously related, he found the balance required for the completion of the purchase, namely six thousand two hundred and fifty dollars (at the then rate of exchange £1,250) and became sole owner of the property. When Frederick went to Leipzig to fit himself for a career in some major American city, it must have been taken for granted by his family that so far as he was concerned Solano Grove had ceased to serve its purpose. It is reasonable then to ask why Julius did not take steps to dispose of it. During the nine years that followed he made no effort to isencumber himself of a possession unwanted by anyone in the Bradford circle, and which he could have sold without sacrifice any time prior to 1896. In 1897 he parted with it to his son and three years later, when making the final disposition of his estate, deducted from Frederick's prospective interest in it not only the full purchase price of the Grove in 1884, but the cost of its upkeep over a period of eleven years. Upon whom should be placed the responsibility for failing to get rid of it? No one assuredly but Julius as the sole person in control. But however this strangest of actions or inactions on the part of a so-called business man may be viewed, its consequences were equally irrational. For his father's mistakes or negligence Frederick must be made to pay, and that to the last farthing of computable liability. I do not scruple to declare this transaction to be one of the most equivocal and inequitable as between father and son of which I have personal cognizance. The only charitable conclusion to be formed is that, at the moment he perpetrated this crowning stroke of parental eccentricity, Julius's mental and moral faculties must have ceased to function normally. The warnings Frederick had received in 1893 from William

Shaw about his father's progressively erratic behaviour may have made some disquieting impression upon him, but he could never have anticipated anything so wildly unexpected as this. It would not of course be difficult to present a few plausible arguments in defence of Julius. Frederick as a son had been a grievous disappointment to him and a recurring cause of worry and perplexity. Worst of all he was an obvious failure, whose absurd pretensions after more than a decade of futility and levity had landed him nowhere. All this had been clearly foreseen by Julius long ago, but his will had been thwarted and his wisdom set at naught. An example should be made of him for the good of the rest of his family. There may be a small glimmer of reason in these hypothetical contentions, but taking everything into account, I am unable to agree that equality of treatment was enjoyed by him. In Julius's will there is reference to a sum of £5,000 loaned some time previously to the husband of one of his daughters and now forgiven. If we compare this generous benefaction with the negligible amount left to Frederick, a son, I find it sufficiently substantiated that a deliberate measure of discrimination was exercised against him.

During the years extending from 1888 to 1894 his modest remittance from home was increased by the benevolence of his uncle, Theodor, but we have no knowledge of how much the contribution was. This came to an end when the pair disagreed in 1895 with the result that Frederick was left only with the £52 a year which he received from home. He would have been in a truly awkward position had it not been for the goodwill of 'Aunt Albertine' who stepped into the breach, with an annual contribution of £60 which continued without a break for over ten years. None the less it has been always a matter of wonder to me how he continued to exist during those lean years 1895–1898, when upon the death of Theodor he inherited the legacy to which reference has been made. Things were bad all round. He was well into the thirties, he had refused to return to America, he scorned the idea of teaching, in fact he declined to do anything at all in the way of augmenting his income, save by the uncertain chance of a successful stroke with one or more of his compositions. He spent most of his time writing operas which apparently no one wanted to produce, and songs that were mostly above the heads of the Public. What could be done with such a fellow? It is little wonder that in spite of his pleasant ways and agreeable disposition, some of his acquaintances began to lose faith in his future. That he had the uneasy feeling of being regarded as one set apart from the rest of his family is confirmed by the long correspondence he maintained with the Trustees of his father's will, for two years after its appearance. By the autumn of 1902 the once prosperous firm had passed into the hands of new owners who discharged its outstanding debts and bought its goodwill for no more than £2,000. The residuary estate of Julius was valued at about £50,000, most of which he had inherited from his brothers Ernst and Theodor. After making a settled provision for the widow capable of yielding £1,200 per annum, there was not a considerable surplus for division among the numerous members of the family.

His prospects looked far from promising. Although he had known for some years that the family fortunes had been declining from their old height of opulence, he had no suspicion that they had dropped to something like zero at the time of Julius's demise. His expectations had never been extravagant; but very probably, and not unreasonably, he had anticipated coming into a modest bequest whose income could have removed from his mind the unpleasant spectre of extreme poverty. But with both Julius and Theodor gone, where was he to look for any support guaranteeing him even a modicum of independence? The answer was nowhere, and for the first time in his life he stood alone, with the stern realization that from now onward he must rely upon himself and no one else for the means of bare subsistence. His world seemed to be falling about him. A few years previously he had suffered a heavy blow in the defection of his favourite goddess Aphrodite Pandemos who had returned his devotions with an affliction which, although temporarily alleviated, was to break out again incurably some twenty-five years later. Solano Grove had proved a fiasco of the first order and all other potential sources of aid had died upon him.

During the next eighteen months he passed through a sustained mental crisis and more than one of those who knew him well in those days noted a gradual change taking possession of him. There developed slowly a higher seriousness of thought, a deeper concentration of method and growing signs of weariness with the kind of life he had been living in Paris since 1888. The several set-backs such as have been related constituted a dividing line that cut across every side of his life, social, artistic and philosophic. His old *laisser aller* habits and his outward joyousness of temper and liberality of mood came to be replaced by a slow hardening of inward fibre and outward expression. Hitherto there had been little sign of the aloof, exclusive and egoistical creature depicted by those whose acquaintance began with him only when he had passed into the fifties and sixties of his later days. But now at last Destiny, which so far had followed him at a casual distance, stepped forward and led him firmly by the hand towards a future which could have been predicted by no one.

18

A *Village Romeo and Juliet* now completed, Frederick looked around for fresh literary material for a new opera, never a light or easy task for him. While he was weighing the merits of half a dozen subjects suggested to him by friends, his attention was directed to an opportunity of making a considerable amount of money, under conditions which included a blaze of publicity. Some twelve years previously the publishing house of Sonzogno of Milan had offered a substantial prize for the best one-act opera written by an Italian composer. The successful competitor was Mascagni who with his *Cavalleria Rusticana* leapt into world fame and fortune. The rival establishment of Ricordi now considered that the time had come for a repetition of this experiment, but on this occasion threw open the contest to foreign as well as to native composers. Frederick decided to enter and proceeded to adapt himself to what he imagined to be essentially Italian requirements, chief among them being a pronounced streak of stark realism. He certainly appears to have assumed that anything other than the Mascagni-Leoncavallo pattern would be unlikely to meet with success, but for my part I believe he was entirely wrong. It was easily within his power to have written a dramatic piece of one hour's duration, that would have successfully held the stage without departing from the principles or guiding influences that had moulded at least three of his preceding operas. In all of them as well as in his instrumental works, such as *Paris* and *Appalachia*, he had displayed an abundance of lyrical invention adequate to meet any demands made upon him.

Valid criticism of the text of *Margot la Rouge* should be concerned less with its melodramatically tragic ending, reminiscent of both *Cavalleria Rusticana* and *Pagliacci*, than with a slow-moving pace which quickens into life and interest only in the last quarter of an hour. In the long scene between Margot and her old sweetheart, where the mood is mainly one of sentimental reminiscence, he apparently found himself incapable of inventing the right sort of music to meet the needs of the situation, fell back upon the use of a little figure already exploited in *Paris* and worked it almost to death. Briefly the piece never really came to life and that, much more than the rather sordid finale, which after all is no worse than the sort of thing to be found in a dozen other successful stage pieces, was responsible for its failure. It is hardly necessary to add that not only did it not win the coveted prize, but that it never had the smallest chance of so doing. At the same time a fair percentage of the music had more than ordinary merit, and the best portions were extracted from it some thirty years later and incorporated in a work of totally different character.

Frederick was unable without some effort to relinquish the idea of writing a one-act stage piece full of excitement and disaster, and turned to Oscar Wilde's drama *Salome*, at that time available only in its original French. This was not a casual whim. He discussed it for months with several knowledgeable and cultured friends, and in the early part of the following year we find him negotiating for libretto rights with Wilde's executors, a well-known firm of London solicitors. But the more he reflected, the less certain he became about his choice, and perhaps he was not too disappointed when Richard Strauss snatched the work from his indecisive hands. I do not know if he ever regretted this lost opportunity, but some of his friends did, for later on we find the gallant Haym, who had developed into the most complete and perfect of hierophants, writing 'What a pity Strauss chose this subject first! Could you not do it in spite of that, and even because of it?'

Perhaps a simpler explanation of the diversion of his mind from the lurid attractions of *Salome* was his increasing susceptibility to two very different sources of influence, the verse of Walt Whitman and the poetic prose of Friedrich Nietzsche. A portion of the first-named author's *Sea Drift* had captured and inflamed his imagination, and before the close of the year, he had made not only sketches for a musical setting of the poem, but had formed in his mind an unusually clear conception of how it should be built. The composer has left us very few comments upon his own works, especially as to how they came to be written, but he makes an exception in the case of *Sea Drift* which has always been looked upon as one of his happiest inspirations. This is how he talked to Eric Fenby about it some twenty-five years later: 'The shape of it was taken out of my hands so to speak as I worked, and was bred easily and effortlessly of the nature and sequence of my particular musical ideas, and the nature and sequence of the particular poetical ideas of Whitman that appealed to me.' He also began to dally with an old friend the *Also Sprach Zarathustra* but did not make his final selection from the text until a full year later.

But surpassing in interest and importance all else that had gone before in either his public or private life, was the announcement of his coming marriage to Jelka Rosen. Nearly seven years had elapsed since their first meeting and more than five since Frederick's return from Florida and the allocation of a wing in the Grez establishment to his use. We know something of the strength and intensity of Jelka's obsession with Frederick in those earlier days, and I have already vented the opinion that Frederick's emotions were far from being on the same exalted level. Indeed I do not think they ever rose higher than a deep friendly affection, coupled with an unbounded respect for Jelka's many remarkable qualities. Certainly he made no serious effort to control his appetite for indiscriminate flirtation, and if the evidence of a couple of ardent but mysterious letters may be accepted, it is likely that he became involved, some time during 1899, in a new entanglement which appears to have been both short-lived and infelicitous. Jelka on her side had by this time her own circle of acquaintances and a small bevy of admirers, among whom was the ageing Auguste Rodin. The great sculptor's part in a charming correspondence which passed between them during 1900 and 1901, clearly indicates how fully he appreciated his young friend both as woman and artist. It would not be surprising if during the intervening years some of her blind devotion to Frederick had abated, to be replaced by a cooler estimate of him as a man and potential lover. But she could not have failed to note and be moved by the trying and seemingly endless material difficulties against which he had been fighting ever since he had landed himself with the wretched Florida encumbrance, while her profound belief in his artistic future never faltered for a moment. I have little doubt that there came a critical moment when Frederick, tired of amatory excursions and commercial alarums, and longing for the sort of peace in which he could work out the new and glowing inspirations which were crowding his brain, turned to the one individual who, like a rock in a troubled sea, bore herself in any emergency with unruffled dignity, and never failed to irradiate sympathy and under-standing.

The material prospect confronting the pair was not overbright. Jelka had a smallish income inherited from her father, and the use of the house at Grez which her mother now permitted her to occupy rent free. While retaining for the time being her ownership of the property Madame Rosen executed a deed in the summer of 1902, under which all interest upon the capital sum she had provided for its purchase was to be discontinued. Frederick had in hand the sum received from his father's estate, a few, indeed a very few occasional royalties and fees, chiefly from songs which were then more freely circulated than today, and the modest allowance from the kindly Aunt Albertine. This good lady, however, was nothing less than horror-stricken at his temerity in plunging into matrimony with so little sense of responsibility. Since those far off days in Virginia he had never made any money, and it looked to her as if he never would. We find her writing to him in a highly disturbed state of mind: 'I advise you seriously not to think of marriage until you have won a secured position;' but wishing to relieve his mind as to her goodwill towards him, adds later: 'For the present I will continue to give you 100 marks (monthly) for another year, but do not let me in for any more.' The wedding took place in the summer of 1903 and now that there was nothing anybody could do about it, there was a general attitude of relief and resignation. Aunt Albertine executed a gracious *volte-face* and Frederick's mother unbent to the extent of sending him twenty-five pounds as a marriage present. The Paris apartment was given up for all time and henceforth Frederick's only known address was Grez-sur-Loing.

So far from his marriage proving to be a burden either to himself or his wife, it looked as if it might be the prelude to the dawn of a modest spell of prosperity that lasted for eleven years. His *Nachtlied* had just been given in a concert at the Basle Festival, and now the welcome news arrived that *Koanga* would be produced the follow-ing spring at the Elberfeld Opera House. While Alfred Hertz was conductor there he had serious thoughts of bringing it out in 1899, but had reluctantly allowed himself to be convinced by his manage-ment that the stage resources of the theatre were unequal to the task of mounting the piece in a style that would do justice to its strange and picturesque character. Since that time a new Intendant had been appointed, Hans Gregor, an ambitious and enterprising type of man, anxious to acquire a reputation with the Public as a sponsor of attractive novelties. There was also another conductor in the saddle, Fritz Cassirer, a young Berliner, who, having been made acquainted with the music of Delius by Haym and Buths, had fallen completely under its spell. The Piano Concerto too was at last to have a public hearing, also at Elberfeld under Haym with Buths as soloist.

Written as far back as 1897 this work like so many of its brethren had passed through a period of some vicissitude. Two years earlier it had attracted the notice of Busoni, who had undertaken to play it at one of his Berlin concerts. Relying upon this assurance Frederick had gone to the German capital, only to encounter a succession of postponements. After several weeks of tedious delay the work without any explanation was dropped from the programme, and he returned to Paris with a feeling of resentment against the great pianist, which for many years he was unable to overcome. To make matters worse Busoni, on a subsequent occasion and presumably by way of compensation, gave a performance of *Paris* conducted by himself of such atrocious ineptitude as to linger also in the memory of its unlucky composer until his last days. It fell once more to the lot of Haym to rescue the piece from oblivion by introducing it to Buths, who in addition to being a capable conductor was an excellent pianist. At first inclined to be lukewarm, he became after some study of the piece quite enamoured of it, and although unable to bring off the first public performance until the following year, he contrived that a four-handed copy should be arranged for two pianos, and industriously advertised its coming birth by playing it in conjunction with Haym or any other pianist capable of rendering the second part both in Elberfeld and elsewhere. Respecting the worth and character of the work as estimated by able and sensitive musicians of that day, it is worth quoting an extract of a letter of Haym dated July 10th:

'We think this Concerto still shows a little of Grieg's influence upon you but only in occasional passages. The main thing is that the whole expresses an original mind. After all everyone comes from somewhere, but while most [composers] keep trotting around a well worn track, you are a pathfinder and I feel it to be an enchanting experience that I am allowed to follow you on these paths.'

Frederick had now reached the age of forty-one. He had written five operas, six large works for full orchestra, several suites of a lighter type, a large number of short pieces, some for orchestra, others for solo instruments, and about fifty songs. Of this imposing output only a score or so of the songs had been published! Not a note of the operatic or instrumental side of it had found its way into print. This curious anomaly is probably without precedent in the case of a composer who within a few more years was hailed in more than one country as a musician of underivative genius. It is not as if publishers were totally unaware of him or his music. I have often heard it said that Frederick after he had completed any work, made no effort to secure either publication or performance of it. To a large extent that is true during the years that followed the recognition of his worth, for the reason that both publishers and performers alike competed for the privilege of being associated with him. But the same thing cannot be affirmed of the fifteen years that linked his arrival in Paris with the time of his marriage. A good proportion of both his larger and smaller instrumental works had gone half-way round Europe, had been submitted to the inspection of most of the leading publishers and scrutinized by a majority of the important conductors of the Continent, England and the United States. Many of these had glanced or affected to glance at the scores before them and, after a decent interval, returned them to their author with expressions of regret and admiration. The fault, if indeed there were a fault, was not wholly on their side. Few of the manuscripts were easy to read, being written in a small and close calligraphy. They contained very few indications of changing time, marks of expression, dynamics or phrasing to guide or instruct the student of them. It needed more than ordinary zeal to penetrate below the surface of what looked like a mass of barely legible hieroglyphics and to discover the half-hidden revelations to be found there. When exceptional men like Schillings, Haym and Buths[1] seriously set about bringing such music to the notice of the Public, they, each one of them, had fresh scores made from the original by first-rate copyists. But granting all this, it is a little surprising that there should not have existed in any publishing house of that time, one person who had the acumen to discern that here he was dealing with material very far removed from mediocrity. It is true that new compositions were not issued with that celerity and indiscrimination

[1] Max Schillings—General Music Director, Stuttgart—opera and concerts; Hans Haym— Director of Concerts, Elberfeld; Julius Buths—General Music Director, Dusseldorf.

which makes the present age almost golden to composers young and old of half a dozen nations; but there was a steady stream of novelty flowing from several reputable firms, and the plain truth is that nine-tenths of it is not only stone dead today but never had a genuine spark of vitality at the time. A single illustration will here suffice. While our composer was vainly knocking at the door of such houses as Breitkopf and Haertel, Peters, Arbol and others, we read of a work by one Karl Blayle on a text from Nietzsche which received instant publication by the firm Kistner, who charged fifty marks for the full score. When *Paris* was first performed in London during January 1908, the only material available was in manuscript, and this piece, which is certainly alive enough today to satisfy the average listener, had been written and made ready for the printer's hand nine years earlier. Three years more had to pass before he secured a publisher with a whole-hearted belief in the value of his work.

19

THERE can be little doubt that 1904 was the year in which Frederick and his work first made a serious impression upon the German musical world. Owing to the conjoint advocacy and enthusiasm of Haym, Buths and Cassirer, Elberfeld became the centre and radiating point of what might fairly be called the Delius movement in the Fatherland. It should be made clear, I think, just what this movement was, as well as the state of musical life in Germany that brought it about. It might be described generally as an opposition or protestant affair, and more specifically a reaction on the part of a group of influential musicians together with their followers against all post-Wagnerian music written by German composers, of whom Richard Strauss was the chief exemplar. Majority opinion was still imbued with the conviction that as Germany during the nineteenth century had produced a generous percentage of the best and most widely acknowledged world masters, this happy superiority could go on indefinitely without serious rivalry from outside. Moreover, was not the new Empire the most powerful state in Europe, and were its nationals not only the most industrious as well as the best educated and cultivated of all modern peoples? Every city and town of substantial dimensions, and some of lesser consequence, had an opera house as well as a concert-hall, and musical societies abounded. A comparison of the formidable Teutonic machine with that of any other country only swelled the national pride and belief in the fancied supremacy of the self-appointed heirs of Greek and Roman civilization. Indeed so far as this majority was concerned it was almost laughable even to suggest that France, Italy, Russia and possibly Scandinavia, were now manifesting signs of an inventiveness in music and other arts equal to if not greater than its own.

But in most European countries there is a leaven of keen and enquiring spirits who look beyond the boundaries of their immediate

Engraving by A. Ouvré

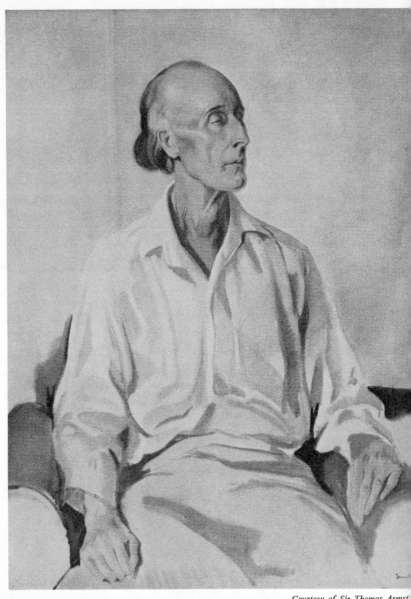

Portrait by James Gunn, A.R.A.

circle, who have the critical and analytical faculties with which to weigh and compare, and this by no means inconsiderable collection of free and unbiased minds had become not only doubtful but even alarmed about the future of creative music in their own German land. While most of the younger generation were pinning their hopes on Richard Strauss and were determined to maintain him in the position once occupied by Wagner, to others both at home and elsewhere it seemed that this effort was mainly an assertion of national pride and honour, which must be stoutly supported in spite of any argument to the contrary. In a letter to Frederick dated September 1st, 1903, Grieg as an onlooker and an admirer of the earlier Strauss writes:

> 'German musicians always put a German arrival on a pedestal so that they can idolise it. Wagner is dead, but they must have something to satisfy their patriotism and they would rather have *ersatz* than nothing at all.'

And so there began to grow and be circulated the suspicion that by the time the *Sinfonia Domestica* had appeared Strauss's inspiration was running all too thinly. As one eminent musician declared—'This time he has cooked in water: nothing new, no profundity: only terrible emptiness.' And another, a famous conductor, on first hearing the washing scene exclaimed—'If all the sacred elephants of India were driven into the Ganges at the same moment, they could not make half the noise as that one little Bavarian baby in its bath.' Just as the anti-Wagnerite had to find a counter-blast in Brahms, so the anti-Straussian prayed for a rival who would be as much of an antithesis to the enemy as possible. To their intense satisfaction here was the very man and they pounced on *Appalachia, Sea Drift, A Mass of Life* and subsequently *A Village Romeo and Juliet* as a perfect justification of the faith within them. Here was poetry in place of rhetoric, sound without uproar, reticence instead of exaggeration, in fact all those aristocratic qualities of which the bourgeois composers of their own people had lost all cognizance or appreciation.

Although it was *Appalachia* first performed by Haym in May 1904 that made a startling impression on musical circles, just as happened later in London, the most spectacular event of the year was the production of *Koanga* in March at the Elberfeld Opera House, with Gregor in charge of the stage and Cassirer conducting.

However important may be the first performance of any piece in the concert-room, it never arouses so much the interest of the Public and Press as a similar occurrence in the opera house. Whether it be a symphony or a shorter work, rehearsals and a concert take up together no more than a few days' time. But a new opera requires several weeks, sometimes months, of preparation; scenery and costumes have to be designed, a small army of supernumeraries are on the move night and day, expectation is generated and excitement stimulated by artful publicity. *Koanga* without question has many moments of charm and originality, with plenty of colour and in the middle and final acts a reasonable amount of action and tension. But it is in more ways than one a less truly Delian work than its predecessors *Irmelin* and *The Magic Fountain*. As already outlined, the overall guiding and controlling influence in each of these two pieces is an element of nature; in the first the Silver Stream and in the second the Fountain itself. The actors in each drama move as if they were in the grip of outside forces, irresistible and unchanging. In *A Village Romeo and Juliet* also we are made conscious that the two principal characters are puppets at the mercy of an unknown power, which from the beginning has ordained their eventual destruction: and a similar impulsion is present in the three chief figures of *Fennimore* who give the painful impression of being pulled about this way and that, without will or power to resist. Little of this inevitability of Fate oppresses us in the case of *Koanga*. It is true that we have the mystical factor so beloved of Frederick in the shape of Voodoo, but its demonstrations are just as likely to provoke risibility as to arouse terror; and although I cannot go along with an ingenious commentator who suggests that the piece might easily prove a rival to *Chu Chin Chow*, there is something of the mood and atmosphere of the operetta or musical play in the setting of the piece, the gaudy garments of the slaves and the pseudo-heroical aspect of Koanga and Palmyra. The two leading characters were played by Clarence Whitehill who, with his splendid voice and towering figure, must have been admirable as the captive Prince, and Rose Kaiser who, according to the composer, was vocally competent and dramatically plausible. The opera was an unqualified success and fired both Gregor and Cassirer with ambition to produce another work of the composer. It had the further effect of reminding a few persons in England of his existence, it now being five years since any of his music had been heard there.

During the last week in May he received a letter from Henry Wood asking for the score and parts of *Lebenstanz*, which he was anxious to give during the Promenade Concert Season beginning in the following August. There being no printed material of the piece Frederick was obliged to collect a manuscript score and set of parts from the last conductor to whom it had been submitted. This took some little time to accomplish and in answer to an enquiry from the composer, Wood assured him that all would be right if he received the material by September 20th. On September 4th he apologized for not answering earlier a further communication from Frederick, but cannot give the exact date of the concert although hoping it will be before October 16th. Meanwhile, public announcements had been made that a new work by Delius would be heard during the current season and on September 18th we find Alfred Kalisch, who in conjunction with Percy Pitt produced regularly the analytical notes for the Promenade Concerts, writing as follows:

'I should be much indebted to you if you would be so very kind as to let me have such details as to the "poetic basis" of your new work *Lebenstanz* as you would wish to have incorporated in our analysis. Any other information which you may feel disposed to give us as to the work will also be welcome—I do not know when your work is to be done, but *it will be soon* and it will be necessary for us to have the information some days before the production to enable it to be printed.'

But by the beginning of October Wood discovers that he is unable to produce the work at all 'owing to great difficulties', but hopes to give it or *Paris* next season. He is returning the score and parts to Elberfeld where Buths is awaiting them for his own advertised performance, which did take place towards the end of November.

Lebenstanz, better known in England as *Life's Dance*, is a fitting companion piece to its immediate successor *Paris*. Although inferior to the latter in breadth of design, melodic inspiration and variety of mood, it hardly merits the all but complete neglect which has overtaken it. In many ways it anticipates its great rival in instrumental brilliance, and with it forms the peak point of purely orchestral achievement in this the composer's second or middle period. Both also foreshadow those later tendencies so fully exploited in *North Country*

Sketches and 'In a Summer Garden' in the way of occasional sallies into what for want of a better word in aesthetic terminology is known as 'Impressionism'. Whether there can exist such a thing in a form of art whose constituents are solely melody, harmony and counterpoint is open to question; but I accept the term provisionally, being unwilling to involve even remotely the indulgent reader in anything approaching that most vain and unprofitable subject, metaphysical controversy. Buths was enchanted with the work, and Haym equally so. The former also fulfilled his promise of playing the solo part of the Piano Concerto and this too was given at Elberfeld under Haym's direction. Here may be the place to mention that the version of the piece played at that time is not that with which the Public is now familiar. This earlier edition consisted of three separate movements, of which the first two did not differ materially from similar sections in the final one. The last however began vigorously in five-four time, with much virtuoso writing for the solo instrument, passed for a while into four-four, then resumed its five-four rhythm and finally ended with a restatement of the principal theme of the first movement.[1]

The production of *Koanga* had brought Frederick into close touch with its conductor Fritz Cassirer, and there developed a warm friendship between them which continued until 1914 and the outbreak of war. Cassirer, about thirty years of age at this time, was a member of a Berlin Jewish family who ran a fine art business with galleries on the Unter den Linden. Possessed of some private means he was ambitious for recognition as a conductor, was fairly well read, and had a naturally good if slightly fastidious taste in music and painting. His acquaintance with *Koanga*, *Paris* and *Appalachia* had begotten in him a fanatical belief in them as genuine music of the present as well as of the future, and he attached himself to their composer with an almost dog-like devotion. It was to him that Frederick first communicated the plan of creating a wholescale work founded upon *Also sprach Zarathustra*, but confessed to finding himself in some difficulty over making suitable selections from the text of this extraordinary and monumental work. This was a task very much after Cassirer's fancy, and upon his offering his assistance, it was arranged by the pair that they should take a bicycling trip through Brittany in the coming August, leaving their respective wives at Grez. It was during this excursion that they solved a knotty problem by a simple process of

I apologize to the reader for this temporary lapse into technical jargon.

devastating elimination, chiefly owing to Cassirer's insistence that what mattered vitally was a musical counterpart, not so much of the text of the work, as of its prevailing character. He expresses himself with some force on this point:

'As Zarathustra is not composed thematically an analysis in this case would be nonsense. . . . These analyses in music are the height of platitude: don't you take any part in them: my aim is the pure and simple rendering of the mood of the poem.'

Frederick was thereby enabled to return home in September with a ready-made libretto for another important musical adventure.

By the middle of the summer a project upon which Gregor, assisted partly by Cassirer, had been working for some time came to fulfilment. This was nothing less than the establishment in Berlin of a new opera house to be run on the lines of the Paris Opéra Comique. Naturally a novel concern of this kind does not come into being over-night. Singers have to be secured, a new orchestra formed, scenery and costumes for half a dozen operas fabricated, and a dozen other operations incidental to the life of a lyric theatre soundly organized. It would take at least several months to get things going with a swing. But whatever might be the first batch of works selected for performance, Cassirer vowed that *A Village Romeo and Juliet* must be included in it. As is usual with such enterprises there arose a score of complications and obstacles, so that it was not until November 18th, 1905, that the Komische Oper, as it was christened, opened its doors with Offenbach's *Tales of Hoffmann*. It was followed on the 23rd by Massenet's *Le Jongleur de Notre Dame* and on December 3rd by Leoncavallo's *La Bohème*. The management not having found it possible to adopt the practice of its French prototype in playing a different work every night of the week, had established the principle of short runs for each opera with repetitions of the most successful pieces, until the repertoire became exhausted. Cassirer had hopes of a production of *A Village Romeo* for the following March of 1906 and with this expectation in his mind we will leave him for a while.

Frederick after his return to Grez from Brittany devoted the re-mainder of 1904 and the greater part of 1905 to the composition of *A Mass of Life*. Meanwhile, his fame begins to transcend the German area, his *Paris* being given in December at one of the Concerts Populaires of

Slyvain Dupuis in Brussels. His songs were circulating now in many countries, even in England for we find Ada Crossley[1] writing enthusiastically to him earlier in the year to relate what pleasure it has given her to sing them. Her two favourites are 'Irmelin' and 'In a Seraglio Garden'. Less satisfactory was a letter from Henry Wood on November 6th, regretting that he had been obliged to drop *Paris* from the Promenade series owing to the lack of adequate rehearsal time. Having regard to an exactly similar experience in the same quarter twelve months earlier, I do not think that Frederick can be criticized for holding the view he was heard to express openly and frequently about this time, that competent planning was not a main British accomplishment.

Another and more melancholy event was the death of his younger brother Max in Canada. For several years past the career of this unfortunate young man had been one mainly of frustration and failure. Although possessed of excellent abilities no opportunity had been granted him to display them to advantage in Julius's warehouse. He had run into business difficulties on his own account and was still heavily in debt at the time of his father's death. Upon the reconstruction of the old company he had made no effort to obtain any position in it, and failing to find any other occupation congenial to himself, had decided to emigrate. But he was already in a poor condition of health when he left England and survived his arrival in Montreal only a few months, dying of cancer. The news of this tragic event was conveyed to Frederick, who was very attached to Max and had been seeking information about him for some time, by an official of the Canadian Pacific Railway. The latter wrote:

'Your brother made a very plucky uphill fight in Canada, and had he lived would have been a success. His chief fault (if it be a fault at all) was his great kindliness towards his fellow creatures, and he would have been far better off if he had not tried to drag other people out of the mire. He was one of the straightest and most generous-hearted men I ever met and everyone who knew him liked him.'

Similar testimony to the excellent qualities of the elder brother had been offered by more than one reliable person twenty years earlier,

[1] With Clara Butt, the most popular contralto of that day.

and it is hard to believe that all the three sons, so much alike in mental and physical endowments, could have been wholly at fault in their various dealings with Julius.

A cheering and significant event marked the beginning of 1906; the first performance of *Sea Drift*. This was under the auspices of the Tonkünstler Verein and took place at Essen under the direction of Georg Witte, conductor of the local orchestra, with Joseph Loritz taking the baritone part. In the preparation of the work things at first went none too easily, Witte finding fault with several passages in the choral sections on the ground of needless difficulty, had suggested some banal alterations in the part writing. As these would all have involved changes of harmony, the proposal aroused in Frederick a state of frenzied wrath soothed only by the calm advice of the resourceful Haym who was luckily in Paris at that moment. He counselled a polite but firm refusal and quoted an apt coincidence in Cyrano de Bergerac which he had lately seen and admired:

'*Il vous corrigera seulement quelques vers*' some officious French Witte recommends. To which Cyrano replies: '*Impossible, monsieur, mon sang se coagule, En pensant qu'on y peut changer une virgule.*'

This event definitely established his reputation in Germany and he became, together with Richard Strauss, the most admired composer of the day. Pamphlets and articles about him began to appear, demands for his music poured in from many sides, and best of all, he found a publisher.

A few years previously there had been established in Berlin a new printing house under the name of 'Harmonie'. It had obtained some celebrity through the handsome style of its issues for which it had received more than one prize in international printing competitions. Its last award of consequence had been the gold medal given by the judging committee of the 1904 St. Louis (U.S.A.) Exhibition. The chief moving spirit of the firm was Alexander Jadassohn who had taken a keen liking to those Delius pieces which he had recently heard, namely *Sea Drift*, *Appalachia*, and the Piano Concerto. Active negotiations began between the two parties, composer and publishers, for the early issue of these three works, starting with *Sea Drift*, which was most in the Public mind at the moment. The Piano Concerto had recently been recast in a new form, that of a single movement in three sections.

The whole of the five-four episode was excised and the work ended with a partial repetition of the first section. A more effective antiphony was established between solo instrument and orchestra, and the general result was an indisputable gain in the directions of conciseness and simplicity. This piece has excited more differences of opinion as to its merits than any other of the composer, with the exception of the 'Requiem'. Frederick himself professed to have grown tired of it and some learned wiseacres have roundly abused it: one going so far as to compare it unfavourably with the *Warsaw Concerto*! Yet it is to be found in the repertoire of most pianists, orchestras continue to include it annually in their programmes and the Public likes to listen to it. Also it might be recalled that fifty years ago it made its way around half Europe and excited admiration and approval everywhere, particularly among the younger musicians of that time in England such as Bax and Vaughan-Williams. I have observed a tendency here and there to look upon it as an orthodox concerto comparable with those of Schumann, Liszt or Tschaikowsky. It is of course nothing of the sort, and I cannot do better than cite the opinion of an excellent musician and pianist of that time, Professor August Schmid-Lindner, who played the work frequently in Munich and elsewhere:

'Felix Mottl informed me today that you were seeking advice about alterations to your Concerto and asks me to reply to you about it. He said he could not see himself what had to be altered. I informed you yesterday that I was more or less of the same opinion. Your work is *not a clear-cut Piano Concerto* and any attempt to stamp it as such would in my view be sure to fail. The amount the piano has to say is already given in the basic plan and can hardly be altered subsequently. At the most the volume of the orchestra might be reduced just a little in a few unimportant places. I appreciate the work immensely as a *melodious* and beautifully *sensed orchestral piece* in which an *obbligato piano*-part is integrated. I do not ask for more nor is it at all necessary to do so. I believe that the work would be bound to lose in naturalness if a more dominant role were forced upon the piano-part than had been allowed for in the basic plan.'

During the summer came worrying news from Grieg about his health. Though always a weakling physically and troubled from time to time with severe digestive disorders, he had never been disabled from giving easy flow to the creative ideas visiting his brain. But on July 21st he writes:

'I am ailing a great deal and unfortunately cannot meet you much as I would like to [Frederick was planning his almost annual Norwegian trip]. Now in old age life has become more of a burden: I cannot compose in my bodily misery although I feel that I have still got the stuff in me. That's what makes life so unbearable.'

Grieg lingered for another fourteen months, hoping until the end for a revival of strength that would enable him to visit both England and Germany. Although this expectation was never realized, the last year of his life was brightened by the introduction into it of that vigorous and joyous spirit Percy Grainger. The vivacity and personal charm of the young Australian must have recalled pleasingly to Grieg memories of that other gifted youth whose personality and talent had made such an impression on him twenty years earlier. I do not think it outside the legitimate scope of this biography to quote fully from a letter (perhaps the last he wrote) to Percy on August 11th, 1907:

'You have become a dear young friend to me who has made more rich for me the evening of my life.

I have always found that they are mistaken who would divide the artist from the man; on the contrary, the two are indissolubly wedded one to the other. In the man can be found the parallels of all the artist's traits. (Yes, even the most minute). Even your stubborn "unnecessary" fifths(!) I could recognize again in my dear Percy Grainger! Not that I cherish the least doubt that they will sound well in your choral treatment. I have again immersed myself in your Folk-song Settings and I see more and more clearly how "genial" they are. In them you have thrown a clear light upon how the English Folk-song (to my mind so different to the Scotch and Irish) is worthy of the privilege of being lifted up into the "Niveau" of Art, thereby to create an independent English music. The Folk-songs will doubtless be able to form the basis for a national style as they have done in other lands, those of the greatest musical culture not excepted.'

I have made reference to this letter not only for the reason that the lives of these three men, Grieg, Delius and Grainger, were closely connected by ties of mutual esteem and friendship, but because of the views held by the eldest of them on the value and importance of folk-music. I confess to sharing the opinion of several other musicians that the fanatical cult of the 'music of the people' has not been an unmixed blessing in its influence upon composers in some countries during the past eighty years. This, of course, is a question inviting any amount of interesting argument; but it may be noted that a large proportion of Grieg's best music is European rather than Norwegian, and that Frederick, once he had got both Florida and Norway largely out of his head, relied less and less upon any source of inspiration other than his own. We may now return to the Berlin scene and observe how the preparations for the promised production of *A Village Romeo and Juliet* are progressing.

20

B Y AUGUST it is evident that they have temporarily slowed down, for we learn from a letter dated the 12th and sent by Cassirer to Delius who was then in Norway, that the Komische Oper is so far without a tenor for the role of Sali. For this reason he writes:

'meanwhile the work on *Romeo and Juliet* is completely held up. In addition, the Oper is in very urgent need of money. Our Director in quest of further smash-hits has decided on *Fledermaus* and *Lakmé*, which latter opera will have an inspired attraction, a female dancer! I think it impossible for *Romeo and Juliet* to be performed during the first half of the [winter] season.'

Frederick does not appear to have been much put out by the continued withdrawal from the light of day of a work completed more than five years before and which had been in Cassirer's hands for two. He was deep in the composition of a new piece, the 'Songs of Sunset'; Jelka was ready with several new canvases for the 'Salle des Indépendants', and the first exhibition on a big scale of Gauguin's works was being organized by the faithful De Montfried in Paris. This took place at the end of September at the Salon d'Automne and 'Never More' was among the masterpieces exhibited.

By the beginning of October the Komische Oper appears to have discovered a new tenor who might prove to be an adequate Sali, but Frederick's relief at this announcement was somewhat qualified by an ominous passage in a Cassirer letter of November 7th:

'For the time being it would be useless for you to come here. Please await my news. Enough to say that Gregor is being influenced on all sides against the performance. Nevertheless Merkel

(Sali), Padilla (Vreli) and Egenieff (the Dark Fiddler) have been studying their parts for a fortnight.'

But three weeks later, on November 26th, Cassirer writes again that all is now well and *Romeo and Juliet* will be given and in the near future. The letter in which he conveys the good tidings is a vivid and not unamusing account of how decisions of this sort were made in a German opera house at that time and is worth quoting at some length.

'Gregor became very hesitant after I had made him read through the Keller short story. The unexpected result was that he told me your libretto had ruined the text of the book by attempting to improve it; he could never produce an opera with such a libretto. Finally it was decided that I should play through the opera to Morris, the chief producer, who did not know the Keller story. He was to decide whether the work was possible for the stage. Gregor was convinced more than ever that a theatrical success was out of the question and said that he was prepared to present *Romeo and Juliet* as an oratorio! At that I suggested to him that he should make a simplified décor (only backdrops) whereby a certain stylization would be possible. At this point *they all* decided most definitely for an artistic simplification of the stage mounting. With these problems to be solved a group of people arrived at my house on the evening of November 15th [a most notable day in the Delius history] who were to decide on the life or death of your work. After a little supper I played the whole opera from 11 o'clock at night until one in the morning before the following judges: Gregor, Mertens,[1] Morris, Chop, Walser[2] and Bruno Cassirer[3] with his wife. After I had struggled through it I disappeared and left them to carry on quarrelling over the subject. But all were *without* exception of the opinion that:

1. The music was magnificent. . . .
2. The text was completely impossible. . . .
3. A success could only be expected with an elaborate and rich production.

[1] A well-known manager and agent in Berlin.
[2] Business manager of the Oper.
[3] Cousin of Fritz Cassirer.

There I stood with my "simplified" décor, and our stock, dear Delius, sank to zero. No decision was reached. We sat until half past two in the morning and thought, drank, chattered and ate. I remained resolutely silent fetching bottle after bottle, Gregor sat over with Chop and held firmly to his point that in any case the entire libretto must be reconstructed. Then they went. Last act. On the following morning they all realized that they had heard a magnificent work! Gregor declared that he was still none the wiser but in order that he could explore all possibilities he would like me to ascertain just how much the thing might cost. As clothes played no part in it perhaps it would not turn out to be so expensive. The last sitting took place at sundown. All the décor was minutely discussed, the production was decided upon, and as Sali and Vreli together with the chorus already knew their parts a performance ought to be possible at the end of January. Not one note of the music will be altered; textual (not scenic) changes must be examined so that we can have a *spoken Prologue* before the first act. Here we must make many, even if only small changes; so, dear Delius, eight more days of patience and then the bags packed!'

And so as the momentous year of 1906 came to a close he could sit down to his Christmas dinner with gratifying content, that with the great north German stronghold of music now penetrated, the latest and ripest of his operas would be seen and heard there in a few weeks' time. If the production which took place in February was not all that his keenest admirers expected or demanded, it was certainly not the deplorable affair stigmatized by some commentators, who never saw either it or any of the subsequent performances given during the few years that followed. The principal elements in any operatic representation are the singers, the chorus, and the orchestra: in a few works only is dancing such an integral part of a whole as to exact an equal degree of excellence. In the case of the Berlin production, of the three principals one was excellent, the second good and the third at least adequate. The orchestra played as well as any other in the city, and according to some accounts produced a more refined tone, owing to the superior quality of instruments possessed by several members of it in both the string and wind departments. Most of the adverse criticism, when not aroused by the work itself, was directed against Cassirer who did not repeat the personal success he had secured with *Koanga*. The written comments of those who heard more than one representation are emphatic that the standard of performance rose perceptibly after the opening night, which suggests that the work could have been more thoroughly rehearsed. This mishap occurs more than occasionally with first performances, and the result is that those who are present receive a misleading impression which it is not easy afterwards to modify.

At the present moment there are two kinds of jarring voices raised in the land; the one declaring that the thing called production has come of age only in the last few years; the other asseverating with vigour that never before have there been so many so-called representations which are outrageous caricatures or travesties of the composer's intentions. Of the second category of pundits I do not desire to speak, but no one who for nearly sixty years has heard the magnificent performances and seen the splendid productions in twenty of the leading theatres of the world, and some minor ones too, with half the works created before the eyes of their authors, will agree for one moment that the regisseur of the latter quarter of the nineteenth century or the first of the twentieth could have had anything to learn from his successor of today. Respecting the ideal or even correct presentation of an opera of the kind under consideration, it should be realized that there is perhaps no theatre at present in the world, with the possible exception of Glyndebourne, where this could be achieved successfully. The characters are frail and intimate creatures who cannot bawl their emotions with gusto, as can be done in heroic music dramas such as *Die Götterdammerung* or *Aïda*. They are almost dream creatures who wander on and off the stage as in a fairy-tale. In a large building they are out of artistic focus and their identities wither, as would those of *The Wild Duck* or *The Cherry Orchard* in the vast auditoriums of La Scala or the Metropolitan of New York. A structure of moderate dimensions is the first requisite for dramatic effectiveness, where the actors are not dwarfed by their surroundings. Unhappily, however, our composer insisted on writing operas which demanded a larger number of instruments than are to be found in *Tristan*, *Die Meistersinger*, *Otello* or any work of Puccini, and no reduction of his score is artistically satisfactory. But here intrudes the irritatingly earthbound side of the question. A smallish theatre for an entertainment of a costly kind and catering for a necessarily limited public is not the sort of edifice that either the hard-headed business man or any public corporation is likely to invest money in. So without doubt performances of the

Delius operas will continue to be given under the imperfect conditions here described, on the principle of preferring the half of something to nothing at all; and the misguided promoter of them will be properly and roundly abused for his perversity in striving to perform that baffling miracle, squaring the circle.

But as it is in no way my purpose to divert the attention of the reader from the main course of this history, I will take him across the Channel and to London, whither Frederick had accompanied the Komische Oper Group under Gregor and Cassirer in a series of performances of *The Tales of Hoffmann*. Possibly he was hoping that if this enterprise were successful his own opera might be given a few hearings. Unfortunately the reception accorded to the Berlin Company was none too cordial, for the Public being of opinion that an Opéra Comique should play comic pieces, failed to discover any occasion for side-splitting joviality in Offenbach's largely tragic masterpiece. He remained in London for a little while after the conclusion of this short season, renewing old acquaintanceships and making new ones mostly with the younger musicians of the day. Henry Wood, anxious to wipe out the slur upon the escutcheon of the Promenade Concert Series self-inflicted by its two lapses of faith in 1905 and 1906, announced his firm intention of including the Piano Concerto in the 1907 autumn season and discussed the possibilities of giving *Sea Drift* and *Appalachia*. Cyril Scott had been useful in finding him quarters near his own in South Kensington, and his old friend of Bradford Grammar School days John Coates introduced him to London club life. In April the Sheffield Festival Committee on the recommendation of Wood accepted his *Sea Drift* for performance in the autumn of 1908, and in return for this service Frederick allowed himself to be persuaded into taking on the task of adjudicator, in company with Granville Bantock, on a Prize Cantata competition sponsored by the Norwich Festival Committee. He returned to Grez in the late spring but not before he had laid before a few sympathetic and respectful listeners the outline of a grandiose project for converting England into a musical country, somewhat on the lines of the abortive opera scheme of 1899, but this time concerned only with music to be played in the concert-hall.

He had been seriously impressed during his visit by the modesty and enthusiasm of a dozen young composers, which suggested to him that something vital might at last be stirring in the land of his birth. As

they all deplored the limited opportunities available for the performance and publication of their music, he broached the idea of a cycle of
special concerts given annually in different centres under the control
of a new organization founded for that specific purpose. After all, this
is only what the Germans had been doing for some time past in cities
such as Munich, Frankfurt, Stuttgart and Essen, under the direction of
their Tonkünstler Verein; and having disseminated the idea with
customary vigour of utterance he departed to the tranquil seclusion of
Grez and the more harmless pursuit of composition. The following
June some of his new-found enthusiasm was a little checked by a letter
from Henry Wood, in which that eminently practical man had something to say about executive standards then prevailing in England:

'Please do not suggest an English Tonkünstler as, if you heard
the local orchestras even in places like Liverpool and Birmingham
you would have a fit. They have improved a good deal in recent
years, but are still incapable of playing a modern work by Strauss
or yourself; why, they cannot even accompany Elijah decently!'

Cassirer had remained in London after the return of the Komische
Oper Company to Berlin, having conceived the curious notion that a
pleasanter and more profitable career could be made in England than
in Germany. He had been encouraged in this belief by Frederick's old
Leipzig companion Robin Legge, who had now succeeded Joseph
Bennett as principal music critic of the *Daily Telegraph*, a position of
genuine consequence in 1907, as that paper devoted more space to
musical matters than any other in the country. Ill-advisedly Cassirer
had refused an offer from the Manhattan Opera House in New York
controlled by Oscar Hammerstein, and was now beginning to feel
that he might have made a mistake. 'It requires very great patience to
achieve anything over here,' he wrote in June. 'In addition the English
it seems, are turning nationalistic and patriotic as well. . . . London as a
city is repellent to me—and so the temptation to stay here is not very
considerable.' (Shades of Samuel Johnson and Charles Lamb!) By
September his prospects had not improved and he returned to Berlin
to secure the assistance of his family for the promotion of a concert on
his own account in London. This being obtained he concluded arrangements for it to be given on November 22nd at Queen's Hall, the
programme to include *Appalachia* and *Ein Heldenleben*, the latter work

'Springtime at Moret-sur-Loing'
Alfred Sisley

'A *café-concert* in the Champs Elysées'
Engraved by M. Coste after M. Morin

A late photograph

chosen for the opportunities it would give him for the exhibition of his virtuosity as conductor. He wrote to Frederick, who was now back in London, for advice about orchestras and choirs, as his agent L. G. Sharpe, the official representative of one of them, the London Symphony, might naturally be a little prejudiced in its favour.

While these preliminaries were being ironed out, the Pianoforte Concerto in its new form had been heard at a Promenade Concert with Theodor Szanto as soloist. No better piece could have been chosen to reintroduce him to London after eight years' absence and to present him for the first time to a Promenade audience. Chevaleresque and brilliant in sound it contained just that modicum of derivative influence likely to catch the ear of a Public whose gods were Beethoven, Wagner and Tschaikowsky, as well as a spice of the real Delius to excite the hopes of his new group of admirers. Indeed most of the latter appear to have been quite carried away, judging from the letters of congratulation that flowed in from all sides, Robin Legge confessing that by the time the slow middle section was over his emotional capacity was strained to such a pitch of exhaustion, that he could neither hear any more nor indeed write about it as he would have wished. It was during October that Frederick made himself known to me after a concert I had been giving at Queen's Hall with a programme of modern French and English music. It appeared that he had consulted Robin Legge about the choice of an orchestra for Cassirer's coming concert, and had been informed that there were at that time two only in London, the Queen's Hall and the London Symphony. But on the previous day he had noticed an advertisement in Legge's own newspaper of a concert to be given with a body of players about whom he had been told nothing, and had decided that he ought to hear what it could do although he had naturally assumed that it must be of recent formation. When I corrected this impression, he commented in a tone of voice that expressed both incredulity and derision, 'London is the only city in the world where an obviously first-rate orchestra can appear many times during a full year without the knowledge of those whose business it is to write about such things.' He advised Cassirer at once that here was the right sort of instrument for their joint requirements, and during the next few days he found it necessary to see me frequently.

Although I had previously heard a good deal about the man, my first impression of him was one of considerable surprise. 'He must be a cardinal or at least a bishop in mufti,' I kept on saying to myself, for his features had that mingled cast of asceticism and shrewdness one mentally associates with high-ranking ecclesiastics. I was also struck by a general air of fastidiousness and sober elegance rarely to be observed in artists of any kind. Unexpectedly contrasting, but not unpleasing, was his style of speech, of which the underlying basis was recognizably provincial. Not for him was the blameless diction so laboriously inculcated and standardized in our leading public schools and ancient universities. He loyally preserved his preference for the Doric dialect of that great northern county of broad acres, which looks down with compassion upon the miminy-piminy refinements of the softer south. Upon this had been grafted a polyglot mish-mash, acquired during his twenty-four years self-imposed exile from England. Both French and German words interlarded his sentences, and he always spoke of the 'orchester'. At times he would invent with comical effect a composite word borrowed from more than one language to express his meaning, and I recall on one occasion later in our acquaintanceship how he complained plangently about the ugly 'ayderadoon' in the bedroom of his hotel which obliged me to think twice before grasping what he meant. He was usually given to confusing the different meanings of hygiene and sanitation in a manner which never failed to upset the gravity of those around him at the moment.

In listening to music of any sort at a concert he sustained an impeccable demeanour of absorbed attention, and anyone who had the temerity to disturb it was rebuffed by a spirited explosion of annoyance. In public he was invariably dignified, reticent and well mannered; and of Bohemianism there was no visible sign. Only in private circles did he let himself go, giving vent with delightful gusto to opinions on music or any other subject. When standing, he never put his hands in his pockets, but let them hang down by his sides with a quasi-military precision oddly at variance with the rest of his posture. No one in those days ever saw him smoking, although I subsequently learned that in his earlier years he had rarely been seen, like Colonel Newcome, without a cigar in his mouth.

The first performance in England of *Appalachia* is one of the half-dozen momentous occasions I have known over a period of more than fifty years. I am thinking here less of my own personal reaction to the music than that of the very considerable audience assembled to hear it. In a word it was one of the few red-letter days in English music, an occasion that the majority of the Press failed to appreciate. Fortunately it is not those who write about music whose opinions ultimately influence its destinies, and one of the anachronisms of our age is the belief, on the part of old-fashioned editors, that it is still necessary to include among their regular staff men who know very little about the fundamentals of music, who cannot distinguish the merits of one work from another, and who rarely lose the chance of mistaking talent for genius and vice versa. None of this complaint, let me make clear, is directed against those few exceptional men to be found in England, both at that time and today, who were and are a credit to their calling. But undoubtedly it was upon the young and progressive composers of the day, together with those executive musicians capable of recognizing beauty and novelty of sound when they heard it, that the profoundest impression was made.

During the weeks following this event the project introduced by Frederick to his new-found friends had taken the shape of an organization, christened The League of Music. Elgar became the President, Delius the Vice-President, and they were assisted by a Committee of ten including Granville Bantock and Henry Wood. Booklets and leaflets indicating the aims and objects of the League were widely distributed, the scheme had the backing of sympathetic journalists such as Ernest Newman, Robin Legge and E. A. Baughan, and the Committee, resting from its preliminary labours, awaited that inflow of financial backing through subscriptions and donations which it was expected would be forthcoming. Unluckily the response to the appeal was disappointing, for this well-intentioned collection of enthusiasts had failed to learn the lesson that the English Public is less interested in promises than in achievements. Had it started with a few privately sponsored concerts, and had these met with a fair measure of success, the Leaguers might have gradually created a worthwhile following. But, speaking generally, the musical world everywhere responds only to definite and tangible results and not to indefinite and intangible propositions. The League struggled through a period of nearly two years of fitful activity, underwent several changes of direction, succeeded in giving one Festival of concerts in the October of 1909, and thereafter sank gently into oblivion. Conceivably had its two leading figures been willing to give a good deal of their time to social contacts and administrative control, something more might have come of it. But each of them thought that in giving his blessing to the affair he had done all that could be reasonably expected of him. It was for the younger men surely to take over the more prosaic duties of management, which invariably involve continual attention to the humdrum exactions of daily routine. Doubtless they were right; for the really paramount need in England was the creation of more first-rate music and this need they alone had the acknowledged genius to satisfy.

21

IKE every other musician under thirty years of age who was present at the performance of *Appalachia* in November, I was startled and electrified. Here at last was modern music of native growth in which it was possible with uninhibited sincerity to take pride and delight. I formed the unshakeable resolution to play as much of it as I could lay my hands on whenever I had the opportunity, and at once included in my coming programmes for the New Year, *Paris* and *Appalachia*. To make myself better acquainted with the composer's wishes concerning the former work whose style, form and colour were wholly strange to me, I accepted his invitation to spend a few days at Grez towards the close of the year. But as there was a good number of friends in and out of the house during this period, I had small chance of learning much from him about his work, or of enjoying any personal intercourse with him. I was obliged therefore to do as well as I could on my own account, and gave *Paris* its first English hearing three weeks later at Queen's Hall with the New Symphony Orchestra, which had established itself with some assistance from me in the autumn of 1906. *Paris* without repeating fully the sensation of the previous November did nothing to diminish the prestige of its composer. From the start it took its place among the 'popular' works of Delius and has continued to maintain that position.

Brigg Fair was produced at Basle in January by Hermann Suter,[1] and February saw its initial English performances at Birmingham under Landon Ronald and at Liverpool under Granville Bantock. In April the provincial début of *Appalachia* took place at Hanley under the auspices of the North Staffordshire Choral Society, the composer conducting; but I regret to say that the execution of this splendid work,

---

[1] Switzerland's most distinguished composer. For many years he lived in Basle where he was active as a conductor. His masterpiece *Le laudi di San Francesco d'Assisi*, an impressive work written for solo voices, chorus, organ and orchestra was written to celebrate the centenary of the Basler Gesangverein.

apart from the small share of the choir in it, was far from satisfactory. The orchestral playing, whether due to the manifest incapacity of the conductor to communicate his intentions to it, or a want of sympathy with the music it was encountering for the first time, was painfully perfunctory and uninspired. The second London performance of the piece was given under my direction a few weeks later at Queen's Hall, this time with the assistance of the Birmingham City Choral Society. But every other Delius event of the spring and summer was eclipsed by the Munich production of the second part of *A Mass of Life* in June, the crowning point of the composer's German career, and the undisputed highlight of the Festival. Perhaps the most interesting comment on the event was that of a well-known writer in a French paper *Lugdunum* the following month, where he compares Delius with Debussy:

> '*Comme lui, il paraît vêtu d'arc-en-ciel dilué: une continuelle pâmoison de delicats frottements d'accords nous chatouille delicieusement et, cependant, quelque chose de fort et de salubre règne dans l'ensemble. L'architecture de l'oeuvre connaît une élévation à grandes lignes audacieuses et un plan large et aéré, mais ferme et defini. On sait d'où l'on part, où l'on va, et où l'on aboutit.*'

It was shortly after this that I accompanied Frederick on a month's walking tour in Norway, and he took me over very much the same ground covered by him on that earlier trip with Grieg and Sinding, as related in Chapter 6. The flight of fifty years has changed much in the scene and life of the country. In those days railways were few (the line between Christiania and Bergen had not then been constructed), and the only means of getting about were walking and driving in little vehicles, with occasional recourse to a diminutive steamboat on one of the fjords. This more conventional method of transport was useful when confronted with the impediment of a long and winding stretch of water, which would take the best part of a day to reach and round, while a few miles away on the other side was our next destination. On one of these excursions I was accosted by a middle-aged Englishman who viewed with much curiosity the appearance of my companion. 'Look at that face,' he said, 'strength and purpose are written on it. I appreciate that because I myself am flabby. Nearly everyone I meet nowadays in Europe looks flabby. This fellow is either distinguished or has a remarkable future.' My interrogator turned out to be an ex-civil servant who had spent twenty-five years in the Near East, and was highly pleased with his acumen on learning that the object of his interest was someone of international reputation and a musician of possibly greater individuality than any other living.

At one of the stopping places on our route, a tiny town with a long pier, we were greeted by the band of the local Salvation Army, comprising a flute, a violin, a trumpet and a harmonium. A young lady completed the ceremony with a couple of hymns, to the astonishment of Frederick, who exclaimed, 'The last time I heard those tunes was when the Negroes sang them to me in Florida over twenty years ago,' and rather wistfully, 'with very different harmonies.' But anything other than unadorned simplicity could not be expected in such a remote part of the land, where in the average home the music library consisted of a hymn-book, a volume of Grieg's songs and (sometimes) another containing a few of his simpler pianoforte pieces.

Frederick was a first-rate and tireless walker, and luckily I was in good physical condition in those days owing to my many long rambles in the countryside on the outskirts of London, where I had been living for the past three years. As a relaxation from our arduous exertions, whether staggering up mountains or slithering over glaciers, he would pick out some little village with a running stream so that he could do a little fishing as well as bathing. At one of these we found a countryman of ours, also an enthusiastic angler. But although he had furnished himself with a piscatorial equipment, which for beauty and elegance would have excited the envy of old Izaak Walton, he had not succeeded during the course of three days in obtaining a single bite. His mortification was doubled by an exhibition of professional virtuosity on the part of our guide, who had conducted us safely down the winding descent from a hazardous mountain range. This worthy, stimulated by the ill success or incompetence of the foreign visitor, ransacked the outbuildings of the inn, and brought forth what looked like a long pole with a piece of string at its end. This he threw with a casual air of indifference well into the middle of the river, and within fifteen minutes had brought off two triumphal captures.

It was towards the close of our tour that I gained an unexpectedly close insight into some of the social customs and practices prevailing in the more out-of-the-way districts of this delightful country. We had been driving nearly all day on a narrow road that ran through a wide and fertile valley, and suddenly arrived at a closed gate, evidently the entrance to a largish-looking farm. On the other side of the gate were two young men engaged in earnest conversation, and not wishing to interrupt we waited until it terminated. I, of course, had no idea what their talk was about, but I could not fail to notice that Frederick showed increasing signs of amusement as it went on. When the gate was opened and we were permitted to continue our way, for the road ran through the farmlands, I asked what it was that had provided him with such an unanticipated piece of entertainment. The pretty little story he told me I have judiciously condensed out of a desire to avoid lacerating the tender susceptibilities of my Anglo-Saxon readers, and paraphrased in the form of a short dialogue.

Quoth Farmer One: 'I want you to do me a favour; lend me a couple of your men for a few days as I am very behindhand getting in my hay. Do this for me and I'll let you spend the night with my sister.'

Quoth Farmer Two: 'Very sorry, old fellow, but I can't oblige you. I am just as much in a mess over my hay as you. As for your sister, I think you ought to know by this time that I can spend the night with her whenever I like.'

Our daily companionship was invaluable to me in gaining an insight into the workings of a highly unusual type of mind. To it the universe, presenting no problems or mysteries, was a vast and beautiful thing, whose secrets were all to be found in Nature and its boundless manifestations of life. Delius was no Christian; neither was he Mohammedan, Buddhist, nor follower of any creed that concerned itself with some form of existence other than that lived on this planet. But his kinship with what the mystical Blake somewhat contemptuously called 'the vegetable universe' was limitless and profound. He revealed a close acquaintance with the literature of at least four European nations, France, Russia, Germany and Norway, and could talk about them with an appreciation and clarity of thought that demonstrated beyond doubt how completely he had absorbed all that he had ever read. Of English letters his knowledge, although less comprehensive, was at least equal to that of most educated persons in this country. The sixteenth and eighteenth centuries appealed to him more than the seventeenth or nineteenth, and his favourite novelist was Fielding. He had scarcely less admiration for Sterne and Smollett, always contending that he found in these three authors more virility and freedom from affectation than in their successors.

I have heard it stated that he was not only an unlettered man, but took small interest in anything but his own music and impressionistic painting. This report emanates mainly from those who knew him only in his later days when blind and paralysed. But the Delius of 1908 and during the few following years was a man of more than average learning, took the keenest interest in the thoughts and actions of every different class of human being, and betrayed nothing of the exclusive aristocrat and scorner of the humble, such as we have been led to believe. That the appetite for deriving pleasure and information from books diminished perceptibly during his final decade cannot be denied; but he was not singular in this respect. At least one famous scientist of the nineteenth century and an almost equally celebrated statesman found it impossible to enjoy poetry after a certain age in their respective lives. My personal association with him was mainly in the days of his zenith as a man and musician, and I have never known a keener and brighter spirit than Frederick at that time. One writer has affirmed that he was no intellectual, whatever that may mean. But the ability to hold clear-cut views about all mankind and its ways, and to utter them convincingly, was as great in him as in any of the acknowledged sages I have known over a period exceeding forty years.

Naturally I did not crystallize inalterably these opinions during the short period of our tour, for the conditions of a companionship à deux offered small opportunity for the display of his more flamboyant gifts. Among these was a highly uncommon talent for controversy, to be seen and heard at its best when prompted by the presence of a small company of acquaintances gathered under his own roof. But about the beginning of the following September I was in Paris on one of my periodical hunts for first edition scores of old French operas, and finding the weather over-warm for that time of year I moved out to Fontainebleau, to become later a favourite haunt of mine. Hearing of my arrival there the Deliuses invited me to an early evening meal at which half a dozen other guests from Paris and the near neighbourhood were present. It was held in their beautiful garden and after a while there started one of those lively discussions I had heard so much about and to which I have made brief allusion in Chapter 13. My expectation of a characteristic performance from Frederick was not disappointed, and he revealed a technique of argument all his own.

Allowing others to start and partly develop a line of talk, he would listen carefully for a while, contributing no more to it than an occasional interjection that did not seem to have much connection with what the rest were saying. Indeed I was reminded of one of those old-fashioned operas of the eighteenth century in which the overture is built on themes which are never heard again in the work itself. But as the controversial temperature warmed up, it began to be evident that through a maze of seeming irrelevancies he was feeling his way to a definite point. When he did arrive there it became instantly clear that here was the crux of the whole matter, and this capacity to hit the nail unerringly on the very centre of its head could be ascribed only to an instinctive logical sense that often confounded the orthodox methods of some of those who passed for skilled and successful debaters. There were of course limitations to this strange accomplishment. Frederick would not have gone far as an orator or impromptu lecturer and some years later he confessed to me that he could not make a speech lasting more than a couple of minutes to save his life. His delivery was spasmodic rather than sequential, and although this debarred him from public appearance, it detracted nothing from the brilliance and appositeness of his utterances when addressed to a select audience *in camera*. I have always been thankful for the chance given me of viewing this robust and resourceful intelligence in action, while yet unimpaired by any sign of decline.

The autumn season in England opened with the long-expected performance of *Sea Drift* at the Sheffield Festival, under the direction of Henry Wood, with Frederick Austin as the baritone soloist. The work was given again by me on two occasions, the following December at Hanley on the 3rd and the next day at Manchester, with the same soloist, the New Symphony Orchestra and the North Staffordshire Choral Society. This choir which two years successively had won the first prize at the National Eisteddfod was at that time in my view the most completely equipped for the interpretation of this particular kind of music. Under its excellent choirmaster, James Whewall, it had a bright ringing tone, undeviating pitch and a sensibility that marked it apart from most other larger choral bodies of the day. Just the organization for the production of *A Mass of Life* when I should be able to give it. *Sea Drift* I repeated in London towards the end of the following February, and not without interest is a judgment upon the work by one habitually sparing in her praise—Ethel Smyth:

'I am a slow listener and whosoever the people may be who grasp very deep and new thoughts, and jump to a new outlook in one minute, I am not one of them. But I felt of course all through the performance pages of such divine exquisite beauty—that I have absolute confidence in the other pages that connect them even tho' their content may be less irresistible on superficial acquaintance. The whole thing remains in one's mind as a great vision—I am longing to hear it again.'

An appraisal of a lighter sort, and which I cannot refrain from quoting, was uttered by a gentleman of the Press, evidently recruited from the Sports section of his paper for the occasion, who wrote: 'Mr. Delius seems to have exhausted the whole gamut of aquatic emotion.'

Frederick can now be said to be floating safely on a wave of prosperity which increased as the year went on in Germany and other adjacent lands. Although the Munich Opera House had postponed for the time being the proposed production of *A Village Romeo and Juliet*, Mottl included in his concerts the Piano Concerto and *Paris*. *Appalachia*, *Life's Dance* and *Brigg Fair* were being given in many of the principal cities, and the faithful Haym was scheming for a performance of the entire *A Mass of Life* at Elberfeld in the autumn: an achievement which, after much preliminary obstruction, he eventually succeeded in accomplishing. But in the steady advance to international fame our attention may now rightly shift to England, where the repeated manifestations of his genius were even more of a revelation than elsewhere. For it was not every day that a composer of the front rank appeared unexpectedly on the scene, with half a dozen or more splendid and exciting scores of which hardly anyone had ever heard a note. The climax in the crescendo of interest was attained in the performance at Queen's Hall on June 10th of *A Mass of Life*; this being the first time the complete work had been given anywhere. The impression created among both amateur and professional musicians was profound. I had full opportunity of discussion with more than a score of composers and conductors, both English and Continental, and the almost unanimous opinion was that the *Mass* was the most impressive and original achievement of its genre written during the past fifty years. The solo singers appearing on this occasion were—Gleeson White, M. G. Granger-Kerr, Webster Millar and Charles Clark; and the North

Staffordshire Choral Society sang with brilliance and conviction the strange-sounding and difficult choral numbers.

After the performance of this, his greatest concert work, it was natural that the thoughts of his admirers should turn towards the operas. Two of them had been given in Germany during the past five years, and both had won either the admiration or aroused the interest of many of the leading German musicians of the day such as Strauss, Humperdinck, Schillings and Mottl. Was the entrance door to opportunity and recognition to be barred against him here? Fortunately an answer in the negative could be given with the least avoidable delay. Circumstances had made it possible for me to take a short lease of the Royal Opera House, Covent Garden, at the beginning of 1910 during which half a dozen works, some of them new or unfamiliars could be mounted. The most obvious choice was *A Village Romeo and Juliet* whose maturity of style would make it preferable to the earlier *Koanga*, and the first performance took place on February 23rd and before a sufficiently large audience. A report, circulated mainly by persons who were not then upon the scene, has given birth to the notion that this event was an unsatisfactory affair which did Frederick little credit. It would be unfitting for me at any time to defend an artistic occurrence for which I was mainly responsible, but I cannot admit that the purely musical interests of the composer here suffered any wrong. Some of our best English singers, and each of them with at least ten years' stage experience behind him or her, were in the cast; and the instrumental part of the score, which had been rather slightingly criticized at the Berlin production of 1907, was executed by an orchestra declared at the time by Richard Strauss to be the equal of any in Europe.

We hear a great deal today in our theatres about the often undefinable part played by production in Opera which in the main is largely a matter of scenery and clothes. This perhaps is to be expected in an age when first-rate singers are scarce and hardly anyone can be found to write an opera even of the third rank. Something has to be done to counter these deficiencies and to sustain the flagging interest of the hearer. But fifty years ago the vocal and instrumental sides of his work were the main preoccupation of a composer, and how it looked, although a matter undoubtedly of some importance, was nevertheless of secondary consideration. Furthermore those who have no knowledge or recollection of the theatre prior to 1913, cannot possibly imagine what a revolution was effected by the coming, first of the Russian

Ballet, and shortly afterwards of the Russian Opera. Elsewhere I have related how almost entirely we were in thrall to a highly realistic, feebly imaginative and almost invariably mediocre style of design in scenic decoration.[1] This state of things had prevailed in England for generations and it was not until the Muscovite invasions to which I have alluded, that the realization of our inferiority dawned upon us. The settings of *A Village Romeo and Juliet* were as conventional and un-inspired as one could expect them to be in those days, but they detracted little from the beauty and charm of the music, and those who saw and heard the piece were genuinely attracted or moved. Nor were they few in number. All the same it failed to create a resounding stir in the Press, for the reason that everything else contained in the repertoire, which included *Tristan und Isolde*, *Ivanhoe*, *Hänsel und Gretel*, *The Wreckers*, *Carmen* and *L'Enfant Prodigue*, was eclipsed in the way of publicity by the notoriety given to Strauss's *Elektra*. The larger music Public talked and thought of nothing else but this extraordinary *tour de force*, whose power, violence and headlong impetuosity made even Wagner by comparison sound like a tranquil idyll. It is hardly a matter for wonder that the average ear, roused and shocked as never before, had less disposition to listen with patience and attention to one of the most completely musical stage pieces written during the past two genera-tions.

In the ten years that followed this first experiment of mine with an opera of his, I had ample opportunity of discovering Frederick's views upon the subject of stage decoration, so far as it concerned this or any other of his pieces. While he desired the most fitting and where possible the most alluring scenic pictures for the background and the move-ments of his actors, he rejected emphatically any over-simplification of the problem such as the use of curtains or singing through gauzes to suggest a condition of other-worldliness or allegory. His characters, as I have already hinted, may tend to be helpless pawns in the implacable grip of an irresistible destiny, but for all that they are capable, when the occasion arises, of expressing themselves with vigour and passion. To reduce them to shadow shapes of an inevitably etiolated or anaemic type would not heighten but lower the effect of his music. I will freely admit that this beautiful work is still awaiting superlative representa-tion. This is no easy task, for reasons which I have already explained. But as much as any other cause of difficulty is that of finding the

[1] In my book *A Mingled Chime*.

right kind of voice for any Delian singing part. All of the various characters in his six operas can be tolerably sung by dozens of well-trained and intelligent vocalists; but as much as any other composer known to me, dead or alive, does his lyrical line demand voices of a definitely special sound or, as some would say, colour. All the great composers I have known have favoured certain singers for the creation or revival of their works, and while there are many accomplishments desirable in the make-up of a first-class stage artist, of which not the least are grace, beauty and nobility of appearance, overriding all else has been the timbre of the voice which can reveal the true character and inner heart of the music. Today there are far more persons at large who understand and love the music of Delius than formerly, and it is not too much to hope that in the none too distant future there will be found among them the voices that we have been awaiting so long.

22

THE year 1910, while it saw an ever-widening prospect for his
work, was one of some anxiety to both Frederick and his
friends. Throughout his stay in London for the production of
A Village Romeo and Juliet it was evident to those near him that he was
far from well, his indisposition taking the form of chronic nervous
indigestion coupled with pains in the back. One of the causes of this
physical set-back was a succession of niggling worries, forced upon him
by importunate and incompetent persons. He may also have been
experiencing a not unnatural state of reaction from so many years of
struggle against frustration and disappointment, as well as unceasing
creative effort. It looked as if nature was beginning to sound an over-
due signal of warning. Long before this he must have begun to regret
that he had ever prompted the foundation and encouraged the development of the abortive League of Music. For something like eighteen
months hardly a week went by without a communication from one of
his colleagues on the Committee, claiming his close attention and urging
immediate response. He was frequently asked to leave Grez and to
come to England for some meeting or other, dealing with the practical
affairs of the League, just when he most wanted to forget about such
side-lines and to concentrate on the tasks he was better fitted than anyone else to accomplish. In England and to some degree also in the New
World, when a creative artist achieves celebrity, there is immediately
set on foot a species of conspiracy to divert him from the work in which
he is engaged, and to propel him into some utilitarian duties or functions which could be performed with greater efficiency by a thousand
other persons of average executive capacity. He is invited to sit on
councils, open festivals, attend public banquets, and worst of all, he
suffers the infliction of a vast correspondence, the bulk of it utterly
inconsequent, and all of it clamouring for instant acknowledgment. If

he ignores it, he is abused and his conscience troubles him more or less acutely; if he copes with it, he has little time for anything else.

The main trouble was that the new scheme had not only proceeded from his active brain, but owed most of its existence to the impact of his personality, together with his swift ascent to fame and recognition in the country of his birth. Movements such as this need constant nourishment from the fountain head and this was something that Frederick had little mind and less time to give. It was a repetition of the Concorde opera project of ten years earlier, when he was content to fly the kite of a new and attractive venture and to watch others perform all those little routine jobs without which no organization that starts from nothing can hope to get on its feet and remain there in security.

Even more irritating was a series of tiresome disputes with his publishers 'Harmonie', against whom after a course of unfruitful bickering he had been obliged to start legal proceedings in September 1909. The major ground of his discontent was the ill-judged and maladroit arrangements made by this firm for the representation of his interests in England. These had been handed over to the London branch of the Leipzig firm of Breitkopf and Haertel, who were not only doing next to nothing in the way of promoting the circulation of his music, but seemed to be placing every obstacle it could think of in the way of its frequent performance. The clash in this triangular dispute came to a head over the London production of *A Mass of Life*. In the several little squabbles, difficulties and controversies in which Frederick became involved, I was not always able to take his part with a clear conscience. He was at times apt to be impetuous, irascible and suspicious of those with whom he had business dealings. But in this instance he had a genuine grievance, inasmuch as the London house was charging about five times more for performing rights and hire of material of the *Mass* than 'Harmonie' itself for similar transactions in Germany. These all but prohibitive costs militated heavily against the chances of performance in a country where the number of organizations able to afford such exactions was less than the figures on one hand. Frederick, in whom there was a definite streak of hard commercial sense, although it rarely came to the surface, insisted that a schedule should be issued indicating at how much each of his works should be priced, so that some rationality of procedure might be established. Until this were done the future of his music in England would be severely hampered, if not halted altogether.

Just as unreasoning was the question of an English translation for the same work, which could be sung before a British audience without creating either amazement or hilarity. 'Harmonie' had not only employed a wholly inefficient person to undertake this task but had actually printed his version in both the full and vocal scores. Fully convinced of this gentleman's fitness for the task, they were now endeavouring to foist it upon me. This I naturally opposed and engaged the best man I knew in London to provide me with something that could be both sung and understood. This was William Wallace, one of the most versatile figures of the day, and I make use of three of his letters to Frederick on the subject, for further clarification of the issue. The first is dated April 6th, 1909:

'I have gone through the Bernhoff text, word by word, and I am convinced that it will stand in the light of your success if it is printed in its present form. The critics are paying special attention to the words nowadays, and the revival of Berlioz's *Faust* is entirely owing, as I think I mentioned, to the fact that the new English text is intelligible and singable. I have nothing to gain in this matter. All I want to see is your work having a chance. But I am certain that its present text would be an obstacle to performances in England. As you know, many a fine work has been killed by a bad libretto.'

Frederick had sent on Wallace's letter to 'Harmonie' and had received a reply which he forwarded to London. On April 26th Wallace writes again:

'It is perfectly absurd for a German firm to speak of Bernhoff as a 'first-class, literary, highly cultivated artist'. Breitkopf had to cancel his atrocious version of Berlioz's *Faust*, and only a few days ago I was told by another German firm that though they had accepted and paid for the translation of a big work, they had to get it done all over again by someone else. It is in the style of inferior ballads and the sooner German firms recognize that English singers are not all uneducated and refuse to sing words that make the audience laugh, the better their sales will be. Every German firm should have an Englishman as adviser as to translations. German or semi-German composers, like d'Albert, who have lived so long out of England that they have no notion of decent

English now, are not the best judges of what a good text is, and though Bernhoff may have letters from many thanking him for his work, they fail to see that the English will be criticized by Englishmen and not by Germans. Take the first line of Bernhoff. This will be sung—"O thou my wi—ill". Page 8; the word "cleped" is obsolete, and probably not one in 100 of your audience will know what it means. Page 14; who will understand what is meant by "prepared to mine ego", etc? Page 56; last line of text "Wilt thou my hound" etc., is not grammar. "That is a dance" is foolish. *Now for a dance* is English. "Pitiless Columbine"! ! ! Page 113; "Rages" has two syllables, not one. Page 131; "ululating, inebriating" is simply putting a weapon in the hands of your critics. Page 180; what singer will have the assurance to get up and declare "I'm a temulent dulcet lyre (liar)"? On Page 184 it is the turn of the poetess to be "temulent"! Page 202; that word "awfuller" gives the text away. You cannot afford to have your critical taste in English shown up with this sort of thing. Every musician who has seen B's text has said that it will damn the work if it is printed in the programme. I understand that "Harmonie" says, "We have no objection to a performance with the new text, on the supposition that it will be sent to us for disposal with all rights". I made the new text for the sake of yourself and Beecham, and I will not allow it to be used for any other performance. If "Harmonie" thinks that it is to their advantage to cancel Bernhoff's, they will have to pay for their mistakes like other people.'

This correspondence terminates on May 5th, Wallace writing again to the composer:

'Many thanks for your letter and the enclosure from "Harmonie". As far as I can see, you are allowed to use and to print in the programme my text for THIS performance ONLY. That is to say, "Harmonie" will not allow the new text to be used at any other performance of your work in this country. *Why do they stand in their own or in your light?* I also gather that they will not pay for the new text, and that they claim to have sole rights of translation. Now I am told by the publishers of the English translation of Nietzsche that there is no copyright, and that anyone can translate and publish his own text of *Zarathustra* in English without hindrance.

I got this information a moment ago from Fisher Unwin, the publisher of one of the English texts of *Zarathustra*, and he is scarcely likely to be wrong. I think it very important that you should have a clear understanding with "Harmonie" as to what they will allow in the case of other performances of your work after Beecham's. It strikes me that "Harmonie" are not very anxious that your work should have the best possible chance, but they ought to realize that whatever we may be as a musical nation, some of us understand what is good English and what is bad. German firms spend thousands in pushing German songs here, but ninety-nine in one hundred are never sung because the translations are so bad. That I suppose is what they call "business enterprise"!!!!'

I have made reference to this incident partly for the purpose of throwing some light on the extraordinary state of German mentality as a whole before the First World War. Briefly, the entire nation was intoxicated with intellectual pride and conceit, and was indulging in the conviction that there was no area of culture great or small of which it did not have a deeper understanding than inferior peoples such as the British, French or Italian. When this delusion found itself allied to deficient commonsense and lack of sound business understanding, such as is evident in the case of this unfortunate firm, we may whole-mindedly commiserate with Frederick at having fallen into such irresponsible hands.

The greater part of the year 1910 was passed quietly at Grez, where he completed *Fennimore and Gerda*, begun during the last months of 1908. Generally he was in a nervous and debilitated condition and towards the close of the year he went into a sanatorium at Dresden with no benefit to himself. A removal to one in Wiesbaden seems to have yielded better results, for we find from a letter in December to Granville Bantock, that he has now taken a turn for the better. I am unable to dissociate this year of uncertain condition both of mind and body with the strange form his latest operatic work came to take. It is divided into two unequal parts, which have next to no connection with one another. *Fennimore*, by far the more important of them, is hardly the sort of opera that could have been expected of him, after several years of work notable for its high lyrical quality. It is unfortunate for the student of Delius that its vocal score contains only the

English translation, in every way below the standard of the German version to which the music was written, as well as totally unrepresentative of the delicate and distinguished mind of Jacobsen. The problems confronting successful production are not few in number. None of the characters (at least on paper) makes a sympathetic appeal to us, and each one of them talks lengthily and monotonously about his or her 'complicated state of mind'. Only towards the end, when it is almost too late, does the piece take on any really dramatic character, as if to remind itself that some sort of action is desirable as well as requisite upon the stage. Except for a little ditty heard (off) in the moonlight upon a fjord in the second scene, there are few lyrical passages and of genuinely vocal melody scarcely a trace. I am aware that the same complaint might be levelled against *Pelléas et Mélisande*; but in Debussy's masterpiece all the figures have either charm or interest and succeed in holding our attention throughout. Although there is no fault to find with the orchestral portion of the score, which is in Frederick's ripest and most sumptuous manner, its attractions do not entirely avail to gloss over the predicament of three rather dreary people who have nothing to sing.

I have to confess a strong attachment to the old-fashioned theory and practice of opera prevailing during the eighteenth and nineteenth centuries, namely that the essential difference between the lyric and the spoken drama was that the former should be sung. Notwithstanding this time-honoured convention, which is still rife nearly everywhere, it is always possible for someone to break entirely fresh ground, provided it be done plausibly and attractively. This has been accomplished, as I have said, with acknowledged success in *Pelléas et Mélisande*, but there are some vital differences between the French and the Anglo-Danish work. In the first-mentioned we find ourselves in the Early Middle Ages, the locality is unidentifiable on the map, and the characters all indulge in a style of diction that evokes the atmosphere of a dream world.

Fennimore, on the other hand, is as modern and up-to-date as anything in nineteenth-century Scandinavian drama, and its speech is almost wholly prosaic. It would seem therefore that an unusual burden of responsibility is placed upon the histrionic capacities of the chief actors to carry off this sort of thing convincingly, particularly in the part of Fennimore. Here is the sort of neurotic and passionate woman of which in our times we have the prototype in Hedda Gabler. But where among the ranks of opera singers past or present may be discovered one with the talent of an Eleanora Duse or a Sara Bernhardt? Unless the conflicting emotions of an Ibsenish heroine be portrayed with an intensity compelling and riveting our interest, it would almost certainly falter and evaporate. But it is only just to add that, despite any critical animadversion that can be directed fairly against *Fennimore*, it stands revealed as the genuine creation of one man alone. Wide as may be the difference that separates it from all its predecessors, the Delian idiom and style are to be discovered upon every page of the score, and it might be unwise to assume that the last word has been said and that the time has come to write it off as an unskilful experiment. There is a way, perhaps the only one, in which the problem might be subjected to a practical test. Return as far as is possible to the original text of Jacobsen's *Nils Lyhne* and let the work be heard with a selected cast of first-rate Danish artists.

Gerda, the second of the two pieces, has little or no connection with the first. It is a separate episode with a happy ending of an almost childishly sentimental turn. There is evidence among his preliminary sketches that Frederick had first intended to follow Jacobsen's novel in consigning Gerda to an early grave, and this would at least have done something to fulfil the author's intention, that love and happiness were to have no part in his hero's earthly existence. It is not easy to decide what should be done with it. There is no action anywhere and it is too brief to stand alone in performance. To couple it with *Fennimore*, as must have been the composer's intention, would only be to produce a feeble and meaningless effect of anti-climax, following upon the powerful and semi-tragical denouement of the greater work.

A final word on the non-lyrical nature of the whole piece. The composer said to me at the time that in his opinion he had eliminated from it all that was unessential to the true development both of the drama and the music. Let us hope that this sweeping elimination may not have been carried a step too far.

23

EXCEPT for a brief visit to London in the summer to hear the first performance of *Songs of Sunset* with Julia Culp and Thorpe Bates as soloists, Frederick spent the rest of 1911 quietly at Grez, where during this and the succeeding year he wrote some of his most remarkable and characteristic works. Indeed during the period following the completion of *A Mass of Life* and the summer of 1914, we have an uninterrupted flow of creation, most of it of high interest and value.

Looking back a little we come to four pieces dating from 1907 and 1908, namely *Brigg Fair*, the First Dance Rhapsody, *Songs of Sunset* and *In a Summer Garden*. Neither *Brigg Fair* nor the Rhapsody are equal in inspiration and individuality to the two others of the quartet. By comparison they sound a little like excellent and occasionally beautiful *tours-de-force* and both suffer from some over-repetition of the principal theme utilized in each instance. Perhaps the greatest compliment that could be paid them is that they should be in the hands of students in every academy, as text books on the art of harmony in its most advanced stage of ingenious development. In *Brigg Fair*, the main source of invention is the well-known popular song discovered by Percy Grainger in a village of north Lincolnshire. That of the Rhapsody is original and for that reason the composer had rather more liking for it. But at no time did he rate either piece among his really serious efforts. All the same *Brigg Fair* is not to be too lightly disregarded, if only for its persistent popularity with the Public in more countries than one. Most commentators, influenced by its title, have sought to perceive in it a picture of our native countryside, though what the middle section has to do either with England or any other specific locality, I have never been able to imagine. For one person well acquainted with the work it irresistibly evokes both the atmosphere and form of a Virgilian Pastoral, more notably the eighth Eclogue with its recurring refrain introduced by a flute.[1]

In quite another class are *In a Summer Garden* and the *Songs of Sunset*. The former is not only one of the most completely characteristic efforts of its composer, but is well-nigh flawless in form and orchestration. The mood has an unimpeachable unity and in it as much as in any other single piece may be found the quintessence of Delius. That it has not earned, nor is likely to earn for some time to come, the acclaim accorded the two other pieces referred to is to be deplored, but this detracts nothing from its merits. *Songs of Sunset* is another truly Delian product although there are inequalities in both inspiration and workmanship. There are also some curiously unexpected reminiscences of other men's music, which may be purely coincidental, although it is hard to escape the impression that the song 'Exceeding Sorrow' lies under a perceptible obligation to the Third Symphony of Brahms. There are also slight echoes of Wagner in the duet 'Cease Smiling Dear', and the concluding phrases of the whole piece. It must be admitted that it is by no means easy to guarantee an adequate performance of it, for the female solo part is to be competently rendered only by a high mezzo-soprano that can cope with the rich middle register of the music. Such a voice is rare to find these days and that of the average soprano is wanting in the voluptuous quality needful for the reproduction of the right kind of sound. The baritone part contains some unnecessarily vocal angularities, notably in 'By the Sad Waters of Separation', but the composer makes amends later on in the eloquent and moving passage beginning 'I Was Not Sorrowful'. The choral portion, once the opening number is out of the way, gives little trouble; at the same time it is essential to emphasize that in no circumstances should a large number of voices be employed. Fifty or sixty at the most are enough; otherwise the extremely personal harmonic sequences tend to be muddied or blurred.

Nineteen hundred and eleven yields another remarkable work, also presenting problems of performance. This is a setting for baritone solo, chorus and orchestra of J. P. Jacobsen's poem *Arabesk*. As in the case of *Fennimore*, it is almost impossible to give this work in any language but that of its native Danish, as both the English and German versions make sheer nonsense of its meaning. If this prescription be followed the number of occasions when it might be heard is likely to

[1] '*Incipe Maenalios mecum, mea tibia, versus.*'

167

be very limited; a matter for high regret, as the work is not only in its composer's ripest style but in point of sheer opulence of sound unsurpassed by anything else he ever wrote.[1]

From this same period date the two little works one of which is easily the best known of all our composer's output. They are *Summer Night on the River* and *On Hearing the First Cuckoo in Spring*. In their respective ways they touch perfection, although I cannot agree with the judgment of one commentator that they display Frederick's powers of orchestration at their best. After all they are miniatures and written primarily for small groups of players. Of far greater importance as well as significance are the two major works, *A Song of the High Hills* and *North Country Sketches*, the latter begun in 1913 and finished the following year. *A Song of the High Hills* is the longest as well as his most impressive work written as a single movement. It is built on an heroic scale and the inspiration is on an exalted level throughout. It has also a certain austerity of manner that we have not encountered before, and which appears to be associated in the composer's mind with the emotions roused by the contemplation of great heights. The ascent of and descent from the High Hills is cunningly depicted in music of a totally different character from that which greets us when the summit has been attained, where we have a magical sequence of sounds and echoes, both vocal and instrumental, all culminating in a great outburst of tone that seems to flood the entire landscape. The first entrance of the full choir singing as softly as is possible is surely a stroke of genius, and of its kind without equal, either in him or any other composer. It may be that the purely instrumental portion of the middle section is slightly redundant, but it is within the discretion of a judicious conductor to effect some abbreviation here.

North Country Sketches consists of four movements of which three are nature pictures. These are more realistic or suggestive of realism than anything that Frederick had yet attempted, and for that reason are of peculiar interest. The visions of autumn, winter and the return of spring are conceived with much the same austerity that governs the atmosphere of *A Song of the High Hills*. There is very little of human contact here and we seem to have left behind the intimate moods that pervade *Sea Drift*, *In a Summer Garden*, *Brigg Fair* or *Songs of Sunset*. We have the clear impression that we are listening to the manifold

---

[1] A gramophone record has been made of this piece, using the original Jacobsen text with both the baritone and choir singing the original Danish version. The effect is surprising and beautiful.

utterances of nature alone: and even in the seemingly irrelevant dance from which outdoor life appears to be for the moment excluded, there is something impersonal in its spirit. A good performance is essential to reveal the unique character of each of the sections: the sombre mood of autumn, with the sound of the wind in the thinning trees, the icily cutting blasts of winter and the strangely contrasted convulsions and ululations of Nature that mark the re-birth of spring-time.

By way of relaxation from his larger labours he produced a handful of songs about this time, of which the more notable are 'The Nightingale has a Lyre of Gold' and 'Hŷ Brasil'. He also wrote for choral societies in England a group of unaccompanied choruses, of which the most striking is a setting of 'On Craig Dhu' by Arthur Symons. In addition he completed his final version of *Life's Dance* (*Lebenstanz*), performed by Oskar Fried in Berlin during 1912.

The private lives of Delius and his wife during the two or three years that preceded the outbreak of war were tranquil and undisturbed. His material circumstances had improved substantially, thanks to a considerable bequest conveyed to him in the will of Aunt Albertine, who had died in 1913. His income from performing fees and royalties had now assumed fairly satisfactory proportions and his disagreements with publishers had apparently been adjusted. He discontinued for the time being his annual summer trips to Norway and broke fresh ground by visiting both Switzerland and Italy. The exotic charm of Venice made an especial appeal to his fancy and it was there he met that remarkable individual Henry Clews, with whom he formed a friendship, which influenced both parties profoundly during the next twenty years.

24

THE outbreak of war in 1914, with the exception of the fatal malady that finally overcame him ten years later, was the greatest single blow he suffered during his long and troubled career. So far as his fame and prestige were involved, these stood in Germany at their highest point. There he was one of the two men of the hour, as well as the elected champion of all that minority to which full reference has been made. Although the interest and speculation he had aroused in England during the seven preceding years had been outstanding, it lacked something of the stability he had secured in the Fatherland. In the former country he had been recognized by the bulk of professional musicians, especially those under the age of thirty-five, as a powerful and original force. But the perception that here at last was music of unmistakable beauty and individuality, and moreover totally unlike anything that had been heard before, was rarely manifest in the attitudes of either Public or Press. Until 1903 Germany had no reason for looking upon the Yorkshireman as other than one of its own composers, he being known there as Fritz Delius. But on the occasion of his marriage he announced that henceforth Fritz should be dropped in favour of Frederick, although he never gave any reason for the sudden change. Not even Grieg, who wrote to him chaffingly about it, could extract a convincing explanation of the transformation. It was not as if he owed some musical allegiance to the country of his birth. He had lived away from it for nearly twenty years: until 1907 few people there knew of his existence and fewer still of his attainments. When at that time he began to play an important part in English musical affairs, it probably never occurred to him that he was indulging in a species of gamble. In common with so many Englishmen in those days, he felt no compulsion to look into the future, for had not the relations between Great Britain and Germany been generally cordial for more than a century and a half? Furthermore, although the substitution of Frederick for Fritz might imply that he was emphasizing his British nationality, this at the time meant little to the German Public, which had been educated in the belief that for centuries past half the men in Europe of inventive genius, even those of Italian birth, had Teutonic blood in their veins.

The declaration of war, despatched by London to Berlin on August 4th, was probably the greatest shock that Germany had ever experienced. It was unexpected, inexplicable and condemned by the entire population as an act of treachery, and therefore unforgivable. From one end of the Empire to the other rose an universal cry 'God punish England', and this denunciation was repeated daily for years on the lips of men, women and children. Whatever claims up to that moment Frederick had upon the esteem and admiration of a large number of Germans, vanished overnight in the emotion of hate that governed the entire country. At the conclusion of the war when mass hysteria had abated, those of his faithful adherents who had survived made energetic efforts to secure for him a return of favour, and for a few years these were tolerably successful. But much of the glamour that had formerly surrounded his name was gone, so far as the general Public were concerned. He was no longer a German composer.

The rapid advance of the enemy had come perilously near Grez-sur-Loing and the Delius couple, burying their valuables and wine in the garden, vacated their home with celerity. Their beloved Gauguin picture—'Never More'—was rolled up into a conveniently portable shape, and taken along with them. They journeyed first to Orleans in a wagon filled largely with manure and there learned the result of the Battle of the Marne. Assuming that this was a decisive German defeat, they took it for granted that the Kaiser's legionaries would now retreat quietly to the Fatherland and sue for peace. Lauding the prescience of an English newspaper which a little earlier had declared that the war could not possibly last longer than two months, they returned to Grez where they remained until the close of the year. But realizing by that time that the struggle would probably continue for years instead of weeks, they packed up again and set out for England. They reached the coast after some devious wanderings on the way and, as the Channel steamers were still making their regular crossings, they arrived safely in London, where it became the concern of their friends that arrangements should be made on their behalf for what might be a lengthy stay. Shortly before this I had taken the lease of a little house a few miles out of Watford; a pretty place well away from main roads and blessed with a mill-wheel to provide soothing sounds both day and night. This I offered them and there they settled and remained for nearly a year. For a while Frederick remained in a highly nervous and agitated state, with small inclination for anything but restless inaction. But by the beginning of 1915 he regained much of his habitual serenity, and started work again. He rewrote a part of *Arabesk* and made sketches of a new orchestral tone-poem —*Eventyr*—which however was not completed until 1917. He then became absorbed in the largest and most important production of this period, a Requiem, which has excited less interest than any of his other large-scale compositions.

Let confession be made at once that here we are confronted with the most curious flight of futility that ever misled the intelligence and deceived the instincts of a great artist. At no point is the invention equal to that of any preceding work of similar dimensions, and for this reason alone, it is not surprising that it has failed to hold an established position in the Delian repertoire. But equally disconcerting was the ill-timed appearance of it, suggesting a strange psychological miscalculation on the part of its author. Ostensibly a lament for the youth of all nations, fallen and still falling in Europe's greatest tribal war, it is in reality a polemical attack upon Christian doctrine and the generally accepted Christian way of life. That Frederick was not a Christian was generally known, and it cannot be counted seriously against him that he failed to share beliefs rejected by the greater number of the inhabitants on this planet. But during the early days of the war there appeared in England, certainly for a time, a strong revival of religious emotion, largely inspired by a conviction that the contest was between one side that was upholding certain principles of supreme value, and another which was shamefully abandoning them. It has been asserted that as a highly egocentric individual, he regarded the war almost as a personal affront to himself, on the score that it was seriously interfering with his own labours. But there were many thousands of others sharing this misfortune, who nevertheless refrained from exploiting it for the purpose of theological argument. It would really seem that his sequestered life at Grez over the preceding period of seven years had not only increased his attitude of isolation and independence, but had bred in him a spirit of growing indifference towards the ways of thought and action to be found in the majority of those around him.

That he was entitled to hold the opinions he cherished so tenaciously was his uncontested privilege, but that he should now and later rarely cease to force them upon others, was an unattractive manifestation of growing egoism. It is typical of the state of self-delusion into which most composers and authors fall over the value of their own works, that three years later, in a letter written to Philip Heseltine, we find Frederick writing: 'I do not think I have ever done better than this.'

His flight from France to England marks a decided break between almost all that he had been striving to accomplish over a period of fifteen years and what he was now about to undertake. With the exception of the tone-poem *Eventyr* and the short Second Dance Rhapsody, both of which he completed two years later, we have nothing resembling the many outstanding achievements of his pre-war life. The spirit that animated the great *Mass*, *In a Summer Garden* and the *Song of the High Hills* had departed for ever. Possibly he felt the lack either of ability or inclination to continue working the rich vein of treasure that had disdained a parallel in the music of any other composer, notably in a structural way. His mind turned to the contemplation of orthodox classical forms, particularly those in which voices should play no part. Yet it was not a wholly unexploited mine of unfamiliarity, for he had experimented with it during his earlier years in Paris; but then in all conformity with the prescribed pattern of his predecessors, as is evident in his First Sonata for Violin and Piano and his Suite for Violin and Orchestra. Now, with a radical metamorphosis of melodic and harmonic resources, he set about the somewhat hazardous task of pouring new wine into old bottles.

During 1916 and 1917 he completed a series of concerted pieces for instruments alone, which comprised a Sonata for Violin and Piano, written for Arthur Catterall and R. J. Forbes of Manchester; a Concerto for Violin and Violoncello with Orchestra; a Concerto for Violin and Orchestra, together with a String Quartet, the third of its kind so far as we know. Of these the only completely successful effort is that of Violin and Orchestra. It is admirably planned for the solo instrument of which he had an intimate knowledge; it has considerable melodic beauty and is structurally entirely logical and effective. It also bears the stamp of genuine originality, in owning no resemblance to anything of the sort written by anyone else before or since. The long accompanied cadenza in the Slow Movement is a piece of musical rhetoric, both unexpected and moving, and it is only the customary diminuendo, tailing off to near inaudibility at the close, that has prevented it from being adopted by all or any of the great virtuoso violinists. As one of the most eminent of them said to me on a certain occasion: 'It is hardly a concerto, but it is a lovely poem.'

Of the three other works the Double Concerto with Orchestra is much the least successful, the composer betraying an obvious inability to handle the violoncello part when it is not playing melodic passages. At the same time it may be admitted that it contains much material that is both beautiful and original, and might be saved from oblivion on the condition that two gifted soloists took it in hand and subjected it to fairly ruthless revision. The Sonata for Violin and Piano is a solid piece of work that suffers slightly from a mixture of styles, the greater part of it having been sketched out or partly written ten years earlier. In spite of this it is fresher in mood and more attractive generally than the two later specimens of its kind. The String Quartet, except for the Third Movement, is wanting in Delian charm; but there can be no quarrel with the line of its architecture, although the composer's hand falters perceptibly in the final movement and yields the impression of an anti-climax.

From this period dates also the Second Dance Rhapsody and four English songs. The Rhapsody, while lacking the variety and brilliance of its predecessor, No. 1, is in some ways a more meritorious achievement in the way of construction; it halts nowhere, all the sections being knit together with a firm and unwavering hand. The texts of the English lyrics were probably suggested to Frederick by Philip Heseltine, as they are all of a period, Elizabethan and Jacobean, with which the younger man had more acquaintance than any other musician then living in England. They are:

> 'Spring the Sweet Spring' (Thomas Nashe)
> 'Daffodils' (Herrick)
> 'So sweet is She' (Ben Jonson)
> 'It was a Lover and his Lass' (Shakespeare).

Although their authorship is unmistakable, particularly in the Ben Jonson lyric, it cannot be pretended that they have the charm of either the Scandinavian or the French songs.

25

THE name of Philip Heseltine recalls an association between two musicians which is rare in the annals of the art. This has excited the attention of several writers, all of whom seem to have discovered something admirable in the long correspondence between the couple, which extended over a period of nearly twenty years. It began in 1911 with a letter from Philip, while still a boy at Eton, and continued on and off until 1930. Upon me the letters from both sides have always made an impression that is far from agreeable. The trouble began in 1913 when an anxious ex-schoolboy, beginning to look upon Frederick as an infallible guide, sought advice as to his immediate future. Frederick gives his views in a letter dated January 11th, 1913, in which he advises his young friend to do exactly what he feels like doing, and to stick to it. If he considers that music is the only thing in the world which interests him, he should take it up to the exclusion of everything else. But he adds that everything depends on perseverance, for 'one never knows how far one can go'. This reads very pleasantly and would be harmless if there had not been a world of difference between the two men. Frederick, once he had escaped from Bradford, not only realized that music was everything on earth to him, but had the iron will to pursue his way towards a definite goal, without hesitations, misgivings, or complaints. By the time he had arrived at full manhood both his mind and character had hardened into moulds that nothing changed until the day of death. Philip was of quite a different type. At that time barely nineteen years of age, and of a mental development which he himself admitted was distinctly backward, he vaguely desired a career with all the intensity of a great longing and a fruitful imagination, but was entirely incapable of either following a fixed course, or doing some of those things which might have expedited the close of a long period of vacillating apprenticeship.

When he first came my way in the summer of 1915 I at once saw that he was a young man of uncommon gifts and capable of going far. At the same time it was strikingly clear that he had no practical acquaintance with musical life as it was in the England of that day, and his attitude towards it was founded on a medley of generalities, most of them highly misleading. A little later on, when I formed the English Opera Company which included most of the best singers in the country, as well as a group of talented musicians such as Percy Pitt, Eugene Goossens, Julius Harrison, and Geoffrey Toye, I offered Philip a position on the musical staff. Here he would have had the opportunity of meeting a group of able and experienced persons, which after a while would have knocked some of the nonsense out of his head. He might not have been able to fulfil for the moment one of his ambitions to become a music critic, for which anyway there was virtually no scope during wartime; but he would have acquired a fund of useful knowledge, not only of what this particular opera company was doing and further planned to do, but how such things as an opera house and its machinery were run everywhere. He declined the offer.

In October 1916 occurs a spate of correspondence between Philip and Frederick, which in my view reflects credit on neither side. It begins with a letter from the former on October 11th, in which he writes:

> 'Quite definitely next March we shall take a small theatre and give a four weeks' Season of Opera and Concerts, with definite artistic policy, and no compromise with the mob.'

Then he adds:

> 'I will try to explain in a few words the general principles which we have arrived at for our guidance in presenting musical dramas. Needless to say they are diametrically opposed to those of Thomas Beecham whose productions, as well as the choice of works, are becoming more and more inferior and artistically valueless.'

The repertoire to which this youth of twenty-two refers so slightingly included Moussorgsky's *Boris Godunov*, Verdi's *Otello* and *Aïda*, Mozart's *Zauberflöte*, *Il Seraglio* and *Le Nozze di Figaro*, two English operas, *The Bosun's Mate* of Ethel Smyth and *The Critic* of Stanford,

Donizetti's *Lucia di Lammermoor*, Bizet's *Carmen* and *La Jolie Fille de Perth*, Wagner's *Tristan und Isolde* and Puccini's *Madame Butterfly*, *La Bohème* and *La Tosca*. The majority of these were looked upon then as masterworks of opera and still maintain a firm place in the international repertoire throughout the world; the Company enjoyed the assistance of such talented scenic artists and producers as Vladimir Polunin, Edmond Dulac, Hugo Rumbold, Nigel Playfair and Adrian Allinson. To outrival this not unsubstantial enterprise the works constituting the Heseltine repertoire were to be Monteverde's *Orfeo*, Purcell's *Dido and Aeneas*, Pergolesi's *La Serva Padrona*, Gluck's *Orfeo*, Mozart's *Schauspieldirektor*, and of course Delius's *A Village Romeo and Juliet*.

The reactions of Frederick, now back in Grez, to this extraordinary scheme, which would be launched and controlled by persons without the smallest experience of theatrical life, are perverse and unaccountable. He begins by saying:

'I know of no artistic musical or dramatic undertaking that has ever come off in England. The great success of the Russian Ballet was firstly because it was boomed by a fashionable clique—it came to London entirely ready to ring up the curtain. Every other enterprise has been a failure, and often a miserable failure.'

Apparently these two musical cave-dwellers had never heard of the Royal Opera House, Covent Garden, where a syndicate had given annual seasons of opera for seventeen years before the war. Each of these was given in the summer and was of thirteen weeks in length. In addition to the standard repertoire of the great masters, a respectable stream of novelty was presented to the Public, who also enjoyed the opportunity of hearing a goodly number of the famous singers of Europe and the New World. Autumn and winter seasons were frequently given in the same theatre, some of them under my own management. During the period 1909–14 London was served with a variety of operatic fare with which no other great city in the world could compete, nearly all of it in the hands of the same promoters. At the same time, Frederick is sufficiently practical to warn Philip of the immense difficulties he will encounter in launching his project, especially in wartime, and advises a postponement of it until the termination of the European conflict. Then follows a surprising exchange of views on the subject of scenic decoration. Adverting to the intended revival of *A Village Romeo and Juliet*, Philip announces:

> 'I propose to have no scenery, that is no set pieces, only plain curtains, possibly a suggestive back-cloth or two, nothing more, costumes of extreme simplicity . . . in any case the stage must be free from disturbing elements—the curtains or back-cloth beautiful, but entirely free from any elaboration.'

Upon this Frederick comments:

> 'I entirely agree that realism on the stage is nonsense, and all the scenery necessary is an impressionistic painted curtain at the back, with the fewest accessories possible. In Germany this has already been tried with success.'

Regarding this amazing statement I can only remark that it is diametrically opposed to everything that the writer had ever said to me about the scenic side of his own operas. When I revived *A Village Romeo and Juliet* in 1920, several letters passed between us touching the whole plan of production, and I received many sketches of scenery designed by Jelka herself. In the case of *Fennimore and Gerda* there are the most detailed directions throughout the score, indicating the kind of décor essential for each of the many scenes, some of which would suffer severely from the lack of appropriate or picturesque background. What would have happened to *Koanga* if produced with such a fantastic economy of accessories I do not care to imagine! Of course the hare-brained proposition never materialized, either then or at any later time, but it is not a little disconcerting to find Frederick lending so much encouragement to it.

By way of partial mitigation it must be allowed that he himself was passing through a very difficult phase, soured by disappointment and assailed by worries of a material kind. The bulk of the investments he had inherited from Aunt Albertine had been made in countries other than Great Britain—some were in Germany itself—and he found it impossible to secure the payment of dividends upon them. He was virtually dependent upon the performing fees which he received from concert performances in England, a state of things which continued for five more years. It argues therefore some want of tact, at the very least, to acquiesce in a policy aimed at depreciating almost everything attempted or accomplished in his own country. As Philip was one of the most loquacious creatures who ever lived, never hesitating to proclaim his views in and out of season at the top of his voice, and who moreover appeared to have Frederick's sanction for much he was saying, the elder man naturally forfeited a little of the goodwill earned by him over several years with those institutions, notably a handful of orchestras, which alone in the world were playing his music with commendable regularity. Unfortunately he was not on the spot to counter with that force of personality and charm of manner, which he could frequently choose to exercise, a perceptible degree of distress and bewilderment among that group of loyal friends, who for many years past had unceasingly proclaimed his merits both as a man and artist.

It is no part of my task to denigrate either the character or abilities of that strange being Philip Heseltine. As I have said I always recognized his undoubted gifts, and did something on more than one occasion to help steer them towards some definite goal. He had a genuine gift for composition, but this did not manifest itself until several years later, when he produced a handful of songs and small choral works, in many ways equal to anything being turned out by his contemporaries in England. This side of his development, however, is not that with which I am at present concerned. It is the string of letters from him to Frederick beginning in 1913 and continuing until 1919, most of which contain a repetitious story of self-impotence, self-distrust and wandering intention. Hardly the most considerate sort of communication to inflict upon a great man, whose health at this time was far from normal, and who had enough troubles to occupy his mind without being harassed by those of others. Even the Olympian Goethe was once moved to say to an indiscreet visitor seeking advice—'take your problems elsewhere, I have enough of my own'. The real culprit, if culprit there be in this tangled affair, is Frederick, who should never have committed the psychological blunder of preaching the doctrine of relentless determination and assertion of will to someone incapable of receiving it. It is hard to resist the impression that Philip's whole life would have been smoother, better ordered and increasingly rational if he had not devoted it wholly to the service in many forms of one art alone. Our history is not poor in examples of men, literary figures mainly, who have been beneficially sustained by the steadying effect of some regular and more mundane employment. The result was that for most of the time he did not really know what to do with himself, and worked off his self-discontent by vilipending diatribes against nearly everyone around him. That he had quite another side to his disposition which abounded in humour (many of his limericks are deservedly still in currency), a more than occasional streak of practicability, and a rousing enthusiasm when his interest was excited, I am happy to bear testimony; and this aspect of him arose more and more to the surface, after the assumption of the second facet of his dual personality as Peter Warlock. It was not until July 17th, 1919, that Frederick began to realize what was really the matter with his young friend, for he writes:

'Do not begin to think, dear Phil, that luck is against you, because the real reason is that you do not push your ideas to their material end with sufficient energy and *suite dans les idées*. You would succeed at anything you take up if you would concentrate on it and not diffuse your energies in so many things. Stick to one thing just for two or three years and see if I am not right. I think you are admirably gifted as a writer; you would succeed either as this or as a composer if you would stick to it and push it through regardless of everything else . . . do not think I want to preach at you, I am so fond of you that I would like to see you become something and assert yourself, and know how gifted you are and what possibilities are in you.'

All quite true and sound, but advice that might have been given a little earlier in the day.

26

THE years 1917–20 inclusive are the least fruitful in the history of Frederick's creative work. To the earlier part of this period we can attribute the completion of the String Quartet and that of a highly interesting piece for orchestra alone. This is *Eventyr*, bearing the sub-title of *Once upon a Time* and described as a Ballad for Orchestra after some of Asbjornsen's popular tales. As I have already stated, it was sketched out in a somewhat casual way during his residence at Watford in 1915, but the revised score is on a considerably larger scale than originally planned. It is not only an effective example of orchestral virtuosity but has much charm and variety of effect. It contains at least one delightful fragment of melody that recalls the Delius of earlier days, and the sort of tune he seems to have had no difficulty in bringing forth, when thinking of old legends and strange adventures. Like some other specimens of his front-rank work it suffers a wholly undeserved neglect; the more unaccountable as there are no accessory forces here, such as large choruses or soloists, to embarrass either the conductor or the concert promoter. Nor is it written for an unusually large number of instruments, as in the case of *Paris*, *Brigg Fair*, or the First Dance Rhapsody.

This was followed by a Sonata for Violoncello and Piano. Designed as a single movement no fault can be found with its structure, and at no point is there any of the casual, fussy and unwanted writing for the solo part, such as we find in the Double Concerto. Yet in spite of its obvious merits there is something wanting; perhaps a certain lack of spontaneity and warmth together with an absence of those characteristic touches to be found in all the other concerted pieces. Also, unreserved commendation must be withheld from a composition of this sort, where the soloist keeps on playing from start to finish with hardly a bar's pause anywhere. The years 1918 and 1919 are especially unproductive, the only piece of any consequence being the charming fragment 'Song Before Sunrise' for small orchestra. This almost takes rank with the little gems 'On Hearing the First Cuckoo in Spring' and 'Summer Night on the River'. The two principal melodies have an out-of-door feeling of dewy freshness, and the only complaint that can be levelled against it is the rather sudden and inconclusive termination, which requires some discretion on the part of the conductor to handle adroitly. There remains for passing mention only the unfinished manuscript of 'A Poem of Life and Love' for full Orchestra, a short dance for Harpsichord and another Verlaine song 'Avant que tu ne t'en ailles', which gives the impression of having been written at an anterior date.

Here may be the place to give some account of his private affairs during the period covered by the preceding paragraphs. A brief reference in an earlier chapter has been made to a striking personality, Henry Clews, whom he first met in 1913. Upon the return of the Deliuses to Grez in 1916, this casual encounter ripened into a friendship, which for the next fifteen years was the most important and valuable event in our composer's personal life. Just as the association with the two Griegs had been his principal mainstay, during the decade following his departure from Leipzig, so in these his autumnal years did the companionship with Clews give him the close intimacy with a man of superior mind and character which for some time had been denied him. Henry, who was an American by birth, is almost unknown in England, but in his own country is now being recognized as perhaps the most individual sculptor it has yet produced. That the realization of his genius has been slow of acknowledgment is due to his refusal to allow any public exhibition of his work during his lifetime. He died in 1937 and, as the world for the next eight or nine years was concentrating on matters in which the arts played a very minor part, it was not until well after the conclusion of the late war that a group of admirers, aided by the devotion of his widow, Marie, determined that the time had come for the recogniton of an artist whose achievement had been hidden from the world far too long. The art of Clews was compounded of a strange mixture of mysticism and humour. He made use of marble, bronze and wood to embody with malice and satire abstract types of such institutions as Autocracy, Democracy and Plutocracy, together with the less attractive manifestations of human nature, such as Greed, Envy and Jealously. On the other hand those objects which extorted his respect and admiration, such as true specimens of manhood and womanhood, he treated with tenderness and reverence. His technique rejected any kinship with that of post-Rodinesque sculpture and clung tenaciously to the tradition of an earlier epoch when high finish and conscientious workmanship, divorced from crudity and eccentricity, were sacred fundamentals.

Frederick had an unaffected admiration for his new friend's art but that alone would not have brought the pair so near together. In Henry he discovered the nearest thing to a counterpart of himself in mind and spirit: in short, another true type of individualism in excelsis. Both men hated democracy with a passionate intensity, both shared the view that Anglo-Saxon vulgarity and materialism were threatening the standards of a way of life created mainly by the beliefs and culture of the 'supreme Caucasian mind', and they saw around them little to praise and nothing to love. Clews, who was the younger by some years of the two men, was the more fanciful and romantic. He lived and found comfort in a remote past, which his more practical companion did not hold in undivided esteem. But each was certain of one thing. The whole world was rapidly going to the Devil and only a miracle could save it from utter catastrophe. In view of the numerous tragic events that have tarnished the name of civilization in the past forty years, the iconoclastic pair can hardly be condemned out of hand, on the score of pessimism. But however harshly they judged the external world around them, they retained the most absolute confidence in themselves, their own occupations and their conceptions of how everything then standing on its head could be forced or induced to resume a more normal posture. It was fortunate that their respective wives were on equal terms of friendship and mutual appreciation, for we owe to their correspondence over several years some knowledge of Frederick's plans and movements.

During the whole of 1917 and until the middle of June 1918 the Deliuses remained at Grez. They then went to Biarritz for two months, where Frederick benefited from the saline baths, returning home about the middle of September. There they were faced with a highly unpleasant surprise, which can best be described in a letter written by Frederick to Henry on August 21st:

'We thought to land in a fairy dell called Grez and we returned to a filthy barrack. All transformed by a few disgusting humans and evidently reflecting the real state of their souls. Well, the place is spoilt for me for ever and we shall try to sell it as quickly as possible and find another spot where we can finish the rest of our lives in our own atmosphere. I hope no one will ever talk to me again about the vandalism of the "Boches". I doubt whether they would have taken so much away with them as our Allies. I won' go into details, but the house is so filthy that we cannot clean it However we are leaving for London on the 29th and we are taking the Gauguin with us in order to try and sell it. Our addres there until the end of September will be 4, Elsworthy Road, N.W the residence of Sir Henry Wood.'

In October they moved to a flat in Belsize Park Gardens where they remained until the early part of 1919. He was warmly greeted every where; past lapses of judgment were speedily forgotten and every musical organization came forward to bring to light his unplayed work of the few preceding years. In November Beatrice Harrison brought out the Sonata for Violoncello and Piano. The following January appeared the Concerto for Violin and Orchestra at a Phil harmonic concert with Albert Sammons as soloist; shortly afterward the String Quartet was given by the London String Quartet, and *Eventyr* was played about this time at a Queen's Hall Symphony Concert conducted by Sir Henry Wood. These were all first perform ances. For a few weeks it looked as if they were likely to be contente in their new surroundings, but Frederick soon began to be irked b what he considered to be the unintellectuality of the English world and its indifference to anything of artistic consequence. Jelka, in ever way a devoted wife, echoed the complaints of her husband, even to th extent of discovering that the repertoire of the English opera compan then playing at Drury Lane contained nothing but works of mediocrity This curious opinion is best countered by the short answer that th majority of the alleged mediocre operas were some of the masterpiece of Mozart, Wagner, Verdi, Puccini and Bizet. It was beginning to b uncomfortably evident that both the Deliuses were well on the wa to losing the capacity to listen with patience to any music but that of Frederick himself, and this joint state of intolerance was to harde rather than soften during the next ten years.

In the early spring of 1919 they betook themselves to Cornwa where at Sennen, in the vicinity of Penzance, they found themselves distant from the uncultured capital as was geographically possibl

There they remained for about two months, returned to London for a short stay and then went on to Norway. But just before this trip to Frederick's real spiritual home, Jelka had paid a flying visit to Grez, to find out if anything could be done about restoring their house to something like its former condition. Although still in a fair state of disorder the process of purification had already begun, and a friendly French officer, who had re-established something like discipline in the neighbourhood, succeeded in recovering for her some of the property filched during the period of occupation. It really began to look as if they might be able to return and take up their old life there once again. While in Norway they read with surprise and delight that the Frankfurt Opera House was intending to produce *Fennimore and Gerda* in the coming late autumn. Since the armistice of November 1918 a complete change of mood seemed for the time being to have taken possession of the German people. The old belligerency had vanished in favour of a simulated spirit of forget and forgive, the songs of hate had been discarded and the national vocal organ was singing soft and low. Upon the conclusion of their Norwegian visit, Frederick and Jelka went through Sweden and Denmark to Frankfort, where they took part in the rehearsals of the new opera. Its première was greeted by the audience with a fair degree of success, and to Jelka's excited mind everything, music, singing and acting, seemed perfection and to constitute an event of epoch-making importance. It is of some interest to note what she has to say about the scenery:

'It is most thrilling, such a heavenly love-scene in the beech forest in orange autumn, and another charming love-scene in a dark old garden with the little harbour town, a lighthouse and water in the distance—a scene in the snow and ice frozen fjord at night. Then the two scenes all bright and spring sunshine with apple blossom everywhere.'

There is nothing here to suggest that recourse had been made to the use of curtains and simple cloths in the backgrounds. On the contrary, a fair measure of 'old-fashioned' realism seems to have been adopted and approved.

The *Frankfurter Zeitung* honoured the occasion with probably one of the longest critical notices that has appeared in print anywhere. A good part of it was devoted to reminding the Frankfurters of

Frederick's past achievements in the Fatherland, and to a slightly exhausting analysis of the new work. As this side of the subject has already been covered in a previous chapter, it may be enough to quote a few extracts from the article to indicate the impressions made upon an obviously experienced and readable musical journalist, some of which so far as the quality of performance is concerned do not endorse Jelka's glowing eulogy:

'The object appears to be to produce a number of scenes of deeply contrasting passions and to create from their sequence an unoperatic but dramatic atmosphere. Delius is not allured by externalities and outward appearances, he is thrilled by spiritual contacts between human beings and those intangibilities which shape human destinies. He exercises an almost ascetic sparseness in his media of expression; in his treatment of the words as well as of the sound. A single word, a single note or a short melodic flourish suffices, and he is always right. Unbound by tradition, guided only by the urge within him he paints his canvas in simple direct fashion. It is a spontaneous creation unaffected by principles. His weakest point, as with all artists of this kind, is one of timing and a certain treatment of the singers who are *made to declaim all the time*, and his use of the orchestra therefore becomes a virtue from necessity.'

Concerning the performance the judgment is less kindly: 'It tried so far as possible to do justice to the individuality of his style without quite being able to capture the particular tone and character of the work.' For some reason, never divulged, a reduction of the score had been made and our critic comments:

'Any reduction in the orchestral scheme would be bound to interfere with the atmosphere and free flow of the music, and this all the skill and conscientiousness of Gustav Brecher could not avoid. So with the soloists, the will was stronger than the deed. Robert Van Schiedt brought a sonorous voice to the part of Niel Lyhne, but in the delineation of the character he was as far apart from it as Emma Holt was from Fennimore.'

The minor characters were more mercifully handled and the long article concludes:

'The audience was surprised and reserved in the early stages but seemed to feel its way gradually into the strange sphere of this work and in the end greeted all those who had taken part in the production, as well as the composer, with lively applause.'

If the foregoing account of the occasion be accepted as generally accurate, I cannot help wondering what both Frederick and Jelka would have had to say, had an English conductor effected a radical alteration in such an elaborate and beautiful orchestral score as that of *Fennimore and Gerda*, and had a London management engaged for the two principal roles singers apparently unfitted for the understanding and interpretation of the drama. I venture to surmise that we should have heard something from one quarter or another about British lack of insight and dilettantism of method.

27

FREDERICK returned to London in January 1920 for the first performance of the Concerto for Violin and Violoncello. This was given at a Queen's Hall Symphony Concert under Sir Henry Wood, with May and Beatrice Harrison as soloists. He also was present at the revival early in March of *A Village Romeo and Juliet* at Covent Garden. The principal soloists were Miriam Licette as Vreli, Walter Hyde as Sali and Percy Heming as the Black Fiddler. The composer seems to have been satisfied with the production and the performance, for neither he nor anyone else was found to utter a serious word of complaint about it. Perhaps he was beginning to appreciate that the company which took part in it had been working together uninterruptedly for the past five years, and had achieved a unity and ensemble which many competent judges declared were at least equal to those of any similar institution functioning at that time. Charles Kennedy Scott with his Oriana Madrigal Society also gave the first hearing of the unaccompanied choruses 'To be sung of a Summer Night on the Water', and thanks to the enterprise of Mr. Cyril Jenkins *Arabesk* was given its première at Newport, Wales, in the same month.

Returning to Grez in March, where he remained until the following November, he made a preliminary sketch of a Concerto for Violoncello and Orchestra at the request of Beatrice Harrison. This talented lady gave a concert on June 8th in Paris when she played the Violoncello and Piano Sonata; one of the few occasions the Public of that city had been granted the opportunity of hearing one of his works. During the late summer he was approached by Basil Dean, a partner in a concern known as Reandean Ltd., lessees and managers of several London theatres, with a proposal that made an instant appeal to him. This organization was contemplating a production of James Elroy Flecker's tragic play *Hassan or The Golden Journey to Samarkand* and a contract, under which Frederick agreed to write incidental music for it, was signed by him on November 23rd in London. The terms and conditions were not unfavourable to his interests: he received an adequate down payment and enjoyed the expectation of substantial royalties during the future run of the piece in Great Britain, the United States and the Dominions. The prospect of association once more with the theatre restored new life to what had seemed to be a declining state in Frederick of the will to write. Twenty-three years had gone by since his modest but bizarre experience with Gunnar Heiberg in the Norwegian capital; but that was a very different sort of affair to a London West End series of performances, with almost certainly a group of the best actors in the country. He threw himself into the task with zest and although the orchestral resources at his disposal were necessarily limited, this did not frustrate the creation of a series of musical pictures, highly contrasted, full of spirit and including two of his most popular melodies, the Serenade, and the choral number 'We take the Golden Road to Samarkand'. Of almost equal merit are the choruses of beggars and soldiers, and the striking orchestral movement the procession of protracted death.

It was about this time that he finally disposed of his treasured Gauguin 'Never More' for which the purchaser paid almost £3,000; and if it may be remembered that in 1898 he had acquired this picture for five hundred francs, or twenty pounds in English money at that time, due credit has to be given him for an unusually lucky speculation, even if it be the only one he ever pulled off. Although he must have hated to part with his most valued possession, this transaction, together with the *Hassan* agreement, greatly relieved the financial stringency caused by the continued difficulty of securing dividends from stocks bought in foreign countries involved in the late war, as well as frozen royalties from the same sources. Characteristically he had refrained from investing any of his modest fortune in England, the only quarter where he, a British national, could have received income due to him without question or delay. In January the Deliuses took themselves off to Frankfort for a few weeks and then returned to London where they rented a smallish but comfortable flat in Hampstead. There Frederick completed the Concerto for Violoncello and Orchestra, working on it uninterruptedly for two months. His music continued to be played frequently in most of the bigger cities and he appears to have been particularly pleased with a performance, at a Philharmonic Concert in

March, of *Appalachia* under Albert Coates, who about this time had achieved considerable popularity as the conductor of the hour. In the summer they migrated once more to Norway, this time to the Gudbransdalen area, and from there Jelka writes on July 31st to her friend Marie Clews, to announce a more satisfactory turn in the Delius family affairs. From London had come the news that the first instalment of moneys due to Frederick from dividends on stocks and shares in the keeping of two New York bankers had now been made available to him. Just as welcome was an official communication, announcing that the French Government was making good 'quite decently' the damage sustained during the military occupation of the house, including the depredations committed by those in temporary residence, and of almost equal interest was the enterprise of the publishing house Universal Edition of Vienna in acquiring from 'Harmonie' all those Delius works issued before the war, together with several that had been given to firms such as Tischer-Jagenberg of Cologne. This meant that the greater part of his output would henceforth be in the hands of a single organization of recognized stability and expanding influence.

Frederick by this time had completed the score of *Hassan* and was looking forward to the production of the piece in the coming autumn. Unluckily the economic position in England had been changing for the worse during the past six months. The Treasury and the Bank of England having taken alarm at the general prosperity of the country had decided that measures should be taken to curtail it substantially. A policy of pressure known in these latter days as 'credit squeeze' was applied with ruthless vigour, with the consequence that a slump descended upon the whole community. It was decided to postpone the appearance of *Hassan* until brighter days returned, and keen as was the disappointment to Frederick, it must be allowed that it would have been a hazardous gamble to bring out such an elaborate and costly production in an atmosphere of gloom and disillusion. He and Jelka returned to Grez where they remained until the end of the year, when the first serious decline in his physical condition became manifest. Growing weakness, accompanied by pains in both arms and legs, increased rapidly, and Jelka took him off in January 1922 to a sanatorium in Wiesbaden. His Requiem was brought out two months later in London at a Philharmonic Concert under Albert Coates.

We now hail the appearance on the scene of two new acquaintances, Bela Bartók and Zoltan Kodaly. Both of them, particularly the former, were admirers of Frederick's music and valued his judgment on that of other men. Bartók grew into quite a habit of sending his compositions for criticism or comment to the elder musician, whom he also endeavoured to interest in both Hungarian and Rumanian popular music. We have no written expression of opinion from Frederick on the music of his two Hungarian friends, but he must have had some personal respect and regard for them, in consenting to extricate them from a legal quandary in which they had become embroiled. This is best explained in a letter of Kodaly who had the practical handling of the absurd affair.

'We must tell you of an incredibly funny thing. Our publisher insists that the name of a foreign musician must be printed on the piano pieces he is now issuing, as "reviser". If that is missing (e.g. revised by F. Delius) then the things are pirated in America as Hungary is not yet a member of this International Convention. (It is the same with Russia.)

If another person's name has to appear on our music there is hardly anyone we would sooner see there than yours. If you do not object (we must accept the matter as a formality or joke) then please write to Bartok just saying "yes". If you were an American citizen it would be no help to us. As the matter is urgent please write as soon as possible.'

Confronted with such a superb example of what man's mind can accomplish in the way of eccentricity (some people might prefer an unkinder term) when it really tries hard enough, there are no words that can fittingly serve for appreciative comment.

Few letters from either of the Deliuses during 1922 have come down to us. Frederick had almost entirely lost the use of his right hand and Jelka was so distressed and preoccupied with his deteriorating condition as to have thoughts of little else. He seems to have obtained some comfort from the friendliness of everyone around him, and the frequent performance of his music, both in Frankfort and neighbouring towns. Bartók lets him know that he has heard *A Mass of Life* in Vienna towards the close of the year, and that he has been deeply impressed with the sections 'Der alte Mittag' (old noon) and 'O Menseh gieb

Acht' (O man mark well). 'These two parts,' he writes, 'are soul-stirring in a very high degree through their simplicity and poetry.' He and Kodaly were both interested in the choruses without words. 'We have heard nothing like it before. I think you must be the first to make such an experiment, and that a lot could be done in this style, achieving quite original effects.' A letter dated January 1st, 1923, from Jelka to Marie throws some light on what had been happening during the preceding year:

'We', she writes, 'are now in Frankfort. Fred has been seriously ill the whole dreadful year of 1922. Now, at last, he is greatly improved. He grew pitiably weak. . . . We went to Norway in the summer and for the winter months we are settled here in a suite forming part of a mediaeval house just under the Cathedral, as there are quite a number of Delius performances coming on. In my opinion there is no doubt that all the harassing cares of the war and the endless after war period (our sequestered money is not all paid back) contributed very much to this breakdown of his.'

On April 4th Frederick dictates a letter to Jelka for Henry Clews in which he says:

'I am still pretty unsteady on the legs and am taking the waters at Oeynhausen near Hanover. After six or seven weeks here we go to Norway for the summer to our little chalet in the mountains . . . we intend to spend the winter on the Italian Riviera or Sicily and shall very likely knock at your door towards the end of October.'

On August 4th Jelka writes to Marie from Gudbrandsdalen:

'I have had to help Fred composing as he cannot write the small notes which he dictates to me. Then I had to copy the whole orchestral score here, fifty-two big pages. These were additions to the music for the drama *Hassan* and they were waiting impatiently for them in London. . . .
Fred's health is so delicate and after a fortnight's lovely summer weather it has been chilly, cloudy, rainy and changeable: we think of leaving quite soon and returning to Grez before we go to London.'

September finds them first in Grez and then in London, attending the final rehearsals of the much-postponed *Hassan*, which celebrated its first night on the 23rd. The success of the piece was unquestionable. A first-rate cast of actors had been engaged including Henry Ainley, Basil Gill, Laura Cowie and Cathleen Nesbitt; the production was in excellent taste; Frederick's music, conducted by Eugene Goossens, took everyone's fancy, and *Hassan* ran for months both in London and the Provinces. This aesthetically pleasing and economically welcome event reacted favourably on Frederick, both mentally and physically. On returning to Grez, he and Jelka bought a small car in which they delighted to make trips around the neighbourhood they loved so well. They planned a stay in the south for the coming winter, eventually deciding on Rapallo where they secured a villa for a couple of months. On the way down they stopped at Cannes, spending a few days with the Clewses who, after several years of residence in Paris, had acquired and renovated a mediaeval castle some five miles to the west of the town and known as the Château de la Napoule. They reached Rapallo and the Villa Reggio just before Christmas, but the house and its equipment alike prove disappointing and Frederick suffered much from an unusually cold spell of weather. February brought with it sunshine by day and warmth at nights, which alleviated his discomfort, and stimulated him to begin work on a new composition.[1]

Their occupation of the villa terminating during the third week of March, they returned westward to the La Napoule region, where a small apartment Les Brisants had been secured for them by an acquaintance of the Clewses. The four friends, reunited after a separation of several years, spent five weeks of joyful content, comparing experiences, exchanging views and all agreeing happily that, with the exception of themselves, the rest of the world was growing daily more irrational and inexplicable. The Deliuses made their way home by car through Avignon, Chalon-sur-Saône and Auxerre, a tour lasting four days, and midsummer found them at Wilhemshöhe, a favourite German health resort famous for its invigorating air. There they discovered a doctor who succeeded in convincing Jelka that Frederick could be wholly cured if placed under his care. 'Had we known of Dr. H——,' she writes, 'when Fred first fell ill, how quickly he would have put him on his feet again.' In August they returned to Grez and we learn from Jelka that 'Delius is much better in every way, can walk

[1] A Violin Sonata.

better, eat better, play the piano better, looks so much better. He does not wear ordinary glasses any more, only ones for reading, and weaker than he has had for five years. . . .' *Hassan* is running at the Knicker-bocker Theatre in New York, a Delius chamber concert will take place in London on November 8th and *A Mass of Life* will be given that winter in London, Vienna, Prague and Wiesbaden.

In November they removed to Cassel to continue under the care of Dr. H——. Frederick's general health is reported to be good but his eyes are beginning to trouble him again. They are not seriously worried, however, and on December 20th Frederick writes to Henry, a short letter in his own hand, confirming Jelka's optimistic account of his improved condition.

28

THERE is more than an ordinary touch of tragedy in the sudden reversal of the hopes and expectations excited during 1924 by the apparent improvement in Frederick's health. Only a short portion of 1925 had run its course when a sudden reaction set in that defied the skill and experience of medical science. This took the form of a general physical enfeeblement, accompanied by rapid loss in weight, and his eyesight, which had been failing day by day, became totally extinguished by the middle of the year. No longer able to walk, or even totter, he had to be carried up and down in the house, and passed most of his day in the garden at Grez, to which he and his wife had returned after the abortive winter ordeal at Cassel. Here they were to remain immobilized for the next nine years except for the adventurous trip to London in the autumn of 1929. In spite of this irreparable disaster his mental faculties, according to each of the numerous friends from various parts who rallied around him in efforts to relieve his sense of isolation, remained unimpaired. Musicians played to him, others listened to his discourses, while Jelka, aided by a young man on the spot, read books to him by the dozen as well as extracts from magazines and daily newspapers.

The kindly ministrations of visiting executive musicians to cheer him up were sometimes embarrassed by Frederick's disinclination to listen to any music except that of a handful of composers. No one earlier than Berlioz made the slightest appeal to his ear, and this limitation of taste eliminated all those either born in or flourishing during the entire eighteenth century. Only Chopin and the later Wagner enjoyed his complete favour, although on a slightly lower level he had an honest affection for much of Grieg. For Verdi, notably in *Aïda* and the *Requiem*, he had an oddly mixed feeling of attraction and repulsion. *Otello* he always ranked below these two masterpieces, and while he appreciated the musicianly workmanship of *Falstaff*, he regretted its lack of true melodic invention and genuine humour. For French composers, as craftsmen, he had a sincere admiration, but with the exception of Bizet the sentiment of their music rarely moved him. His great contemporary Debussy he once disposed of rather summarily as 'pâlement lascif'. It may be gathered from this list of predilections and aversions that chamber music parties found their efforts to please far from easy. Some accounts have come down to us of occasions into which the spirit of comedy found its way, and on one of these I was privileged to be present.

There arrived one late afternoon a string quartet of some fame who, after being introduced to their host, proceeded to set up stands and place a selection of pieces upon them. The leader then announced in tones of awe-inspiring solemnity: 'Herr Delius, we shall first play you a quartet of Beethoven.' To their consternation, from a remote corner of the large studio where sat the spare and shrunken figure of the master came a roar of anguish and terror, 'Oh no, you don't!' There followed, as might be expected, a decidedly awkward period, during which equally vain attempts were made to conciliate the agitated lion with specimens of Haydn, Mozart and Brahms; and it began to look as if the party would break up in hopeless confusion. Fortunately, one of the distracted musicians remembered that they had left in the hall below stairs another small pile of parts, and I went down with him to see what it contained. To my great relief I found two quartets of Debussy and Bartók respectively, and these I carried back with me to the upper room. I whispered to Frederick the nature of my discovery and asked him to be gracious and listen to the Debussy quartet with as much tolerance as he could command. Luckily, by this time he had become just a little ashamed of his intransigent behaviour, and steeled himself to sit through the ordeal with an admirably simulated expression of content and pleasure.

At its conclusion, Jelka suggested a little light refreshment, and I, taking it upon myself to spin out this respite as long as possible, managed to steer the musicians for a while into the garden, where they could admire the view of the old castle, the picturesque church, with the pretty Loing in the background. On our return to the house we found that Frederick had disappeared, and learned that as this was his customary hour of repose, he had been removed to his bedroom on the other side of the landing. Jelka, however, assured the musicians that with the two connecting doors to the bedroom left open, Frederick would be able to hear every note they played, and I instantly suggested the Bartók quartet, as its composer was a great friend of 'Herr Delius'. But before they started on the piece, I went into the bedroom to find out what was really going on. Frederick had been placed on the bed, was looking very sleepy and hinted that he would like a short nap. This I enthusiastically encouraged because it seemed fairly certain that while he was in that blessed condition, nothing very untoward was likely to happen. It was therefore agreed I should return to the music-room and guard its exits and entrances so that no unwanted intruder could cross the landing without my giving due warning; Jelka, on her part, would remain with Frederick, and when I gave the signal that the music was about to start, would close both communicating doors as well as the windows. The Bartók was played very much more understandingly than the Debussy, and as its last note died away I was vastly relieved to hear the voice of Jelka calling across the landing, 'Splendid, Frederick is enjoying himself tremendously.' With unfailing resource she had opened the closed doors at just the right moment. I left the musicians alone for a few minutes and went across the landing to decide what was the next thing to do. Frederick was fast asleep and had been so for a full half-hour. I was therefore able to return to the studio and inform the players that their host was having a thoroughly delightful time, and that his wife had asked me to express her gratitude to them. I trust that the observant reader will admit that neither she nor I had yet offended any of the canons of strict accuracy. The players declared themselves to be highly gratified and it all too soon became uncomfortably manifest that they were itching to play a third piece. But by an unexpected stroke of luck at that very moment the house was invaded by a small group of rather noisy neighbours whose conversation put any music out of question for at least a further twenty minutes.

Feeling that the occasion must be rounded off to everyone's satisfaction, I first satisfied myself that Frederick was still asleep and warned Jelka to close the communicating doors again. I then requested the musicians to play a Haydn quartet (the shortest in their repertoire), hinting that by this time 'Herr Delius' would be much rested and tranquillized. The visitors wandered into the garden and I remained the sole member of the audience, but always on the alert. As the piece finished, all reassembled in the music-room to the accompaniment of further hospitality, and by the time this was over and the moment of the departure for the quartet had arrived, our eyes were gladdened by the reappearance of Frederick in wheeled chair, and creating the impression of a veritable *Deus ex machina*. Evidently well coached by Jelka, he beamed beatifically on everyone present and warmly complimented the quartet on its beautiful interpretations. The latter, overwhelmed by such condescension, departed in trailing clouds of self-congratulation, extolling the grace of the hostess, the impressive dignity of the host and promising to return, if invited, at an early date. I accompanied them a fair way down the street to make sure they were really going, and returned to the house, feeling very much like a good boy scout who had performed worthily his one brave deed of the day.

And thus a couple of years passed by; years in the main of tranquillity, with little outward sign of unhappiness. The finely tempered spirit of the stricken man rejected the very idea of sorrow or regret. Resignation after a while he achieved, with praiseworthy success, and with it developed gradually an outward appearance of serenity, both impressive and pathetic. Although one side of his personality became stoical, there was no lessening of the old epicurean Adam. Good food and wine appealed to him as strongly as ever, laughter was just as frequently upon his lips and his sense of sardonic humour remained unblunted. The invention of radio, which at first he had viewed with some apprehension, came to be a heaven-sent gift, and a splendid instrument he had managed to obtain enabled him to hear with enjoyment performances of his own music, given regularly in a score of musical centres.

Jelka procured some relief from her arduous and exacting duties in a helpless man's home by making a German translation of Henry Clews's satirical comedy, *Mumbo Jumbo*. This amusing piece exposes with pungent effect, the aesthetic follies and snobberies of so-called High Society in the great capitals of Europe and America, as well as the unscrupulous manipulations of art dealers and their lackey followers in the more venal or credulous Press. Henry had an unquestioned talent for firing off this lively kind of literary squib; perhaps a little too specialized for the ordinary reader or auditor, but vastly entertaining to that comparatively sane minority which had some actual acquaintance with the International Smart Set of the 'twenties and 'thirties, and its almost incredible fads and transient enthusiasms. The play is prefaced by an immense foreword which it would have been better strategy to have issued separately. It is such an out-and-out onslaught on virtually every side of modern society that the appetite for vituperation and invective is almost satiated by the time the comedy itself is reached. Of course only an endearing streak of naïveté in the characters of both Frederick and Jelka could have led them to imagine for one moment that a public representation of such a work could have taken place in a land where nearly all the theatres were at that time controlled by Jewish owners or managers. The principal characters in *Mumbo Jumbo* were of Hebraic origin and, although amiable and kindly after their fashion, had too large a spice of roguery in their make-up to recommend themselves to the approving attention of their fellow religionists. Meanwhile, it must have been some gratification to Grez that so many representations of Frederick's more important works were taking place. *A Mass of Life* was given in Berlin in the October of 1927, *A Village Romeo and Juliet* in Wiesbaden in November and *Hassan* was being mounted at Darmstadt.

Nineteen-twenty-eight rolled along with nothing new or out of the way to vary the pattern of the two preceding years, until the latter part of it. During the Leeds Musical Festival of September–October I first heard of a young man reputed to be a Delius enthusiast. He had been moved deeply by the unhappy plight of a great musician, whose brain might still be teeming with creative ideas, but who appeared powerless to transmit them into written shapes through a crushing physical infirmity. He had decided to offer his services to the composer as unpaid amanuensis and to do anything that might be of service in helping him to continue, if possible, those labours of composition that ill-fortune seemed to have thwarted. The offer had been accepted by Frederick in a letter dated August 29th, and the noble-minded youth made his way to Grez during the first week of October, where from the beginning he was received and treated as a member of the family. Eric Fenby has depicted, in a book of his own, his experiences extending over a period of years in the Delius establishment, and with a wealth of detail that it is beyond the scope of the present narrative to rival. I shall have occasion later on to make reference to a remarkable collaboration, undoubtedly unique of its kind: but for the moment I shall pass on to the year 1929, which contained a few events memorable in our composer's life.

On January 1st, he was created a Companion of Honour, and although he received the award with a calm and dignity, wholly at variance with some of the inflated accounts appearing in one or two Press interviews, I think he was on the whole gratified by this token of official recognition. He was sufficiently man of the world to know that any distinction of this kind raises the recipient in the estimation of the general Public, with a corresponding increase of interest in his work. Moreover, in a country where titles and orders are regarded with traditional respect, it is accepted as a proof or token that a newcomer to the circle of the elect has definitely and unquestionably 'arrived'. The immediate result was a ripple of curiosity in circles wider than those of the musical profession itself. Very few of the general Public had ever seen Frederick Delius, and not a great many more were really familiar with his music. There grew rapidly a desire to know more about the mysterious Englishman who had lived his life far from home, and who, according to experts, had written a mass of strange and beautiful music, which for some reason or other had failed to achieve the popularity of those respectable expressions of the national taste, 'Land of Hope and Glory' and *Merrie England*. The story of his romantic life and courageous fortitude in the face of a disaster that would have shattered the will of most men, became a legend that appealed to the imagination of thousands. Briefly, Frederick, in journalistic jargon, became 'news'. It seemed not only timely but fitting that some weighty demonstration should be forthcoming, to enable the man in the street to become better acquainted with both the personality and the music of one of the few truly original geniuses the country had produced during the past hundred years; and as some individual has always to start anything of the sort, I took upon myself to organize a festival of his music, to be heard in London at six concerts during the coming autumn. Considerable doubt was expressed in many quarters about the chances of success of such an unusual and massive enterprise, but the sceptics were eventually and happily proved to be in error.

I enlisted the aid of Philip Heseltine in the task of organization, the writing of biographical matter, programme notes and any other supplies of information deemed essential to enlighten the prospective audiences. Philip, it may be remembered, had been from the beginning the apostle in print and word of the Delius cause, but latterly he had modified materially his 'first fine careless rapture' and had grown openly critical of the worth of much that his old friend had written. But for all that he knew far more about the composer and his music than anyone else in England and possessed a skilled and facile pen, together with a capacity for fiery energy, when his interest was aroused. Plans were completed by the early summer, programmes drawn up and one question alone remained for decision. Would it be possible for Frederick to be present? Obviously there was a risk in transporting anyone in his debilitated state from Grez to London, with the complication of a Channel crossing thrown in. Was it worth trying? Perhaps the novel excitement as well as the acclaim he was certain to receive might have a stimulating effect that nothing else could equal. It was left to the principal personage involved to answer the question, and to it he returned an emphatic affirmative. The Deliuses set out on October 6th, made two stops on the way, and reached Boulogne on the 8th. They crossed the Channel on the night boat, rested a part of the next day at Folkestone, and went on to the Langham Hotel, London, where they remained throughout the three weeks' duration of the festival.

In view of what the London *Times* in its issue of October 12th described as an event 'without exact parallel in the history of British music', I trust I may be excused if I think it worth while to give in full the programmes of the six concerts.

DELIUS FESTIVAL: OCTOBER–NOVEMBER 1929

Artistic Director and Conductor-in-Chief—Sir Thomas Beecham, Bart.

PROGRAMMES

Saturday, October 12th, at 3 p.m. at the Queen's Hall

(Under the auspices of the Columbia Graphophone Company)

Orchestra of the Columbia Graphophone Company

Brigg Fair.
A Late Lark (First Performance) (1925).
Dance Rhapsody No. 2.
Sea Drift.
        Soloist—Dennis Noble. The London Select Choir.
In a Summer Garden.
A Village Romeo and Juliet (excerpt).
        Soloists—Pauline Maunder, Heddle Nash. The London Select Choir.

A Song Before Sunrise: for small orchestra (1918).
  (led by Charles Woodhouse)
Seven Songs: for voice and pianoforte:
'Heimkehr' (1889) (translated from the Norwegian of A O. Vinje).
'Verborg'ne Liebe' (1890) (from the Norwegian of Björnesterne Björnsen).
'Beim Sonnenuntergang' (1888) (from the Norwegian of A. Munck).
'Sehnsucht' (1888) (from the Norwegian of Th. Kjerulf).
'Le ciel est pardessus le toit' (1895) (Paul Verlaine).
'In the Seraglio Garden' (1897) (from the Danish of Jens Peter Jacobsen).
'Eine Vogelweise' (1899) (from the Norwegian of Henrik Ibsen).
Sonata for Violoncello and Pianoforte: in one movement (1917).
Summer Night on the River: for small orchestra (1911).
Air and Dance: for String Orchestra (1915) (First Performance).
  Vocalist—Olga Haley. Violoncello—Beatrice Harrison. Pianist—
  Evelyn Howard-Jones.

Six Songs: for voice and pianoforte:
'Black Roses' (1901) (from the Swedish of Josefson).
'Chanson d'automne' (1911) (Paul Verlaine).
'Silken Shoes' (1897) (from the Danish of Jens Peter Jacobsen).
'Ŷ-Brasil' (1913) (Fiona Macleod).
'Das Veilchen' (1900) (from the Danish of Ludwig Holstein).
'Spielmann' (1890) (from the Norwegian of Henrik Ibsen).
  Vocalist—John Goss.

Nine Pianoforte pieces:
Three Preludes (1923).
Dance (originally composed for the Harpsichord) (1919).
Five Pieces ('Mazurka and Waltz for a little girl', 'Waltz', 'Lullaby for a modern baby', 'Toccata') (1923).
  Pianist—Evelyn Howard-Jones.

Six Songs: for voice and pianoforte:
'Irmelin' (1897) (from the Danish of Jens Peter Jacobsen).
'To Daffodils' (1915) (Robert Herrick).
'The Nightingale has a Lyre of Gold' (1908) (W. E. Henley).
'Il pleure dans mon cœur' (1895) (Paul Verlaine).
'So white, so soft, so sweet is she' (1915) (Ben Jonson).
'Let Springtime come then' (1897) (from the Danish of Jens Peter Jacobsen).
On Hearing the First Cuckoo in Spring: for small Orchestra (1912).
  Vocalist—John Armstrong.

(Given by the British Broadcasting Corporation)

B.B.C. Orchestra (Leader—Arthur Catterall)

Eventyr: Ballad for Orchestra (1917).
Cynara: a poem by Ernest Dowson, set for baritone and orchestra (1907)
(First Performance).
        Vocalist—John Goss.
Concerto for Pianoforte and Orchestra (Revised Version 1906).
        Pianist—Evelyn Howard-Jones.
Arabesk: a poem by Jens Peter Jacobsen, set for baritone solo, chorus and
orchestra (1911–12) (First Performance in London).
        Vocalist—John Goss. The London Select Choir.
Appalachia: Variations on an old Negro Song for orchestra and chorus (1902).
(Royal College Choral Class and the B.B.C. National Chorus)

Wednesday, October 23rd, at 8.30 p.m. at the Aeolian Hall

Three unaccompanied Choruses:
'The Splendour Falls' (1923) (Tennyson).
'On Craig Dhu' (1907) (Arthur Symons).
'Midsummer Song' (1908) (Anon.).
        The London Select Choir. Conductor—T. Arnold Fulton.

Four Songs: for voice and pianoforte:
'The Nightingale' (1888) (translated by W. Grist from the Norwegian of
Welhaven).
'Autumn' (1900) (from the Danish of Ludwig Holstein).
'La Lune Blanche' (1910) (Paul Verlaine).
'Klein Venevil' (1889–90) (from the Norwegian of Björnsterne Björnsen).
        Vocalist—Dora Labbette.
Sonata No. 1 for Violin and Pianoforte (1905–15).[1]
        Violinist—Arthur Catterall.
        Pianist—Evelyn Howard-Jones.

Three songs: for voice and pianoforte (1891):
'Indian Love-song' (Shelley).
'Love's Philosophy' (Shelley).
'To the Queen of my Heart' (Shelley).
        Vocalist—Heddle Nash.
Two Unaccompanied Choruses (to be sung of a summer night on the water).

[1] Actually No. 2.

Four Songs: for voice and pianoforte:
'Twilight Fancies' (1889) (translated by F. S. Copeland from the Norwegian of Björnsterne Björnsen).
'Am schönsten Sommerabend war's' (1888) (from the Norwegian of Paulsen).
'Margaret's Lullaby' (1889) (translated by William Archer from the Norwegian of Henrik Ibsen).
'Spring, the sweet Spring' (1915) (Thomas Nashe).
      Vocalist—Dora Labbette.
String Quartet (1916–17).

           Virtuoso String Quartet
    Marjorie Hayward   Raymond Jeremy
    Edwin Virgo   Cedric Sharpe

Thursday, October 24th, at 8 p.m. at the Queen's Hall

(Choral and Orchestral Concert, given by the Royal Philharmonic Society)

Royal Philharmonic Orchestra

North Country Sketches.
Songs of Sunset (Ernest Dowson).
      Vocalists—Olga Haley, John Goss. London Select Choir
Violin Concerto.
      Violinist—Albert Sammons
Dance Rhapsody No. 1.
Gerda (First Performance in England).
      Vocalists—Pauline Maunder, John Goss. London Select Choir.

Friday, November 1st, at 8 p.m. at the Queen's Hall

(Choral and Orchestral Concert, given by the British Broadcasting Corporation)

B.B.C. Orchestra (Leader—Charles Woodhouse)

A Mass of Life.

    Philharmonic Choir (Conductor—Charles Kennedy Scott)
    Soloists: Soprano—Miriam Licette.
              Contralto—Astra Desmond.
              Tenor—Tudor-Davies.
              Baritone—Roy Henderson.

The success of the Festival was unquestioned and at none of the six concerts was there a seat unoccupied. Nor was the great interest in it limited to the devotees of the music. After each of the Queen's Hall concerts, notably the final one, a large crowd assembled in the adjacent streets to cheer the hero of the hour as he emerged borne on his litter back to the Langham Hotel. It is a distinguishing mark in our public life that hardly any gathering organized for a serious purpose proceeds in an orderly way as planned to its termination, without at least one person present providing an exhibition of outstanding eccentricity or ludicrous fatuity. To this accepted pattern our Festival conformed loyally, and the necessarily solemn atmosphere that prevailed throughout was tempered by a few humorous incidents, one of which it may be worth recording.

A friend of mine who sat in a Grand Circle seat directly behind two ladies at one of the Queen's Hall concerts could not fail to observe their curious reactions to all that was going on. About half-way through the first part of the programme, they began to betray unmistakable signs of discomfort and bewilderment at the sound of the music and directed their attention to the vast audience, which appeared to be listening with every indication of pleasure and appreciation. Finding this equally inexplicable, they next opened the voluminous book of analytical notes, presumably in the hope of finding there some explanation of the mystery. This they read carefully from beginning to end, not omitting even the advertisement pages, to which Samuel Butler has confessed he always turned when the music failed to hold his interest. Just before the interval the strain of preserving silence over a problem which seemed insoluble proved too much for them, and they broke into a low-voiced colloquy of which a revealing portion made itself clearly audible. 'This is really a remarkable festival, isn't it? Just look at all those people who seem to like it, or are they pretending to?' 'I have no idea,' replied her companion, 'but I am quite certain that I don't and what I have been wondering for the best part of an hour is why they have not been playing the music of some other composer.'

According to all those who were with him constantly, Delius was both moved and impressed by the warmth of his welcome in London. On his homeward trip across the Channel he asked that his deck-chair should be turned toward the fading shores of England, the scene of the greatest of all his artistic successes. I cannot help feeling that even Jelka, in spite of her anti-British prejudices, must have shared some of his pleasure at such an unexpected climax to his career, although there is no reference to it in any of her letters during the weeks following the Festival.

29

WE ENTER now upon the final chapter of Frederick's life, and it tells a story strange without parallel in the annals of music. By the beginning of 1930 Fenby, who by his own account had been gradually and painfully adapting himself during the preceding year to his host's exacting requirements, resumed his complicated task with fuller confidence. Milton, in spite of his blindness, was able to articulate the spoken word; and Beethoven, although totally deaf, had the free use of all his limbs. But how is a man, both blind and paralysed everywhere, to convey to another the sounds which are thronging in his head? It would not be difficult to hum or intone a single line of melody. But what happens to its accompaniment, particularly if that contains the delicate harmonic sequences characteristic of this composer? And most mysterious of all, how is a full orchestral score to be put together if it comprises perhaps as many as thirty separate instrumental parts? Superficially it would seem impossible. Thanks, however, to the iron resolution of one man, and the almost angelic patience of another, the incredible task was accomplished. Two preliminary and fairly successful experiments had been made in 1928, with the completion of the unfinished songs 'Cynara' and 'A Late Lark', both of which had been heard at the Festival. I say only fairly successful because it is evident that neither of the two pieces betrays the certain touch of the old Delius. In spite of this the result is remarkable, and even more so in the case of the unfinished tone-poem 'Life and Love', begun in 1918. This ingenious effort of reconstruction, to which a new title was given—*A Song of Summer*—owes a good deal to Fenby and received its first performance at one of Sir Henry Wood's concerts in 1931. The long-forgotten *Margot la Rouge* was now disinterred and some of its better pages were married without incongruity to Walt Whitman's poem 'Once I passed through a populous city'. This, the most authentic of the several resurrections effected during this period, was arranged for soprano and baritone solo voices and was also first performed by Sir Henry Wood in 1933.

Added to these were a small interlude based on two themes from *Irmelin*, a Caprice and Elegy for Violoncello, a Violin Sonata—number four—and a Fantastic Dance for strings played in 1934 under Adrian Boult. Lastly, and interesting in one way at least, are the four settings of words also from Whitman entitled *Songs of Farewell*, performed by Malcolm Sargent in 1932. Unexpectedly under the circumstances, we find in them a streak of hard masculine vigour, reminiscent in mood and fibre of some of the great choral numbers in *A Mass of Life*. On July 5th of the same year Frederick received the freedom of the City of Bradford, which by this time had become aware that it had given birth to a man of genius.

In the late spring of 1933 a new visitor made his way to Grez— Sir Edward Elgar. The relations between the two men had begun in the days of the League of Music, some twenty-five years earlier, but until this moment had not become cordial. Frederick had an unqualified respect for Elgar as a craftsman but looked upon his music as essentially traditional. What baffled him particularly was its undue leaning towards that (to him) incomprehensible branch of the art, oratorio. Elgar on his part had a deep admiration for the poetry and romance informing nearly all that Delius had written, which sometimes surprised many of those who are apt to forget that opposite poles, either of thought or religion, have a strong attraction for one another. But the reunion of these two men, the one aged seventy-six and the other seventy-one, in the quiet seclusion of an old and beautiful French village, seems to have forged between them a new and charming link of fuller mutual appreciation. The admitted champions of music in England, both of them could look back with satisfaction upon a long service in the cause of their art, and were now better able to estimate the value of each other's contribution to it. At the conclusion of the visit a series of communications passed between Grez and Worcester of which we unluckily have only one end. On May 31st, Elgar, now in Paris, writes:

'Before boarding the aeroplane for England I send a note to thank you and Mrs. Delius for your charming welcome. It was a great privilege to see you and I was delighted to find you so much better than the newspapers had led me to expect.'

On June 8th, another letter sent from Marl Bank, Worcester, contained an interesting request:

'I wish you would think out (I tremble in making any suggestion) some small composition suitable, as regards difficulty, for small orchestra—your 'Cuckoo in Spring' is naturally very much loved, and is within the capacity of some of the minor organizations. We did it in Worcester which, apart from the Festival, boasts no great equipment. I want three movements—any poetic basis you like: Fontainebleau, Grez, your own surroundings. You cannot help being a poet in sound and I say no more on the matter. Something, or things such as I have had the temerity to name, would bring your wonderful art among the devoted people who mean (and do) well in small things and cannot aspire to perform your large works. Do not be angry.'

Frederick responds by sending him the *Song before Sunrise*, which Elgar finds 'delightful'. By October the latter has had to enter a nursing home from which he writes on the 13th:

'Thank you and Mrs. Delius for your telegram of good wishes: it gave me great joy to know that you thought of me in this distressful time. I am supposed to be improving and want to share a few more years with you and hear your "brave translunary things" and to see and talk once more with the poet's mind in the poet's body—you in fact.'

On December 4th he takes up his pen to say that an operation which he had just undergone appears to have passed off very well, but that his main trouble is still 'an appalling attack of sciatica'. He continues, 'I am glad to think that you are really coming to London in the spring' and mentions two visits he has had from their ever faithful friend Granville Bantock: 'We have talked much of you and made the old days live again with joy.' On December 25th he refers again to the chance of Frederick's going to London and hopes that in the proposed series of concerts to be given there *A Mass of Life* and *Paris* will both figure in the programmes. He adds:

'It has been a matter of no small amusement to me that as my name somewhat unfortunately is indissolubly connected with

"Sacred" music, some of your friends and mine have tried to make me believe that I am ill-disposed to the trend and sympathy of your great work. Nothing could be farther from the real truth of the case. I admire your work intensely and salute the genius displayed in it. This recalls an incident which happened to me in New York, where I was conducting the inevitable oratorios. Richard Strauss's *Salome* was being given to the horror of some (presumably) ultra-moral good folk. A deputation from these astounding people waited upon me and urged me to lead a prayer meeting to pray specifically for the failure of Richard's opera. A proposal which was so staggeringly and screamingly absurd that I don't think I have recovered from the shock even now. I do not hope to look back on the past year with any great satisfaction, but a few events stand out far apart. My visit to you is still a vivid thing in my memory and is one of the things which will endure. The kindness of Mrs. Delius and you to me lifts 1933 out of the ordinary Anno Domini.'

This is the end of the correspondence. *Sunt lachrymae rerum.* The expectations of the two men were not be to fulfilled, and hardly six months went by before they both passed into the world of shades, accompanied by Gustav Holst and Norman O'Neill.

During these few last years Frederick's health had experienced the customary ups and downs incidental to his affliction, with a few brief moments of visual recovery. There seemed at one moment, a faint possibility that he might regain a dimmed but genuine sight of near objects about him, but this was of brief duration. By July 1933 Fenby had gone back to Yorkshire and this placed an added responsibility upon Jelka who, with the exception of a male attendant, was Delius's sole companion. Few women have been subjected to such a lengthy period of sustained distress and worry, and its consequences had become apparent to all her relatives and close friends. Often adjured to escape for a while from the cheerless monotony of her environment, she refused, knowing how entirely dependent upon her Frederick had become, to absent herself from him except for a single short breakaway. She paid for her devotion by a sudden decline in strength at the beginning of 1934 and the ominous signs of a cancerous growth. But she struggled bravely against her rapidly growing malady and the apprehension that at any moment she might have to give in and be removed to a hospital. By a lamentable stroke of fate Jelka's troubles coincided with an alarming deterioration in her husband's condition. By the spring it looked as if the long-feared end was at last in sight, and the climax came swiftly at the beginning of June. Frederick grew daily weaker and finally expired in the early morning of the 10th. I cannot do better than quote Jelka's own account of these sad days, to be found in a letter to her friend Marie Clews of the 22nd:

'He died in his sleep, surrounded by us all and without feeling the end just as he would have wished. . . . He looked so natural, beautiful and calm after all this pain, unrest and sleeplessness that one could only feel thankful. . . . It was of course the most dreadful tragedy that Fred's progressing illness coincided with my operation for a large tumour. I had hoped to be first with him at the end and then to look after myself. So I waited till the very last moment and had to be taken away hurriedly. When he got worse I was in agony alone in the clinic. Our doctor saw that Fred must have me back and heroically pulled me out of my bed with the wound not healed and brought me home. I owe it to him that I had a few days with Fred and to have seen his happiness about it. . . . I am getting better, but shall never be my old self again—but what does it matter now?'

The most fitting epitaph upon this pathetic end of a great spirit is a pregnant line of the greatest of poets: 'The wonder is he hath endured so long. He but usurped his life.'

Frederick was temporarily buried in the village churchyard pending his final removal to England. Jelka struggled gallantly with all the formalities of procedure arising from his demise, and the handling of his estate, of which she was the sole beneficiary. Bewildered by the complications of French law dealing with the affairs of an alien resident deceased in France, she crossed to England in the autumn and consulted a London solicitor. Her main concern was that the property she had inherited should be ultimately devoted to the best interests of Frederick's music. I took upon myself to advise that in view of the short expectation of life which Jelka herself anticipated, she should create a trust whose main objects should be the gradual issue of a re-edited and model edition of his important works, and the recording for the gramophone of such of them as would be effective on this medium of sound. To facilitate this latter purpose a Delius Society was formed in November under the protection of the Columbia Graphophone Company, and an album of records was released early in 1935. This first volume contained *Paris*; *Koanga*—Closing scene; *Eventyr*; *Hassan*—Interlude and Serenade; Songs—'To the Queen of My Heart' and 'Love's Philosophy'. The Public was invited to join the Society by paying a subscription which would entitle each member to receive a copy of the album. Two other albums appeared before 1939 under the same auspices and conditions. Volume II contained *Sea Drift*; *Over the Hills and Far Away*; *In a Summer Garden*; Intermezzo from *Fennimore and Gerda*; Volume III contained *Appalachia*; *Hassan*—La Calinda; *Irmelin*—Prelude.

Her business satisfactorily completed for the time being, she returned to Grez, and was joined there at Christmas by the ever-devoted Fenby. Her health was visibly declining and it began to weigh on her mind that Frederick's wishes as to his final interment were not being carried out. A good deal of useless and slightly indecorous comment was made around this time about his choice of burial-place. I am able to assert that there was never the slightest uncertainty upon this point, and that he passed on his wishes to those nearest to him and in his confidence with characteristic lucidity of utterance. His last home was to be a quiet country churchyard in a south of England village. I can understand that to some persons this decision seemed at the time to be unaccountable His only solid association with England had been during the days of his youth in the north; almost all the remainder of his life had been spent in France, and most of that at Grez. But it is impossible to see very far into the depths of a man's desire, and when such a one as Frederick, with his uncommon strength of conviction, made up his mind about something which, after all, concerned himself alone, it was bordering closely upon insensibility to argue about it, as was done almost interminably in one quarter that should have known better.

Jelka planned to leave France on May 22nd and to be present at the reinterment which was to take place on the 24th at Limpsfield near Oxted in Surrey. A section of the London Philharmonic Orchestra journeyed down to play a few of Frederick's short pieces, during the service in the little church, and a large number of persons from many parts gathered round the graveside, where a short *oraison funèbre* was pronounced. Prominent among those present was Vaughan-Williams, now the undisputed leader of music in England. Yet one figure whose appearance had been expected was absent, Jelka. On the way over she had contracted a severe attack of pneumonia and had to be rushed to a hospital. Four days later, resigned but contented that her last wifely duty had been well and truly fulfilled, she died, and was at once buried by the side of the man whose welfare and art had been the mainspring of her life for all but forty years.

30

AS INTIMATED in the preface to this book, little attempt has been made to 'explain' the art of Delius or to dig deeply into any of those esoterically aesthetic puzzles and problems, which delight and sometimes bemuse, the professional writer on music. The day has gone by for further justification of his mysterious ways. He has been accepted as a master in most of those countries where music is understood and practised, even though some of them are still ill-acquainted with many of his greater works. Recently I read in two separate extracts from the English Press that he was being played less frequently than ten years ago. This is not so, and can be easily confuted by the legal successors of himself and his wife, who are able to state by an appeal to figures that the performances of his works (including broadcasts) during this period have doubled in number. As nearly everything he wrote of merit dates back forty to fifty years it would appear that Delius has come to stay.

Half-way through the 'twenties there began in most parts a reaction against what had been looked upon as modern music, and the atmosphere of torrid enthusiasm that had warmed the pre-war days declined gradually to one of chilly distrust. Delius was one of the few composers born later than the middle of the last century who was not affected too adversely; but since that time a more cautious appraisal of his music has prevailed, together with a recoil from any decisive or positive evaluations of it. The single instance of *A Mass of Life* may illustrate what I mean.

In 1923 we find Heseltine comparing *A Mass of Life* favourably with the great Mass of Bach in B Minor, and the first natural reaction to this claim is 'Why not?' Twenty years later Professor Arthur Hutchings finds the comparison absurd, and the equally reasonable comment on that is 'Why?' It is a pity that the learned Professor does not condescend to advance any argument in support of his opinion, which is hardly respectful to his reader. It may therefore be worth while to go abroad and hear what a well-known German musicologist, Hans Schingeler of Hagen in Westphalia, had to say about this work in particular, and Delius in general, as late as 1929:

'The *Mass of Life* can be considered the climax of Delius's creative achievement. In this monumental masterpiece we can sense the nature and value of his music at its best. Everything here is vibrating, ethereal and floating in soft-coloured sublime harmonies; it gives you the feeling that nothing should come between these wonderful sounds and the listening ear. Conductor, musicians, singers, all those who take part in the interpretation should avoid interference as little as possible with this dream-like music. For it is full of thought and poetry, born under the magic of blue skies, sunshine, in the scenery of colour and fragrance, where the coolness of the night is the true complement of the day. But not only beauty is represented in this music. The score of the Mass has its powerful moments as well as its lyrical. There the composer tightens the rhythm and unites orchestra and chorus in grand dramatic climaxes.' As for the composer himself, the writer goes on to say: 'It is for history to pronounce the last word about the value of his work. Independent of fashionable trends this verdict should certainly place Frederick Delius among the very greatest.'

It is no concern of mine to support or qualify this striking and forthright tribute from a German to the genius of an Englishman. I am neither critic nor prophet. Although I have vented some views in the course of my story about many of Frederick's compositions, I have instituted no comparisons between them and those of other men; and I shrink from any attempt to foretell dogmatically the judgment of distant posterity. But many years ago when this music was less known, I placed complete confidence in its future, and as time rolls on it would seem that such confidence has not been wholly unjustified. This is gratifying for more than one reason. A certain amount of his output still remains unpublished and consequently unplayable, while the bulk of his greater and finer work is cast in shapes that present material difficulties to the average concert organization or conductor. *Appalachia*, *Sea Drift*, *A Mass of Life*, *Songs of Sunset*, *Arabesk* and *A Song of the High Hills* all necessitate the use of choirs and solo singers. The performance of a symphony or even that of a famous and popular oratorio does not baffle or even trouble the soul of the typical *entrepreneur*. But when it comes to the added provision of other forces taking part in pieces so far removed in style, sentiment and technique from the half-dozen choral favourites which dominate and haunt most churches and concert-halls in any land, the work and expense created in making a satisfactory job of the task repel and daunt all but the more enterprising.

Another and even more serious obstacle is the comparative ignorance of this music professed or demonstrated by the majority of latter-day conductors. This is not easily explicable. I am aware that a good part of the Delius canon offers fewer opportunities for virtuoso display than are presented in the work of many other great composers. But this disability does not apply to such pieces as *Paris*, *Appalachia*, *A Mass of Life* or the First Dance Rhapsody. We know that to some audiences, our composer's almost invariable tendency to end a piece with cadences that have 'a dying fall', is as disappointing as the absence of a resounding top note at the conclusion of a soprano or tenor aria. But so rapid has been the advance during recent years in general musical culture that this hypothetical deficiency should soon be regarded without offence. It does indeed seem all too clear that few professional musicians have taken the trouble to look beneath or beyond the mere notes of the score, and although I admit that most of the early published editions, many of them the only available ones, are badly edited and dotted with misleading directions of time and nuance, I venture to think that these are the very shortcomings that the truly enquiring mind might find gratification in overcoming. For no one has yet seriously disputed that the leading qualities of this music, as Sir Edward Elgar has so warmly testified, are beauty and poetry, qualities by no means common in most of that produced during the past forty years; and surely it should be a matter of pleasure as well as duty to ensure that its finer attributes are made evident to the Public. All that is really wanted is the insight to comprehend and reveal the infinite wealth of nuance inherent in nearly everything that he wrote. Renan has reminded us that '*la vérité consiste dans les nuances*', and to no composer does this dictum apply so aptly as to Delius. But a word of warning may not be wholly out of place. It is imperative to maintain a tight control over the motion of the melodic line: otherwise there may be created an unpleasant sense of lassitude or shapelessness.

A word of explanation concerning the earlier editions, many of which are still in active circulation, may here be fitting. It appears to have been Frederick's belief that once he had set down the mere notes of a score, barring the occasional inclusion of a few ambiguous hints as o tempo, his task was fully accomplished. I take leave to quote a brief extract from a monograph written many years ago which commented fairly, if a little severely, on this strange conception of the needs and requirements of both performers and publishers:

'Other musicians of eminence have expressed the view that in respect of his art this is a dangerous delusion. It is well known that although he has the ability to inscribe on paper a combination of notes capable of yielding delightful effects if adequately rendered, he is wholly unable to instruct his interpreters how to obtain the desired results. And I am credibly informed that when he attempts to do so, either by oral advice or by the addition in his own hand to his scores of any of those indications of time, expression and phrasing, which we see so liberally scattered upon the pages of other men's work, he is so invariably in the wrong that he only succeeds in adding to that obscurity of comprehension which his peculiar attitude towards the responsibility of composition has automatically created.'

Such directions as are to be found in the editions referred to are mainly those of the first group of interpreters into whose hands they had fallen, and it is to be regretted that their skill failed to equal their zeal.

The best of Delius is undoubtedly to be found in those works where he disregarded classical traditions and created his own forms. Nearly all of these, his masterpieces, were written during a period of fifteen years, the middle part of his life. His revived interest in the sonata and the concerto, active mainly between 1915–21, fails with one exception, the Violin Concerto, to command undivided esteem. Save for the several slow movements in the String Quartet, the Violoncello Concerto and the Double Concerto, in which his true self often rises to the surface, his peculiar melodic and harmonic singularities do not there seem to move with ease and certainty. It is possible to trace an inner sense of relief when during the above-mentioned period he diverts to the media of his earlier days in the instances of *Eventyr* and *A Song before Sunrise*. And with what a zest he returns, if only by a sort of back door, to his great love, the Theatre, in his *Hassan* music!

A short reference must be made to the series of pieces he turned out between 1929 and 1933 in conjunction with Eric Fenby. The only

epithet that can be applied to this strangest of collaborations is—heroic
But it would be idle if in our admiration for the remarkable qualitie
of the two participants we ignored the plain fact that it gives us littl
of Delius that we did not know before; and even that little does no
ring with the sound of unadulterated inspiration. Let us honour it a
a noble experiment and leave it at that. It remains only to say somethin
about the man himself.

No analysis or comprehension of his character is possible unless it b
recognized that we are here dealing, during the course of a life lastin
seventy-two years, with two almost different personalities. They di
not exist side by side but were separated one from the other by cause
which have been outlined in a previous chapter. It is natural, of cours
that there should be occasional traces of his later phase in his earlie
and vice versa; but these are incidental and influenced hardly at all th
main disposition of either. Abundant testimony is forthcoming as t
what sort of person Frederick was up to his thirty-eighth or nintl
year. Handsome, open-hearted, loquacious, amorous and gay, he too
pleasure in performing little services for those around him, straightene
out more than one complication troubling a friend who was not o
the spot to handle it himself, and never thought twice about assistin
impecunious fellow musicians out of his very modest resources. On on
occasion he turned aside for weeks from his own works to organiz
the first Paris exhibition of the paintings of Edvard Munch,[1] whos
reputation during the closing years of the century was extendin
beyond the narrow bounds of Norway. We have seen how definit
was the severance from this first phase of his career and how he har
dened gradually into an almost totally dissimilar sort of being, i
whom were discernible few of the traits that had marked the joyou
spirit of olden days. As nearly everything that has been written abou
him dates from this later period, it is hardly surprising that we shoul
have been viewing for so long an incomplete picture of the whol
man.

He has been represented by some as a hedonist and a devote
follower of Aristippus of Cyrene. We hear from others that hi
material difficulties were few and that he never had real cause fo
worry about ways and means. To any of this it may be answered tha

[1] The greatest of Norwegian painters. No less than forty-five of his pictures are to be see
in the National Gallery of Oslo. A disciple during his early career of the French Impressionisti
School, he later completely emancipated himself from its control. Delius was among his firs
and active admirers.

Frederick led on the whole a hard and laborious life; for many years in straitened circumstances, and during clearly defined periods 1895–1898 and 1914–21 never free from anxiety about preserving mere existence. At no time could he afford to indulge in any but the simplest luxuries, and during the final years, 1924–34, most of his exiguous capital and income went on medical treatment, cures and attendance incident to his helpless condition. There came a time when his wife was forced to sell her house, which was bought by their good friend Balfour Gardiner, who allowed them to occupy it rent free. The imputation of hedonism comes inevitably from English sources, to which the spectacle of a man who writes neither oratorios nor symphonies is both novel and disturbing. That he was a confessing non-Christian helps to make the matter worse; for an absolute devotion to nature, divorced from any sectarian religious belief, is regarded as an indulgence in which morality has no part. If by any perverse or puritanical twist of definition Frederick is to be accounted a specimen of that allegedly inferior section of humanity, dubbed hedonist, he is to be found in the company of the majority of our best poets, painters and philosophers of the last three hundred years.

If we are to look among ancient philosophies for the origin or inspiration of Frederick's outlook upon the world, we are more likely to find it in Pyrrhonism, whose founder was the first of all avowed sceptics to establish a practising school of unbelief. An immense impetus was given to the revival of this creed (or negation of creed), in the middle of the nineteenth century, by the publication of *Natural Selection* and *The Origin of Species*. The result was a vast wave of agnosticism which still dominates a great part of the western world, and it was almost inevitable that Frederick who was born into that era should be no other than a child of it. Too much stress has been laid on his alleged subservience to the teachings of Friedrich Nietzsche. Let it be freely admitted that he admired more than in any other modern thinker the literary style, the persuasive method of argument and the more than occasional psychological illuminations of the great iconoclast; but he certainly did not owe to him the discovery that there were dangerous fallacies inherent in the bulk of democratic doctrine, and that most of the world's significant changes had proceeded, not from the collective inaction of the masses, but from the inventions and ideas of extraordinary individuals. All this he had heard pronounced with telling force by the greatest dramatist of the century, some time well before he had dipped into *Also Sprach Zarathustra*, and it fell like soothing balm upon the distractions and indecisions of his youth.

For my part I doubt whether the spirit of Delius was ever seriously touched by any philosophic influence: encouraged or fortified perhaps, but not moulded, and certainly never deflected. His actions, decisions and development were the consequences of an inner force, that needed little or nothing of an externally intellectual kind to quicken them. I cannot help thinking that future commentators, should there be any, would lose nothing by ignoring much of what has been written about his beliefs or unbeliefs, and concentrate mainly on the real key to the man, his music.

I venture to remind the patient reader of the letter from Grieg to Percy Grainger (quoted in Chapter 19) in which the former insists upon the absolute bond uniting the artist and his work. The two entities are one and indivisible. This view is admirably illustrated in the instance of Frederick and his music. What I said in Chapter 10 about his slow progress in achieving full maturity was concerned less with the character of the music itself, than his difficulty in finding moulds or shapes into which he could fit his ever-widening and richer conceptions. These, as we have seen, are mainly self-created; indeed it could not be otherwise, and it was imperative they be constructed with an architectural mastery that would place them 'beyond the reach of time and change'. But during the twenty years that followed the creation of *Irmelin* there is little change in the sentiment and style of the music itself, and its main qualities, an inward warmth and delicate tenderness, prevail throughout. Here and there is an elegiac strain, which too often has been identified with nostalgia. It goes deeper than that. Not only in his operas which are so replete with it, but in certain of his non-dramatic works there is a quiet but unmistakeable undertone of tragedy. Not, however, the violent demonstrations of it that so many have been led to believe are indispensable elements in lyrical drama, and without which no stage piece can hope to succeed. Of terror there is nothing: only a profound and moving pity. After a performance of *A Village Romeo and Juliet* given many years ago by the students of the Royal College of Music, Sir Hugh Allen, at that time Principal of the College, said to me: 'This is the most heartbreaking music in the world.'

Several other eminent musicians of equal sensibility have been affected similarly, yet death or disaster do not create with Delius the impression of hopeless and irremediable loss. Indeed in three of his operas the fall of the last curtain leaves us with the strange consolatory reflection that Destiny may not have said the last word about its victims. Undoubtedly, until a definable point in his life Frederick was a man overflowing with kindness and affection for his fellow creatures, and he has bestowed upon the unhappy puppets of his imagination a moving compassion which seems to hint that all is not yet over. And this is communicated not through the words, or even the stage action, but the music alone; which, speaking eloquently and revealingly to us, thanks to the wealth of nuance to which I have alluded, makes crystal clear everything taking place in the minds and hearts of the personages in the drama.

Grieg's theory concerning the inseparability of the man and his music receives some confirmation from the change in character and feeling of the latter which coincided with the period of Frederick's metamorphosis of mind and spirit. The iron which had begun to enter his soul about 1902 had become firmly set there by 1911, and from that time on we hear gradually less of the poetry and charm which delighted us in *Sea Drift* and *In a Summer Garden*. In their place we have hitherto unfamiliar elements of austerity and impersonality, as if the composer had grown tired of interpreting the joys and sorrows of human beings and had turned to the contemplation of Nature only. This is markedly observable in the two great works of transition *A Song of the High Hills* and *North Country Sketches*, and although there is no falling away here of power and mastery, we do not find it easy to suppress a twinge of longing for the fragrant and affectionate intimacy of an earlier day. It has to be admitted that the final spell of his creative activity, 1915–23, is one of progressive decline. The ancient fire burns brightly for a few rare moments, as in *Hassan*, but by slow degrees sinks to eventual extinction. This must be charged to the account of failing health and vitality, which, in their turn, may indict the revival, first visible shortly after the outbreak of war, of the fatal ailment which continued to undermine insidiously his strength and powers of resistance until the ultimate collapse ten years later.

What is his future to be? Opinions are bound to differ and widely. For myself I cannot do other than regard him as the last great apostle in our time of romance, emotion and beauty in music. We are living today in an age of transition and disintegration; there have been several like it before. A distinguished Frenchman, the Prince de Ligne, in the early part of the last century, lamented that he had lived to hear Napoleon termed a coward and Talleyrand a fool. Similarly, I have read during the last two decades many unsavoury attempts to belittle most of the outstanding figures in music of the past two hundred years. Even such charming masterpieces of the operatic art as *Carmen*, *Manon* and *La Bohème* have been summarily dismissed as of negligible value, and the Requiem Mass of Mozart has recently been found to be entirely wanting in inspiration. On the other hand, numerous experiments, that have not five years of real life in them, have been hailed with satisfaction or at least serious respect. But through the vast cloud of mental obfuscation hovering over the present musical scene peeps the modest visage of the average man of common sense, general culture and musical sensibility, to affirm in quiet but firm tones his preferences and predilections. Generally, if sometimes belatedly, he is on the side of the angels, and I venture to hope—and indeed think—that the future of Frederick Delius may rest securely in his hands.

Index

226